WITHDRAWN
HARVARD LIBRARY
WITHDRAWN

CONSCIENCE

Published by Midsea Books Ltd.
3a Strait Street, Valletta, Malta

© Fabio Attard, 2008

No part of this publication may be reproduced,
stored in a retrieval system or transmitted
in any form by any means, electronic, mechanical,
photocopying, recording or otherwise,
without the previous written permission
of the author.

First published in 2008

Produced by Mizzi Design and Graphic Services Ltd.
Printed at Gutenberg Press Ltd, Malta

ISBN 978-99932-7-190-1

Conscience
in the
Parochial and Plain Sermons
of
John Henry Newman

FABIO ATTARD SDB

midseaBOOKS
2008

BX
4705
.N5
A883
2008

*In remembrance of
my Mother and Father
Stella and George*

Contents

Contents vii
Acknowledgements ix
Abbreviations xii
Introduction xiii

The discovery of Conscience 1816-1825 3
Advocacy of Conscience 1825-1832 55
Advocacy of Conscience 1833-1843 111
The reason behind the sermon 165
Analysis of the term 'Conscience' 187
Conclusion 223

Appendix 231
Bibliography 234
General Index 240

Acknowledgements

This work could only see the light of day because it was made possible through the contribution of so many people. I am here presented with an opportunity to look back with gratitude.

My first steps in studying John Henry Newman were taken in the Accademia Alfonsiana, in Rome, where Rev. Sabatino Majorano C.Ss.R. encouraged me to study the theme of conscience in Newman. I am most grateful to him for the guidance, as well as his keen interest and concern in my work.

Throughout my undergraduate and post-graduate years I have received continued encouragement from the late Rev. Achille M. Triacca S.D.B., of the Università Pontificia Salesiana, in Rome. The theological insights he shared with me go beyond their purely academic parameters. He has been a teacher, a friend and a mentor to me. May God reward his kindness.

During my two and a half years of research, I felt at home in Milltown Institute of Philosophy and Theology, in Dublin. I would like to express my heartfelt gratitude to Rev. Dr. David Smith M.S.C., then Dean of the Faculty of Theology. He has followed my research with brotherly interest.

I also had the opportunity of benefiting from the scholarly expertise of Dom Placid Murray O.S.B. of Glendstal Abbey, Limerick, Ireland. Sharing the aims of my work with this great

Newman scholar has been a great learning experience. His words of encouragement had a determining and lasting effect on the development of the present work.

I am also indebted to the Fathers of the Birmingham Oratory. During my research and consultation of the Newman Collection, I appreciated their readiness to assist me. My meetings with Rev. Fr. Gregory Winterton and the late Mr. Gerard Tracey, archivist of the Birmingham Oratory, deeply strengthened my love for Newman.

The founding of the Newman Society of Ireland in 1996 gave me the opportunity of contributing to the study sessions that were held in Newman House. The sharing of ideas with the members of the Society and the discussions that followed constituted a most enriching experience.

I have to express a special word of gratitude to Dr. Teresa Iglesias, of the Department of Philosophy, University College Dublin. I recognise that the impact of her contribution cannot be limited to these printed pages. Thanks to Dr. Iglesias I could use the facilities of the Newman Trust, at Oriel House, Dublin.

I have to thank Rev. John Horan SDB, the Provincial of the Irish Province, of which Malta is part. His unfailing support in my research gave me the needed energy required in this kind of work. The Salesian Communities in Crumlin, Dublin and Savio College, Malta, provided me with the right environment to proceed with my work until the end.

A word of thanks to the Faculty of Theology of the Università Pontificia Salesiana, Rome. When I was asked to belong to the staff of this faculty I was made welcome and encouraged by Mons. Angelo Amato SDB, then Dean of the faculty. I have benefited from his support and encouragement both on the intellectual and the human level.

Finally, a word about my family. My mother and father have a very important part in this work. To them it is dedicated. Since I started this research till its present publication the Lord has called them both to Himself. Their generous love, hard work and profound faith, transmitted to me and to my sisters and brothers, can be considered to be the foundation of this research and a lasting heritage. Their contribution is rooted deep within. The void left in my life through their physical absence is abundantly filled with the memory of what they have been to me and my family.

Fabio Attard SDB
31 January 2008

Abbreviations

Apol.	Apologia pro Vita Sua (1873)
AW	John Henry Newman: Autobiographical Writings, ed Henry Tristram, 1956
Diff. I-II	Certain Difficulties felt by Anglicans in Catholic Teaching, 2 volumes (1879, 1876)
GA	An Essay in aid of a Grammar of Assent (1870)
HS I-III	Historical Sketches, 3 volumes (1872)
LD I-XXXI	The Letters and Diaries of John Henry Newman. Volumes XI-XXXI (Nelson, London - Clarendon Press, Oxford 1961-1977); Volumes I-VIII (Clarendon Press, Oxford 1978 – 1999).
PS I-VIII	Parochial and Plain Sermons, 8 volumes (1868)
US	Fifteen Sermons preached before the University of Oxford (1872)

Introduction

A theme, which is rightly associated with the personality of John Henry Newman, is surely that of conscience. To the general reader, Newman's whole life story comes across as a witness of someone who followed the light of his conscience wherever it lead him. Yet, for him or her who decides to enter into a more familiar knowledge of the man, it will soon become clear that the meaning of conscience in his life goes much deeper than was originally thought.

1. The main question

The main aim of this work is to discover what Newman understands by the term conscience in a particular period of his life, that which stretches from 1816 to 1843, his Anglican period. Within this particular period we find two sources which are intimately linked one to the other. They are his sermons, the *Parochial and Plain Sermons*,[1] and the varied biographical events as they come

---

[1] *PPS* I-VIII; «Six volumes of Newman's *Parochial Sermons* appeared between 1834 and 1842, and, in 1843, he contributed a volume to the Tractarian series *Plain Sermons*. Most are acquainted with these as the eight-volume series *Parochial and Plain Sermons*, which was the form in which they were published (to such a surprising reception) in 1868, edited by W.J. Copeland...

across to us through his *Letters and Diaries*.[2]

Our aim is to find in these two sources the answers to the main question which guides our investigation: «How is Newman's own understanding of conscience within the *Parochial and Plain Sermons* related to his personal life story?» This question is dealt with from the standpoint of the biographical events and that of the written word. For this reason we divide our work in two parts. The first examines the whole domain of the events, aiming to highlight the importance they hold for the theme of conscience. The second is directly concerned with Newman's writing on conscience within the *Parochial and Plain Sermons*.

2. Why the *Parochial and Plain Sermons*?

The *Parochial and Plain Sermons* constitute only one in three sermons that Newman wrote as an Anglican. While these eight volumes contain 191 sermons, the whole corpus of sermons belonging to this period is made up of 604 sermons.[3] Besides publishing these eight volumes, Newman himself also published two other volumes, *Sermons on Subjects of the Day* and *Fifteen Sermons Preached before the University of Oxford*.

The eight volumes of *Parochial and Plain Sermons*, our area of research, can claim to represent Newman at his best. As we enter

---

The volumes of the *Parochial Sermons*, and those of *Plain Sermons* and *Sermons on Subjects of the Day*, were a selection which Newman made from his large corpus and include 217 of the sermons which he wrote during these years», in P. MURRAY – V.F. BLEHL (eds.) *John Henry Newman: Sermons 1824-1834. Volume I: Sermons on the Liturgy and Sacraments and on Christ the Mediator; Volume II: Sermons on Biblical History, Sin and Justification, the Christian Way of Life, and Biblical Theology*. (Clarendon Press, Oxford 1991, 1993) p. V; this note by Gerard Tracey, Archivist of the Birmingham Oratory, is taken from the *Preface* to both volumes. It gives the historical background to Newman's sermons. The above mentioned volumes, to be followed by other three, will bring within the reach of Newman scholars all those sermons which still survive in manuscript form in the Archives of the Birmingham Oratory.

[2] *LD* I-XXXI

[3] The complete list of Newman's Anglican sermons is found at the end of both volumes of Newman's unpublished sermons; see note 1.

into more detail about his sermon writing, we become aware that the sermons he wrote were not all to his liking. Those he initially published were the ones he identified with most and the ones who succeeded to express what was most profound and deep within him.[4] His own letters, during the time of publication, give witness to the importance he attached to these volumes. This does not deny the fact, though, that when he published them as a Catholic, he was hesitant about some of the sermons,[5] although this hesitancy was counterbalanced by testimonies of gratitude and appreciation by those who bought and read them.[6]

The sermons succeed in reflecting the journey Newman was undertaking, a journey of development and growth. C.S. Dessain thinks that in tracing «the difference between the earlier and later volumes of *Parochial Sermons* we must point to the greater mastery and completeness. It is substantially the same teaching, the same concrete "personalism", the same psychological insight into other minds, but now more confident, with more experience behind it».[7] He also sees in these sermons an expression of «English Christianity at its noblest, for Newman preaches not a theory or philosophy of his own, but the Christian Revelation: not Christian doctrine in the abstract, but the truths of faith as bringing us into new and close relations with God. He had a horror of "unreal words" and professions».[8]

---

[4] «There is very little in them which I should not say now, altering some forms of expression», in *LD* XX, p. 449.
[5] *LD* XXIV, p. 65.
[6] *Id.*, pp. 177, 274; «according to numerous testimonies of his contemporaries such as Richard Church, Principal Shairp, Anthony Froude and Henry Wilberforce, Newman's preaching in St Mary's had a profound spiritual effect upon his hearers and contributed greatly to the Oxford Movement. The publication of these sermons on almost a yearly basis spread Newman's influence far beyond Oxford. When the *Parochial and Plain Sermons* were republished in 1868, they had large sale particularly among Dissenters», in V.F. BLEHL, 'The Intellectual and Spiritual Influence of J.H. Newman', *The Downside Review* 111 (1993) 255.
[7] C.S. DESSAIN, *John Henry Newman* (Adam and Charles Black, London 1971) pp. 47-48.
[8] *Ibid.*

Of the same opinion is O. Chadwick who qualifies these sermons, together with the *University Sermons*, as «Newman's chief work. He never wrote better; never more powerfully, never more persuasively. These books of sermons made the heart of that body of thought which came in history to be known as the Mind of the Oxford Movement».[9] Chadwick points to the historical importance of what Newman preached and how he preached it: «the power of the sermons is at bottom the quest for reality in religion. The eighteenth century used a lot of religious language that was sacrificial, and was comfortable in not practising what it preached».[10] The moment Newman came into the scene and sat behind the pulpit, «he articulated what they felt, drove it home, and spread the discontent to an ever-widening circle of minds. This was what led some of his followers to ascribe vast consequences to his words, and to believe that he altered the entire feeling among the English people towards religion».[11]

Newman shared his journey. He «was convinced of the truth of what he said... understood the moral and personal predicaments of the human race... (and) commanded a simple style which was the perfect instrument in language for what he needed to say».[12] In this sharing he does not come across as the protagonist in other people's lives, rather he «created his effect by disappearing into the reality of which he spoke, as though he must get out of its way».[13]

---

[9] O. CHADWICK, *Newman* (Oxford University Press, Oxford 1986) pp. 18-19, 21
[10] *Id.*, p. 19.
[11] *Ibid.*
[12] *Id.*, p. 21
[13] *Ibid.*; another reflection from the same author concerns the value of the sermons in relation to the whole *Oxford Movement*: «are not the Parochial Sermons of Newman the "typical" doctrine of the Movement at its highest, contributing to, rather than creating, a body of theological and devotional thought? It is of the essence of the Movement that its best writing should be enshrined in parochial sermons», in *The Mind of the Oxford Movement* (Adams and Charles Black, London 1960) p. 42; «even more successful were the sermons, especially the *Parochial Sermons*, which from 1834 spread Newman's fame to larger than university audiences... To J.C. Shairp they were, with Keble's *Christian Year*, one of the two permanent monuments of

3. The Reason of the Present Work

The aim of this work is to examine the use of the term "conscience" in Newman's *Parochial and Plain Sermons*. Were this to be the only aim, the end result would not do justice to Newman as a person. E.J. Sillem, in his study of Newman's philosophy, starts his very first chapter with the following statement: «most people who settle down to a careful reading of the works of John Henry Newman begin to feel sooner or later as though they were in the presence of a very powerful personality who lives within his writing, almost as if there were so many animate parts of his bodily frame».[14] While fully agreeing with this statement, we furthermore share the feeling of finding ourselves in the presence of someone who transcends his own writings. This feeling cannot be contained within a sentimental alcove. In our case, this feeling finds an expression within the following pages.

To help us in our efforts, we are privileged enough to benefit from the recent publications of the volumes *The Letters and Diaries of John Henry Newman*. These primary sources, together with other sources already published, namely *Apologia* and *John Henry Newman: Autobiographical Writings*, give us nearly all the necessary information that is available on the Anglican period of Newman's life, right from his childhood.

The value of the present study lies precisely in the fact that up to now the theme of conscience has not been dealt with in the way we are proposing here. The various studies available, regarding

---

genius from the Oxford Movement. In them, to use Newman's own motto, *Cor ad cor loquitur*. Doctrinal matters were in abeyance, or implied only. 'He laid his finger,' says Shairp, ' – how gently, yet how powerfully, - on some inner place in the heart's heart, and told him things about himself he had never known till then», in ROBBINS, W., *The Newman Brothers* (Heinemann, London 1966) p. 70, quoting from J.C. SHAIRP, *Studies in Poetry and Philosophy* (Edinburgh 1872) p. 248; see also C.S. DESSAIN, *John Henry Newman* (Adam and Charles Black, London 1971) pp. 44-45 and by the same author 'The Biblical Basis of Newman's Ecumenical Theology,' in *Rediscovery*, pp. 100, 101.

[14] E.J. SILLEM, *John Henry Newman. The Philosophical Notebook.* 2 volumes (Nauwelaerts Publishing House, Louvain 1969) p. 1.

the theme of conscience in Newman, have not yet treated the subject in these texts and from this perspective. One could easily give a reason for this missing analysis. Up to a few years ago, the possibility of working with the necessary primary sources was rather difficult to achieve. Now, thanks to so many scholars who have dedicated their time and energy to working on Newman's unpublished material, we are in a better position to do so.

Ultimately, this means that, from now on, any study on Newman cannot claim to be fully researched, unless the events of his life, as portrayed in his *Letters and Diaries*, come into play. The need for this is by no means a recent discovery. We limit ourselves to justify our approach by referring to two writers towards whom all Newman students and scholars owe a great deal.

Jean Guitton, in his work on Newman's philosophy, recognized this need way back in 1933. In presenting the various works by and on Newman, he expresses the following wish in a footnote form: «une étude intéressante consisterait à chercher dans chaque sermon le reflet des événements de la vie de Newman connus par la correspondance».[15] Guitton, already then, became convinced of the internal connection that exists between Newman's life and his writings. His visits to the Oratory in Birmingham brought him in contact with the correspondence that was still not available to the general reader at the time. Guitton foresaw, then, that time would come when this aspect of Newman's life will need to be explored so as to do justice to his teaching and ideas.

C.S. Dessain expressed the same wish in one of his essays on Newman's philosophy and theology: «clearly more examination of his sources and the influences that affected him is needed, which will show his place in the English tradition without thereby diminishing our sense of his originality»; and he continues «the more Newman is studied for his own sake as he really was, and in his own setting, the more he will be understood». The way

---

[15] J. GUITTON, *La philosophie de Newman: Essai sur l'Idée de Développement* (Paris 1933) p. 196.

Dessain traces for all those who would like to achieve this is the study of his correspondence: «undoubtedly one of the best ways to know not only Newman but also his philosophy and theology is to read his letters, which correct false impressions and answer criticism based on insufficient knowledge». By way of concluding his essay, Dessain quotes the review of one of the volumes of *The Letters and Diaries of John Henry Newman* which says: «a lesser man than Newman would undoubtedly be diminished by the publication of his complete letters in a 30 volume series, each running to more than 600 pages. But as this series grows (...) Newman's true stature becomes apparent (*Times Educational Supp.*, 1968)».[16]

4. The Structure of the Work

Chapter 1 looks into the important events of his childhood and youth, those that make up his whole formative period, from 1816 to 1825 ca. This initial study attempts to discover not so much what happened but rather the meaning of what happened. Through Newman's own witness, we come to terms with how these events effected him.

The critical study in Chapter 1 reveals three dimensions: first, the identification of those initial influences that had an effect on Newman's thought. Secondly, we discover a conflict of ideas, together with a process of development that this conflict necessarily brings with it. Thirdly, we already see the initial signs, the first indications, of his methodological approach, especially in controversy. This third dimension, methodology, is extremely relevant in relation to the whole of Newman works. It runs like a golden thread, witnessing its strength in works of a

---

[16] C.S. DESSAIN, 'Newman's Philosophy and Theology', in DE LAURA, D.J. (ed.) *Victorian Prose - A Guide to Research* (The Modern Language Association of America, New York 1973) pp. 183-184.

more philosophical nature, for example *Fifteen Sermons Preached before the University of Oxford* and *An Essay in Aid of a Grammar of Assent*. The overall aim of this chapter is to meet Newman in his life story. Searching within the store of his experience, we come to know who is Newman before the sermons, that is to say, to discover the person before the preacher.

Chapter 2 and Chapter 3 examine the period between 1825 and 1843. These years are divided into two periods: 1825 to 1832 and 1833 to 1843. This division takes the tour of the Mediterranean as the dividing event between the two. The aim here is to further explore the events of his life. The interest is more centred on the aspect of complementarity: that is, the relationship that exists between the events which deal with issues of conscience and the general notion of conscience as presented within the sermons. Through the *Letters and Diaries* we discover how intrinsically related are the sermons to the events of his life.

On a personal level there is a journey, both spiritual and human, in which growth can be felt. On an intellectual level, these same experiences preceded the sermons in helping Newman to clear his own ideas to himself and to formulate a vocabulary and a method in relation to the notion of conscience.

In exploring the background to the sermons, these chapters present the sermons as reflections of high spiritual and intellectual value, rooted in the day to day experience.

Chapter 4 presents what are Newman's own ideas about sermon writing. Taking his correspondence at the time of his preaching ministry, we examine what Newman thought of his sermons together with the answers received from his correspondents. This interesting collection of thoughts and ideas, both his and others in reaction to him, brings us closer to Newman, the man of faith.

Chapter 5 offers a literal appraisal of the term "conscience". It is a detailed examination of the term from three different but related angles. First we analyse the term from the aspect of identity, "what conscience is". Secondly, we study the same term from the aspect of action, "what conscience does", that is, we explore the use of the verbs which express the action of conscience. Thirdly, we find out "what conscience has", what does it contain within it that reveal more its identity and its actions.

This analysis is separately applied to the two different periods: 1825 to 1832 and 1833 to 1843. This comparative study, as a diachronic analysis, focuses more on the development that takes place in Newman's notion of conscience.

The structure of this work does not favour the analysis of the term «conscience» simply *ad intra*, by curtailing the study from any contact with the rest of the Newman's personality. This option has been taken in order to explore as much as possible the wider spectrum against which the notion of conscience is found. There is a clear choice in favouring a dialectic approach. The ideas and the teachings of Newman are constantly read against the day to day experience. This experience becomes the necessary background to meet the real Newman.

The other methodological choice is the adherence to the chronological sequence of events. This chronological method, complementing and enriching the dialectic one, favours the appreciation of the vocabulary and the style of the controversies. While avoiding the danger of presenting Newman purely as a collection of ideas and convictions, unconnected with his real life experience, the chronological reading presents his life as a journey of growth and development.

CONSCIENCE

CHAPTER 1

The discovery of Conscience
1816-1825

John Henry Newman's early youth is surely a most interesting period. It could also be the least known. An examination of the events that make up this period, besides offering a deeper understanding of his method of thinking, will also unearth Newman's reflection on conscience at the time.

The publication of Newman's *Letters and Diaries*, undoubtedly a most useful and indispensable tool, further enlightens this period of his life, the understanding of which proves to be a very valuable instrument in relation to that further development of his thinking.

The study of the *Letters and Diaries*[1] opens before us a wider spectrum. What Newman goes through when writing his letters sheds light on his later works like the *Parochial and Plain Sermons*, *University Sermons* and *Essay in Aid of a Grammar of Assent*.[2] Those

---

1   P. ZENO, way back in 1952, when he was studying the not yet published material for *AW*, writes: «Another remark to be made beforehand is this: Newman's biographers have not given much information about his inner life during his boyhood; they have copied without much commentary what the *Apologia* and Anne Mozley's *Letters and Correspondence* tell us. Some statements, however, by these authors receive quite a different colour from the private diaries and appear to be inexact or sometimes altogether untrue', in 'Newman's Inner Life up to His Election as Fellow of Oriel College», *The Irish Ecclesiastical Record* 78 (1952) 256-257.

2   «Newman draws heavily on personal experience in his attempts to elucidate the Christian faith. The *Grammar of Assent* is, at the same time, one of the

principles which at this period start taking shape can be witnessed through a consideration of the contents of his letters and the methodological approach contained therein.[3]

1. Ealing: Conversion and Inwardness

On examining the early writings of Newman, which are mainly in letter form, one is immediately presented with that keen sense of a student, endowed with a certain awareness regarding all that is around him. The Ealing period,[4] rendered famous because of the event of the first conversion,[5] contains other important elements which are directly related to the way Newman's mind reacts to the reality around him, to all that of which he becomes part by way of conversation, by way of witnessing or by way of reading.[6]

---

most personal and one of the most analytic of Newman's works. Next to his professedly autobiographical work and his letters, however, it is in Newman's homilies that his heart is most revealingly open to us. Therein... we become "conscious of the presence of one active principle of thought, one individual character, flowing on and into the various matters which he discusses, and the different transactions in which he mixed" (see *HS* II. p. 227)», in T. MERRIGAN, '*Numquam minus solus, quam cum solus*. Newman's First Conversion: Its Significance for His Life and Thought', *The Downside Review* 103 (1985) 105; «We shall never understand Newman until we are prepared to relate his thought to a thorough analysis of the biographical sources», in J. COULSON - A.M. ALLCHIN - M. TREVOR, (eds.), *Newman: A Portrait Restored*. (Sheed & Ward, London - Melbourne - New York 1965) p. 6.

3 «The doctrine of conscience elucidated by Newman in his major works represents the maturation of an insight first gained in the summer of 1816», in T. MERRIGAN, '*Numquam minus solus, quam cum solus*. Newman's First Conversion: Its Significance for His Life and Thought', *The Downside Review* 103 (1985) 113.

4 Approximately up to June 1817 when he «came into residence» (8th June 1817) in Oxford, see *LD* I, p. 34, although Newman «entered at Trinity College, Oxford» on 14th December 1816, see *Id.*, p. 28. He continued his correspondence with Mayers well after he left Ealing.

5 See *Apol*. p. 4.

6 The continuous soul-searching which accompanies this intense self-consciousness manifested itself early in Newman's life. H. Tristram points out to Newman's «natural tendency to introspection» and recalls the description of him as the boy «full of thought». According to TRISTRAM the boy «grew into the introspective youth», see *AW* p. 143; see also T. MERRIGAN,

1.1. Myself and My Creator

On consulting these sources, the first important event is that of «conversion» which Newman experienced at the age of fifteen: «when I was fifteen, (in the autumn of 1816) a great change of thought took place in me. I fell under the influence of a definite Creed, and received into my intellect impressions of dogma, which, through God's mercy, have never been effected or obscured».[7]

In the *Apologia*, writing about the event of the conversion, Newman evokes the background of this event by presenting the interaction of his own mind with that of Walter Mayers - «the human means of this beginning of divine faith in me».[8] Without underestimating the quality of the contents that this event brought with it, this reflection, written years later,[9] exposes in a synthetic way, the outline of a mind in relation to another. There is a clear awareness of an intellect which discovers itself as different in relation to another. The recognition of an «outside reality» as «diverse» is, in a contradictory way, an affirmation of «self» as «inwardness», something which is «other than».

What is crucially important at this stage is Newman's ability to enter in contact with a diverse reality as presented through a person, in this case Mayers, and with which Newman can identify. This is a constant feature in these formative years which will repeat itself more than once.

What enhances this «diversity» is the fact that the «reality» being dealt with transcends the instrument through which, or through whom, it is offered. Thus, at once, the reality is personal but not identified with the person. The realm of which Newman

---

'*Numquam minus solus, quam cum solus*', p. 106; C.S. DESSAIN, 'Newman's First Conversion', *Newman Studien* 3 (1957) 37-53.
7   *Apol.* p. 4.
8   *Ibid.*
9   *Apol.* was published in seven parts between 21st April 2nd June 1864, see *Preface*, p. x.

speaks, the realm of «Creed... impressions of dogma»,[10] is already the stage of transcendence.

In a quick succession, he moves from the immanent, the purely human aspect of the experience, to the transcendent: from the visible reality to the invisible. This interpretation of the event is very much in line to what he himself writes in the *Apologia* in 1864: «in isolating me from the objects which surrounded me, in confirming me in my mistrust of the reality of material phenomena, and making me rest in the thought of two only absolute and luminously self-evident beings, myself and my Creator».[11]

The language here reflects a journey which will influence, amongst other works, his sermons and the *Essay on Development of Christian Doctrine*. He is writing not about an event in a historical and impersonal way. He is rather re-interpreting the fact of the conversion as the main event which was to influence all that followed. For Newman, the event of the «conversion» is a milestone in his early years, important in itself not much because of what it contained but more so because of the meaning it was to have in relation to what followed afterwards.

1.2. Relatedness with the Invisible

For Newman, the conversion event means that his mind, at that age, is able to be aware and understand a reality distinct from «self» but in relation to it. We can say that the whole process is far from passive. His mind receives impressions that have a definite,

---

10 C.S. DESSAIN describes this event as «no mere abstract speculation he had discovered, but a saving relationship with Father, Son, and Holy Spirit. His was now a religion of persons. He understood the meaning of loving God»; and that this «central truth of revelation which Newman first began to grasp at the age of sixteen... he developed so persuasively in his *Parochial Sermons*», in 'The Biblical Basis of Newman's Ecumenical Theology', in *Rediscovery*, pp. 102 and 121.
11 *Apol.* p. 4.

precise quality about them and since they are recognized as such, therefore they have to be treated accordingly. The actual conversion that takes place is not simply a shifting of opinions, or added knowledge. The recognition of a «creed» presupposes an ability of understanding it as such, which in turn asks for the respect of the intellect in its treatment and assent to it, if it is to be admitted and accepted as a permanent influence.

This event means for Newman the beginning of a feeling of «distinctiveness»: him and impressions of dogma. Louis Bouyer is of the opinion that this event revives «in the mind of the adolescent a conviction, an idea prematurely implanted in the mind of the child... it would not only reawaken, it would transform, what, in the child, was merely a passive impression, into a reasoned belief that was destined to remain an enduring factor in the life of the man».[12]

Terrence Merrigan treats the whole area of the meaning of «impressions» in relation to their effect on consciousness. He writes that Newman «distinguishes two sorts of conscious experience, (i) the experience of a world external to oneself, and (ii) the experience of one's inner world... a world of mental 'impressions'».[13]

If what Merrigan writes is taken as a tool to understand the duality that Newman's conversion contains, than Newman does not simply become aware of the exterior aspect of reality but, in accepting the knowledge as distant from «self», he is able to bridge that same distance and get enriched in return. The originality of the event lies in the fact of recognizing «otherness» and being enriched by it.

The distinctiveness of the two experiences not only dismisses their separation, but confirms their relation: «the experience of

---

[12] L. BOUYER, *Newman: His Life and Spirituality*. (Burns & Oates, London 1958) p. 19.
[13] T. MERRIGAN, *Clear Heads and Holy Hearts: The Religious and Theological Ideal of John Henry Newman*. 'Louvain Theological & Pastoral Monographs, 7'. (Peeters, Louvain 1991) p. 23.

one's inner world is an irreducible source of information and a vital source of knowledge. Along with the data of sense experience, mental impressions constitute the media through which the mind perceives specific objects, distinct from itself».[14]

The confirmation of this comes in the *Apologia*, in that this whole experience «isolated» him from «the objects which surrounded» him and in confirming him in his mistrust «of the reality of the material phenomena», and «making me rest in the thought of two and two only absolute and luminously self-evident beings, myself and my Creator».[15]

This second element of the conversion complements the first, since the diversity witnessed and felt by Newman is not simply on the level of knowledge, a passive acceptance of «otherness». It is rather the occasion which causes something in his inwardness.

The invisible world and the visible world are there to interact and not to take the place one of the other. This dimension is of crucial importance considering the different intellectual currents he will come in contact with. Besides, it is an underlying attitude that will be discovered in the sermons. Bouyer connects this relatedness with the invisible when he considers the «consciousness of self»: «for him (Newman), the invisible world is not substituted for the visible, but added to it, and hopes, hitherto vague and undefined, are now steadily focused on the expectation of the Divine Vision».[16]

1.3. Uniqueness and Distance

It is in examining the meaning and the effect the conversion has on Newman that its contents can be better appreciated. The

---

14 *Ibid.*
15 *Apol.* p. 4.
16 L. BOUYER, *Newman: His Life and Spirituality*, p. 15.

event was an awareness of diversity, «a world external to oneself», indicating to a «change of experience of his inner world».[17] This process of the conversion will be witnessed in those future reflections that Newman shares in his sermons. For this reason, J.M. Cameron sees in this event a methodological imprint: «this is Newman's method... to begin with what is inward and from this inward consciousness to go straight to God. This Newman traces back to his 'childish imaginations'; and the effect of his 'inward conversion' at the age of fifteen on his later opinions consisted 'in isolating me from the objects that surrounded me, in conforming my mistrust of the reality of material phenomena, and making me rest in the thought of two and two only absolute and luminously self-evident beings myself and my Creator'».[18]

At this stage of his life, Newman, therefore, acquires a dual notion both of his own uniqueness in relation to the divine and, also, of his distance from the material world. His is a world in which «he» is «alone». His is a world made up of two beings. In his *Autobiographical Writings* he writes: «The reality of conversion: - as cutting at the root of doubt, providing a chain between God and the soul».[19] Bouyer presents this awareness in the following words: «this consciousness of self, more astonishing, when we come to think of it, in the child than in the adolescent, has, no doubt, something disquieting about it... It comes under the category of the 'natural' in the strict sense of the word. It is perhaps that which constitutes the peculiar genius of Newman, if genius be an

---

17 T. MERRIGAN, *Clear Heads and Holy Hearts*, p. 23.
18 J.M. CAMERON, 'Newman and the Empiricist Tradition', in *Rediscovery*, p. 88; T. MERRIGAN, in *Clear Heads and Holy Hearts*, p. 83, thinks that Cameron is wrong in asserting that where revelation is concerned the «consequence of Newman's use of the empiricist model is that we begin from what is within: the impression». What Cameron seems to be concerned more about is the method, rather than the object, of faith; see *Rediscovery*, pp. 82-83.
19 *AW* p. 150. In 1874, ten years after the writing of the *Apologia*, in the same *AW* everytime Newman refers to this event he, more or less, insists on the same dynamics: «he fell under the influence of an excellent man, The Revd. Walter Mayers, of Pembroke College, Oxford, one of the classical masters, from whom he received deep religious impressions, at the time Calvinistic in character, which were to him a beginning of a new life», see *id.* p. 29, see. also pp. 150, 181.

exceptional concentration, a more than ordinarily intense glow, in something that is no more than a natural attribute, or faculty of the human mind».[20]

The Flemish author, A. Janssens, dwelling on the same idea, employs the term «autocentrism»: «Newman has such a vivid, constant, and sharp realization of a special divine guidance and a correspondingly special destiny that he became and had to become, one of the most independent, and autocentric personalities possible; independent in thought, research, opinion and deed».[21]

Thus, from this «real» experience of the conversion, Newman's way of relating to all that is around him takes on a particular form. There is a pattern of a mind forming itself which is not limited to the accumulation of quantitative information. The mind process in Newman is rather a process of assimilation through understanding, reasoning and reflecting interactively. He does not move forward to have information, but he moves around to dialogue with what is around him. He allows into his world whatever his innate tools of observation and intuition succeed to assimilate.[22]

---

20 L. BOUYER, *Newman: His Life and Spirituality*, p. 23.
21 This quotation is taken from T. MERRIGAN, '*Numquam minus solus, quam cum solus*', p. 111, n. 93, who translated it from the original Flemish contribution by A. JANSSENS, *Newman: Inleiding tot zijn geest en zijn werk*. (N.V. Standaard Boekhandel, Brussles 1937) pp. 136, 138-139.
22 «L'idée comme pouvoir de vision inclut indissolublement le jugement et l'imagination dans une contemplation de l'idée comme chose vue, rassemblant tout l'être conaissant en faveur et au nom de tout l'objet connu. Cette puissance totalisante, voire totalitaire, permet de rendre compte de la 'persuasion de sa réalité' (*Essay on Development*, p. 115), d'une certitude qui tient tout ensemble de la conviction intellectuelle et de l'évidence de la constatation directe», in Y. DENIS, "Les mécanismes mentaux du développement doctrinal d'aprés *L'Essai sur le développement de la doctrine chrétienne* de Newman', *Bulletin de litterature ecclésiastique* 80 (1979) 182-183.

1.4. Conscience as Guardian

The way Newman's quest is enfolding is that of somebody who is on a journey. This he is conscious of. He is also aware of the dangers of journeying by himself. It is at this very moment, when his mind is constantly searching and moving, that, for the first time, we encounter the use of the word «conscience»: «for indeed I find I have very great need of some monitor to direct me, and I sincerely trust that my *conscience*, enlightened by the Bible, through the influence of the Holy Spirit, may prove a faithful and vigilant guardian of the principles of religion».[23]

The word, in all probability, making its first appearance in all Newman's writings,[24] is full of meaning. Newman uses the word not simply as a passing remark. The context, as we have seen, is one of extreme importance to his future development. The reference to «conscience» is one which points towards a frame of mind. The inclusion of the term conscience at this stage is an expression of awareness about how important his personal situation is - «myself and my Creator».[25]

---

23 *LD* I, p. 30 (italics added).
24 Reference needs to be made to what is reported in the *AW* pp. 152-154; in these three pages another, almost similar, reference to «conscience» is found, in p. 153: «Although it is far from pleasant to give my reasons, inasmuch as I shall appear to set myself up, and to be condemning recreations and those who indulge in them, yet, when I am urged to give them, I hope I shall never be ashamed of them, presenting my scruples with humility and a due obedience to my parents, open to conviction, and ready to obey in a matter so dubious as this is, and to act against my own (judgment), if they command, thus satisfying at once my own conscience and them...». The date given to this entry is «End of 1816». Yet, the context within which this reference is found, is the same one of the letter in *LD* I, p. 30, that is, «Revd Walter Mayers, on his giving me Beveridge's Private Thoughts, January 1817», in *AW* p. 152; while Mayers letter, in *LD* I, p. 29, is entitled «Ealing 31 Decr 1816», Newman's answer to him is «January 1817», in *id*, p. 30.
25 «The argument from conscience is nothing but a meeting of man with his Maker, an interpersonal relationship with God, mysterious but real, this cannot be and should not be lost sight of in our moral life and ethical considerations», in A.J. BOEKRAAD, 'Conscience in the Vision of John Henry Newman', *Divus thomas* 82 (1979) 243.

A situation in continuous movement is coming in contact with new realities and new questions. At this moment he understands conscience not as a faculty providing him with information, as to what has to be done and avoided. He, rather, understands conscience as a «guardian», «faithful» to the truth and «vigilant» because of the dangers that he may encounter in discovering the principles of religion.[26] It is in reality a discovery not of a word, but of an experience.[27]

1.5. The Seeds of Evangelicalism

Attention to the role Evangelicalism plays at this stage of his life is necessary if the development of Newman's religious ideas is to be understood. H. Tristram refers to it as «simply a phase through which he passed in the course of his development, due to the influence exerted on him by an Evangelical master, Walter Mayers, at Ealing School».[28]

The Evangelical influence has two effects on the personality of Newman. H. Tristram in his presentation of Newman's journals highlights the importance of one of them, the psychological one.

---

[26] «This basic insight and first principle in Newman is the voice of his conscience, which itself grows in the process of a faithful and self-reflecting life, he interprets the general phenomena of human nature and experience by a circumspect application of logical procedure», in J.H. WALGRAVE, *J.H. Newman: His Personality, His Principles, His Fundamental Doctrines: Course Delivered by Professor J.H. Walgrave, Katholieke Universiteit Leuven 1975 - 1976 - 1977.* (Printed Manuscript, K.U.L., Leuven, Belgium 1981) p. 19.

[27] «It is our suggestion that the foundations of Newman's religious philosophy, and more specifically, his doctrine of conscience, can be unearthed in the discussion of his basic psychological orientation and its development as a result of his first conversion», in T. MERRIGAN, *'Numquam minus solus, quam cum solus'*, p. 99; also «Newman's experience in the years following his conversion strengthened his convictions about the nature and role of conscience», in *id*, p. 112; and also: «There is a real continuity here. The doctrine of conscience elucidated by Newman in his major works represents the maturation of an insight first gained in the summer of 1816», in *id*, p. 113.

[28] *AW* p. 142.

«Our interest [here] is psychological rather than doctrinal, in the effects upon his character rather than upon his beliefs; and here we may allow that his Evangelicalism did in fact intensify in him a certain natural tendency to introspection».[29] This piece of insight helps us to focus better on how some evangelical elements do remain with him, even after he starts drifting away from, and eventually gives up, the Evangelical idea of Christianity altogether.[30]

The other aspect of his Evangelical tendency, the doctrinal, is best explained by I. Ker who interprets the doctrinal effect not simply on the level of contents but, more so, on the level of religious attitudes. Ker's reading can be summed up in the following stages: first of all, the 1816 conversion ushered «a commitment to a doctrinal religion».[31] As Newman himself acknowledges, «it made me a Christian».[32]

Secondly, there was the «significance of conversion. Looking back at the end of his life, Newman found it 'difficult to realise or imagine the identity of the boy before and after August 1816' - he seemed 'another person'».[33] Newman understands his conversion in line with what happens afterwards, and not as an isolated event. Dessain, on his part, is convinced that the 1845 conversion «was to him a mere corollary of the conversion by which he gave himself to God at the age of sixteen».[34]

---

29 *Id.*, p. 143.
30 «It lasted for no more than six years, from the autumn of 1816, when he was converted, until Easter of 1822, when his success at Oriel introduced him into the 'noetic' circle of the Common Room. That moment marked imperceptibly at first, the opening of another phase, which culminated, after a slight deviation in the direction of the 'liberalism of the day', in his reception into the Catholic Church on October 9th 1845», in *id.*, p. 142.
31 I. KER, *Newman and the Fullness of Christianity*. (Clark, Edinburgh 1993) p. 19.
32 *AW* p. 268; «Newman's first conversion endued him with 'formed religious convictions' which lasted for the rest of his life», in D. NEWSOME, 'The Evangelical Sources of Newman's Power', in *Rediscovery*, p. 20.
33 I. KER, *Newman and the Fullness of Christianity*, p. 19; quote from *LD* XXXI, p. 31.
34 C.S. DESSAIN, *Newman*, p. 85.

Thirdly, the Evangelical idea helped him develop «a personal, living faith».[35] Although Newman, through his pastoral ministry, is saved from distinguishing Christians into two categories, regenerate and unregenerate, yet «a preoccupation with a *real* Christian faith runs through his Anglican sermons... In this kind of insistent preoccupation with a *real* Christianity one can see very clearly the formative influence of Evangelicalism».[36] D. Newsome, on the same line of thought presented by Ker, sees this «real Christianity» as «quest for holiness». Newman brings with him «this compulsive urge to attain holiness» which is «derived from Thomas Scott, but the medium and the theological context have completely changed».[37]

In this respect we witness that what Newman goes through in this «Evangelical phase» touches a personality both in its psychological and doctrinal sphere in the long term: «certain Evangelical attributes were carried by Newman into a rival tradition, and because none of these qualities were alien to that tradition, they were accordingly transformed».[38]

---

35   I. Ker, *Newman and the Fullness of Christianity*, p. 20; O. Chadwick defines the Evangelical Movement «more a movement of the heart than of the head. If the generalisation be allowed, it was primarily concerned with the law of prayer, and only secondarily with the law of belief. It was aware that creed and prayer are inseparable», in *The Mind of the Oxford Movement*. (London, Adams and Charles Black 1960) p. 11.
36   I. Ker, *Newman and the Fullness of Christianity*, p. 20.
37   D. Newsome, 'The Evangelical Sources of Newman's Power', in *Rediscovery*, p. 25.
38   *Ibid*.; «upon that great change which took place in him as a boy, there were four doctrines all of which he forthwith held, as if certain truths, viz. those of the Holy Trinity, of the Incarnation, of Predestination, and of the «Lutheran apprehension of Christ, the first three, which are doctrines of the Catholic Religion, and, as being such, are true, and really subject of certitude and capable of taking indefectible possession of the mind... the fourth, which is not true, though he thought it was so held, did in the event, as is the nature of mere opinion or untrue belief, take its departure from his mind in very short time, or rather was not held by him from the first», in *AW* p. 81.

1.8. The Importance of Ealing

The Ealing period is short in its duration. Yet it has, in its own way, an undisputed role on the future development not only of Newman's ideas, but even more so on the imaginative process which will turn out to be the tool through which Newman's ideas get conveyed.[39]

During this conversion experience, in one of his letters home he reminds his sister, Harriett, about the nice memories at their grandmother's cottage at Norwood. The language Newman uses reveals as much about his sister as it does about the way he was dealing with himself. He invites her to «ruminate in her brain and digest it well».[40] This «rumination» can well synthesize the whole process which starts at Ealing during his conversion and which continues afterwards.

Newman's ability to «ruminate» the events around him is to be further developed in his Oxford years. So will be that of «digesting».[41] Newman is sensitive to what is happening around him. He comes in contact with it and makes sure that he is not a stranger to it. What he goes through is not what he takes on

---

[39] «If it be true, as he was now beginning to feel that it was, that all complete consciousness of self is moral consciousness, he realised that moral consciousness is the consciousness, the awareness, of Someone, of God», in L. BOUYER, *Newman: His Life and Spirituality*, p. 24; also «not a mere discovery of God that he bore in remembrance. He tells us that God took possession of him in this direct and intimate manner, personal in the fullest sense implied by the words 'Myself and my Creator', bringing him thus to realise and embrace defined dogma», in *Id*, p. 25; see also D. NEWSOME, 'The Evangelical Sources of Newman's Power', in *Rediscovery*, p. 22 about conversion giving a direction to a personality already formed.

[40] *LD* I, p. 27. The date was 30th October 1816.

[41] See how the same word is further explained later in his *Idea*: «The enlargement consists not merely in the passive reception into the mind of a number of ideas hitherto unknown to it, but in the mind's energetic and simultaneous action upon and towards and among those new ideas, which are rushing in upon it. It is the action of a formative power, reducing to order and meaning the matter of our acquirements; it is a making the objects of our knowledge subjectively our own, or, *to use a familiar word, it is a digestion of what we receive*, into the substance of our previous state of thought; and without this no enlargement is said to follow», p. 134 (italics added).

board. What he ruminates in his brain, first he makes sure to digest it well, and, only afterwards, appropriating himself of it as an acquired data. His rumination is the work of the imagination, his digestion leads to the acquisition of «impressions».[42]

2. Oxford: Student at Trinity

Newman, the student, who arrives at Trinity is already the person equipped with growing convictions regarding his own «self». He is also aware of certain attitudes his character is slowly forming. This period in his life is marked by this substantial development in the awareness of «self» in relation to outside reality.

2.1. Aloneness

The awareness of being alone is highlighted by Newman in the first month of his stay in Trinity. The reflections shared with his parents contain the same sense of «aloneness», essentially different from «loneliness». It seems that it is a habitual sense that Newman always carries with him, more so in moments of difficulties or trials. His mother, on her part, comes out as the person who is most aware of what her son is going through. In her letters to him she demonstrates a keen sense of understanding

---

[42] See T. MERRIGAN, *Clear Heads and Holy Hearts*, pp. 56-57. See also the contribution by P.A. EGAN, 'Lonergan on Newman's Conversion', *The Heythrop Journal* 37 (1996) 437-55, especially pp. 449-450, where the author interprets Newman's conversion as a process. He gives some insights to the theological and psychological aspect of both conversions – 1816 and 1845. «His conversion had certain transitory effects... What was permanent and fundamental was the acceptance of the Revealed Religion, and the giving of himself to God in consequence. Let us keep to Newman's own words. He was made a Christian, he began a new life. That was the simple, profound, and lasting result; it was the turning point of his life, which gave the rest of his earthly course its unity», in C.S. DESSAIN, 'Newman's First Conversion', *Newman Studien* 3 (1957) 53.

and exceptional far-sightedness: «I think you stood the *foreign* attack capitally. From that specimen of firmness I am convinced you will easily withstand others more formidable and alluring, *with which you must expect to be assailed*».[43]

H. Tristram, paints a clear picture about how the boy turning student gets even more introspected: «the boy 'full of thought', as his sister Harriett pictured him in her little book *Family Adventures*, grew into the introspective youth, isolated by his conversion from the world of things and the world of men, and driven in upon himself».[44]

In one of his letters to Mayers, he expresses his joy in this «aloneness»: «I am more happy here, than I suppose I ever was yet; for the comparative freedom from temptation I enjoy in having hardly any one near me (I hope I do not speak presumptuously) leaves me at greater liberty to look into my heart, and to keep my thoughts on God».[45]

His father, detecting the way his son was concentrating on himself, warned him of the dangers that can follow: «Have a guard. Your are encouraging a nervousness and morbid sensibility, and irritability, which may be serious. I know what it is myself, perfectly well... Religion when carried too far induces a softness of mind. Take care, I repeat. You are on dangerous ground. The temper you are encouraging may lead to something alarming».[46]

---

43   *LD* I, p. 35 (italics added). Mother also advises him that a «change of society, even if agreeable, is trying to a feeling mind», in *id.*, p. 38. To his Father he writes the following: «I am not noticed at all, except by being silently stared at. I am glad they do not wish to be acquainted with me, not because I wish to appear apart from them and ill-natured, but because I really do not think I should gain the least advantage from their company», in *id.*, p. 36; «Whenever I go I am stared at», in *id.*, p. 40.
44   *AW* p. 143.
45   *LD* I, pp. 86-87.
46   *LD* I, p. 117.

His father's words, besides containing value in relation to the immediate period we are dealing with, do acquire a deeper meaning when we keep the whole of Newman's life in mind.[47]

2.2   The Talented Mind

One of Newman's greatest natural talents, of which he becomes gradually aware, is his ability to comprehend and to think and, at the same time, to express this thought process in writing. To his father he acknowledges this fact: «I think (since I am forced to speak boastfully) few have attained the facility of comprehension which I have arrived at».[48] A case in point during these years is a «projected letter» for the *Undergraduate*.[49]

The following verses expose a mind that is quick in understanding the apparent, visible, reality. He accepts it and is able to dialogue with it and the consequences it will pour forth. Yet, he goes even deeper. The apparent argument does not carry him along. He is in constant search of that depth which, although not immediately perceived, offers strength to any argument. And it is at this depth that he arrives, because it is this depth he has looked for from the beginning.

His aim, in this letter, is to propose the founding of a debating society. He moves in the following way: first he unfolds his ideas, he calls them dreams; secondly, he comes to terms and accepts the first reactions, or consequences, which are ones of derision; and, thirdly, he is able to go beyond and foresees that the ultimate

---

[47]   H. BREMOND, qualifying Newman as «le plus autobiographique des hommes», and explaining away his introspection as «autocentrisme», says that the written reflections and letters are an extension of self, in *Newman. Essai Biographique*, p. 42. See also H. TRISTRAM in *AW* p. 143; T. MERRIGAN, 'Numquam minus solus, quam cum solus', p. 106.
[48]   *Id.*, p. 125.
[49]   Newman was editor of this periodical which «began and ended in February 1819. It sold well, but, to his great disgust, Newman's name got out, and this was its death blow», in *AW* p. 41.

position a person would take is one of appreciation: and this is the depth not immediately perceived, but captured by Newman. This particular event shows Newman's ability to move among apparent contradictory realities, from ridicule and non-acceptance to appreciation and belonging: «if a society were instituted for debating on literary topics... If I were allowed to indulge the sweet dreams of imagination to their full... Men may laugh at this letter, and perhaps they would laugh at the first introduction of such a club, but custom would soon disarm ridicule, and those who before reviled it would be glad to join in it».[50]

The people who understand Newman and are witnessing the development of his personality, hint at this talent. His mother, ever so sharp in understanding her son, writes to him: «It is one of my greatest delights to anticipate that, however chequered the scenes of this life, your well-regulated mind will ever support you under its disappointments, and increase its rational pleasures».[51] Rightly she speaks of a well-regulated mind which his father, different from his mother, does not fully discover, and yet recognizes what it can do, only at hindsight. In a letter to his son he appreciates the contribution Newman gave to his brothers and sisters: «amongst *them* let *this* be a consolation to *you* that as the Eldest you have by example as well as by precept and instruction so greatly contributed to the Moral Beauty as well as to the cultivation and enlargement of their minds».[52]

---

50 *LD* I, pp. 63-64; it is important to keep this point in mind since it is the same conclusion that Walgrave arrives at when he writes how Newman foresaw the dangers of liberalism, see J.H. WALGRAVE, *Newman the Theologian: The Nature of Belief and Doctrine as Exemplified in His Life and Works*. (London, Geoffrey Chapman 1960) p. 33; see also *LD* V, p. 136 in a letter to H.E. Manning about a sermons delivered by the latter where the same line of thought is followed: «It will interest me much, if you have any thing to tell me concerning its reception by hearers or readers, though I know the good done by such testifyings does not show itself at once or to the person making them. Those very men who are ultimately most influenced by them object to them at the time and play the critic – but haeret lateri, whatever they may say or think, and at length they yield. But besides all consideration of effects, a protest is a good and right thing in itself».

51 *LD* I, p. 62.
52 *Id.*, p. 114.

O. Chadwick in his short study on Newman, shares a very dense reflection on *The nature of Newman's mind*. Chadwick's reflection fits perfectly well at this stage in bringing forth, as well as in focusing, on Newman's experience as a unity in continuous development and growth: «let us take him as a mind of unity; growing, articulating, arranging, acquiring new truth from meditating an old truth or even, though more rarely, from new information found in books; but a man with the same mind all his life; the same despite one conversion at the age of fifteen and another conversion at the age of forty-four; a mind with principles formed early, and then expanded, adapted, recast, and yet recognisably the same principles... This is not to say that the mind stood still; never was a mind so unceasingly in motion. But the motion was always growth, and never revolution».[53]

2.3. Reasonableness of Religion

A very important letter written by Newman during this period provides us with some interesting insights about the method of reasoning that he already possesses, this time in religious matters. Studying the main elements of this letter, written to the editor of *The Christian Observer*, in May 1821,[54] we find a collection of logical and systematic convictions in their embryonic state.

The main scope of this letter is to show that as in scientific matters we can confirm the existence of «contradictions and impossibilities», so, through analogy between mathematics and Christianity, we can also establish that the existence of

---

[53] O. CHADWICK, *Newman*. (Oxford University Press, Oxford 1986) p. 5; for a wider exposition on the concept of 'growth' see R. BOUDENS, '*Growth*: A Key Concept in understanding Newman', *Ephemerides theologicae lovanienses* 69 (1993) 335-353.

[54] *LD* I, pp. 102-104. This letter contains the prelude of a methodological approach which will be typical of Newman in any controversy later on in his life.

such «contradictions and impossibilities» cannot be used as an argument against religion, but, if anything, as an argument for. Furthermore, this analogy draws its own strength from the existence of a proper disposition of the mind, rightly cultivated, which helps one to approach the subject with «consistency and impartiality».

The parting shot of the letter is a statement that «it has often been said» that «mathematical studies prepare the mind for scepticism in religion».[55] Newman, as will be typical of him later on in his life, cannot see any contradiction between scientific knowledge and religion. Yet, at this early stage of the letter, he is not concerned in defending the value of this position. He prefers, rather, to expose the different elements of the argument, thus coming to terms with them.

Through the systematic exposition of the proposed principle, he can then proceed immediately to the primary cause, the root element, which alone dictates the direction of an argument: «no science perhaps is more adapted to confirm our belief in the truth of Christianity than that of mathematics, when cultivated with a proper disposition of the mind».[56] The last few words are the centre piece of the argument. They will be the focal point of the whole letter: the «proper disposition of the mind».

What follows is underlined by this basic truth, serving like a silver thread going through the whole. Having cleared the air and avoided getting caught up in matters of a secondary nature, Newman goes to the root cause from where he can follow the development of the argument. He moves from the apparent argument to the invisible core of the whole issue.

The second point that follows is a presentation of what mathematics is in itself and what kind of relationship exists with the person who is interested in it: «in studying the mathematics,

---
55 *Id.*, p. 102.
56 *Ibid.*

passions and feelings and prejudices are excluded: there is nothing to excite hope, or gratify desire; nothing to be gained or to be lost... and yet even here, when there is no temptation to be dissatisfied with the truth... (as, often unhappily, is the case in matters of religion,) many things occur, at which we cannot but wonder, and for which we can give no reason».[57]

This relationship between the knowledge and the knower leaves space for uncertainty and unanswered questions. It does not satisfy the appetite of wanting to know more.

Newman, in pointing out what mathematics is, is more concerned with how the knowledge, or rather the lack of it, affects the knower; how easy it is for the knower «to think, had we the power to effect any alterations which might appear to us expedient, the arrangements of nature could be rendered far more regular and its machinery less complicated».[58] In other words, the danger is that, even in this sphere of scientific knowledge, we are in a state of not knowing everything.

The real danger is that of falling into «rashness and arrogance... attempting to give an opinion respecting the propriety of the plan approved by the Creator, while our judgement is in its present feeble state, and our knowledge of the system of the universe, and of the adaptation of its parts, is even more limited than that of the fly in the fable, who saw it fit to find fault with the architectural proportions of one of the noblest buildings in the world».[59]

This second point is the turning point of the whole argument. In it Newman examines all the implications of knowledge and its consequences. In exploring truths about mathematical knowledge and helping the reader to accept those same truths, he is simply preparing the ground, in the reader's mind, to accept the conclusion as soon as he moves to the third point. In other words, the second point prepares the strength of the third point

---
57 Id., pp. 102-103.
58 Id., p. 103.
59 Ibid.

which is that of analogy: «apply this confession to religion - how little do we know of the ways of God, and how unequal are our faculties to judge of what we *do* know! Shall we then presume to say, Why was man allowed to fall?... Why is the truth of Christianity allowed to rest so much on historical evidence rather than the sensible perception of miracles; on moral rather than direct mathematical demonstration?»[60]

The whole of Newman's strength is drawn from this analogy. This framework of reasoning gives him enough space to move like a pendulum, to and fro, to strengthen one point by referring to the other and vice-versa. And it is precisely at this point that Newman's methodology tends to demonstrate all its weight and convincing power. Once he is sure of the fixed points, than he moves around like a spider, one move prepares the ground for the next, while each move completes what the previous one has started: «besides the objections arising from the *difficulties* of revelation, a second species of objections may be answered from the same analogy; for we may extend our argument to a defence of those mysteries which have been said to involve *contradictions* and *impossibilities*. How can the Divine Being exist in three Persons? How can God and man be one in Christ?»[61]

The depth and importance of the analogical argument lies on the conditions it presupposes for its fruitful application. «If persons would but consider this analogy, if they would but apply something of the same temper and calm judgement which they do not refuse to science, there would be but few objectors to the truths of the Bible».[62] In examining the difference between truths in science and those in religion, Newman detects that the only difference that exists in their being accepted, or otherwise, is the condition of the knower in dealing with truth. Since scientific

---

60 *Ibid.*, n. 1 Newman himself wrote this footnote: «Many of these questions in religion, and of those above in mathematics, may perhaps admit of a probable answer; there are *some*, however, which cannot be answered».
61 *Id.*, pp. 103-104.
62 *Id.*, p. 104.

truths do not affect the inquirer, therefore they are approached with no prejudice whatsoever: «the conclusions of Newton are implicitly believed, because the arguments which prove their truth are sound. The nature of those conclusions makes no difference in our belief; we acknowledge them whatever they may turn out to be; be they difficult, mysterious, incomprehensible, seemingly contradictory, it matters not: they are *proved*».[63]

Newman at this point asks what would happen, in the scientific realm, if this disposition of the mind were not put into practice: «what would be said to the man, who, instead of sifting the proofs on which these propositions are built, and beginning with the demolition of the premises, should commence with asserting the falsity of the conclusion from some à priori conception of his own fancy, and then proceed, by the help of this assumption of error in the conclusion, to overthrow the reasonings on which it is founded?»[64]

Newman is keen to explore the full consequences of an unproper disposition of the mind in the sphere of science, so that he can transfer the strength of its conclusion to the sphere of religion. Then, he just lets the reader arrive at the conclusion which he himself is heading towards: «yet this very thing is done daily with the Bible. Men begin at the wrong end of the scale of reasoning; and having refuted as they conceive, a doctrine by arguments resting on the basis of pre-conceived ideas, they proceed up the ladder, and arrive at once at the portentous determination, that all the proofs which had been advanced in support of that doctrine, and the book which contains an avowal of that doctrine, must be erroneous».[65]

---

[63] *Ibid.*; Newman himself added the following note: «Footnote: I should add, however, that Christianity does not require us to believe any thing absurd or contradictory: its most incomprehensible doctrines are not opposed to reason, nor are they in reality more calculated to awaken just incredulity than many demonstrable propositions of human science», in *ibid.*, n. 2.
[64] *Ibid.*
[65] *Ibid.*

The Discovery of Conscience

Having arrived at this point, one would think that the point has been made. Yet for Newman the conclusion of any argument does not lie solely in the fact of affirming the truth, but rather in exposing the mechanism of that machinery which can produce other untruths. The reasoning so far is centred on the issue of truths in both science and religion. The final point, by way of conclusion, highlights the reality that is contained behind the application of an unproper disposition of the mind: «it is in this spirit they lay down the unphilosophical axiom, 'a true religion can have no mysteries'; and then infer either that Christianity is not a true religion, because it contains mysteries - or that it contains no mysteries, because it is a true religion. Nothing can be more illogical, more unworthy of a person of science than such conclusions; but where the passions of men are aroused, and their interests concerned, little regard is paid to consistency or impartiality».[66]

This letter, containing, as it does, important elements that will develop later on in Newman's life, is of great value for various reasons. First of all, it outlines the basis of his methodological approach in controversy; secondly, this letter offers, for the first time, the argument of analogy; thirdly, it points to the introduction of that theme, «faith and reason», that will be treated later on in the *University Sermons*, in some *Parochial and Plain Sermons*, and further developed in the *Essay in Aid of a Grammar of Assent*.

This letter does present some questions about when did Newman really encounter for the first time the two principles of «analogy» and the «logical cogency of Faith». We are told that «it was about this date (1823), I suppose, that I read Bishop Butler's Analogy; the study of which has been to so many, as it was to me, an era in their religious opinions».[67]

---
66 *Id.*, pp. 103-104.
67 *Apol.* p. 10.

Yet in his *Letters and Dairies* we find that the date when he «began Butler's Analogy» is June 25th 1825.[68] After the examination of the letter to the *Christian Observer* of 1821,[69] one is tempted to ask certain questions not only about the timing of these fundamental moments of his life, but even more so about how and when the encounter with Butler and his ideas did actually take place.[70]

2.4. Graduality as Basis for Development

It will be one of Newman's features to insist on the «gradual growth» of the Christian within his *Parochial and Plain Sermons*. The theme cannot be simply understood from a quantitative point of view, the growth of holiness. In Newman it needs to be seen against a wider spectrum, the qualitative one, growth in holiness, growth towards the wholeness of truth, growth as «change» in the sense of the person being in and towards «development».[71] It is against this background that the notion of «graduality» contains its real meaning.

In a letter from his «dear Friend» Walter Mayers, in June 1817, Newman receives the following advice: «(I) shall rejoice to hear your views are daily clearer and brighter, the slow and gradual progress to Divine truth is the favourite with me, it is I am inclined to believe the most certain and lasting, add to which

---

[68] *LD* I, p. 238; similarly, in his *AW* p. 78 Newman wrote the following: «Besides Sumner, Butler's celebrated work, which he studied about the year 1825, had, as was natural, an important indirect effect upon him in the same direction, as placing his doctrinal views on a broad philosophical basis, with which an emotional religion could have little sympathy».

[69] «My opinion of the Christian Observer is this, that it is a humbug. You must use exertions. That letter was more like the composition of an old man, than of a youth just entering life with energy and aspirations»; this is what his father told him about the letter, in *AW* pp. 179-180; see also *LD* I, p. 117.

[70] On this subject T. VARGISH has come out with the conclusion that «Newman like Whately, enjoys demonstrating that most of our certitudes rest ultimately on convergences of probabilities, and that religious convictions are therefore as 'reasonable' as most assumptions held by sceptics... Whatever one thinks of the validity of this argumentative gambit, it seems likely that though

it is the usual mode of God's proceeding».[72] This becomes for Newman, as it is already for Mayers, one of the frequent truths in his sermons and later on it will feature both in his *Essay on the Development of Christian Doctrine* and *Essay in Aid of a Grammar of Assent*. The more he advances in life, the more «graduality» takes the shape of «development». The whole notion, thus, is further enhanced when it is later used as a tool applied to the development of ideas. The sense of progress and «graduality» which we encounter at this stage, is enhanced in the sermons, and will be the basis for the idea of «development».

The notions both of change and «graduality» are part of Newman's mental mechanism at this time. Twice, in his *Early Journals* and *Autobiographical Memoirs*, he refers to a meeting with his father where, amongst other things, the latter told him: «depend upon it, no one's principles can be established at twenty. Your opinions in two or three years will certainly, *certainly* change. I have seen many instances of the same kind. Take care, I repeat. You are on dangerous ground... Do not commit yourself. Do nothing ultra. Many men say and do things, when young, which they would fain retract when older, but for shame they cannot».[73]

This notion of change must have certainly hit him hard because, later, in his *Autobiographical Memoir*, he returns on this event and writes that: «Yet very few years passed, before,

---

Newman's ultimate source for the argument for probability was Butler, his polemics came from Whately», in *Newman: The Contemplation of Mind*. (The Catholic Book Club, London 1973) pp. 13, 14.

71 The following quote from *GA* expresses well how *growth* and *development* are compatible in Newman's idea: «It is that, though man cannot change what he is born with, he is a being of progress with relation to his perfection and characteristic good», in *GA* p. 349

72 *LD* I, p. 37; the following is to be found in a letter by the same Mayers, probably around mid-June 1821: «I am glad to perceive that the Lord is leading you into all truth and that you are brought to bow to the decisions of Scripture, it is my dear friend the triumph of grace, and hence so many wise in this world are in the worst sense fools», in *id.*, p. 109.

73 *AW* pp. 179, 82; see also *LD* I, p. 117.

against his confident expectations, his Father's words about him came true».[74]

It is worth quoting from a letter, written in 1837, in which he recalls this period and the developments that have taken place in the meantime. Newman is writing in response to a letter accusing him of unfairly criticizing the Evangelicals for not insisting «on the object and fruits of faith». The answer to that accusation contains the same truth about the growth of ideas and their necessary development that he experiences at the stage of his life under examination. «I will add, as may naturally be surmised from my acquaintance with Mr. Scott's writings, that I have not always held my present views. It is now above fourteen years since I first *began* to hold them; but they have been the growth of years. They have formed within... At last they burst these external bonds from their increase in strength and definite proportions».[75]

This letter, in retrospect, confirms what will be later termed by Newman, in clear and precise terms, as the «gradual advancement to the fulness of one's original destiny». «It is his gift to be the creator of his own sufficiency; and to be emphatically self-made. This is the law of his being, which he cannot escape; and whatever is involved in that law he is bound, or rather he is carried on, to fulfil».[76]

---

74 *AW* p. 82; other events in Newman's life are characterized by the idea of *graduality* in the sense of change and development. One such event is the influence exercised on Newman through his friendship with Hawkins which he termed as having «a great and gradual effect» upon him.
75 *LD* VI, pp. 129-130.
76 *GA* p. 349; Newman recognizes that the Oriel experience «opened upon him a theological career... bringing him across those various influences personal and intellectual, and the teaching of those various schools of ecclesiastical thought whereby the religious sentiment in his mind, which had been his blessing from the time he left school, was gradually developed and formed and brought on to its legitimate issue», in *AW* 63; «Newman himself had always behaved in a manner more consonant with belief in progressive sanctification than in a sudden and irreversible assurance of salvation», in M. TREVOR, *Newman, the Pillar of the Cloud*. (Macmillan, London 1962) vol. I, p. 58.

2.5. Meeting of Opposites

One of the areas which has created difficulties in studying Newman has been that which concerns the study of his character and, in a more accurate way, how his mind proceeds. Studies so far have dealt with the study of his character in a general and global way.[77] Through the same methodology adopted by Walgrave in analysing Newman's character, the wealth that is found in any source belonging to this period can be further highlighted.

Walgrave starts by interpreting the notion of «polarity» as two communicating poles, negative and positive, between which electricity is created. He is indebted to other authors for this application, namely to Coleridge,[78] and recognizes in it a model through which we can understand Newman's mind.

Walgrave writes that «polarity» «is the basic inner law of all that happens».[79] The first polarity that exists at this very level, that of «understanding and reasoning», is the way through which the mind tackles an outside reality. Both are needed, both are different. Understanding «is the faculty of abstraction, conceptual definition and articulation, discursive inference, etc. It is the lower faculty of knowing».[80] Reasoning being «the higher faculty of metaphysical intuition or the all penetrating speechless awareness and contemplation of the ultimate dimension of depth in all nature. The relation between reason and understanding is already a relation of polarity».[81]

Polarity can also be termed as dependence of one element on the other, whereby understanding, not simply taken as

---

77 See J.H. WALGRAVE, *J.H. Newman: His Personality, His Principles, His Fundamental Doctrines*, pp. 9-20; P. SOBRY, *Newman en zijn Idea of a University*, as quoted by J.H. WALGRAVE, in *id.*, p. 15; R.C. SOLBY, *The Principle of Reserve in the Writings of John Henry Cardinal Newman*. (Oxford 1975) as quoted by J.H. WALGRAVE, in *id.*, p. 16.
78 See O. BARFIELD, *What Coleridge Thought* (London 1972).
79 J.H. WALGRAVE, *J.H. Newman: His Personality, His Principles, His Fundamental Doctrines*, p. 11.
80 *Ibid.*
81 *Ibid.*

accumulation of loosely connected ideas, leads to the enhancement of reason. Thus, reason is dependent on understanding for its call to elaborate the collected data.

This first mode offers an explanation how the unity of the mind necessarily presupposes two forces «which, through tension or opposition, have to keep one another in balance and continually to restore this balance in all processes of nature and thought».[82] What is more important is the realization that these opposing forces are intimately connected not only between themselves but also with a basic antecedent unity: «this dynamic duality, springing from a basic antecedent unity, is the condition of possibility of all creative processes».[83]

Applying this method in Newman's case, evidence can be seen of how, even at this early period of his life, there is the forming of this mental attitude for which he will become notorious later on in his life. He is aware of the opposing elements that exist within him when he looks and ponders on idea – the understanding of it and the reasoning about it. Moments of crises become privileged moments where this attitude comes out in full force. His letter writing proves to be a privileged source where this whole inner reality continuously comes out without being mediated.

The examination for his 'BA' degree is a particular case in point. He is aware of the event in itself and at the same time he is conscious about how this event is going to affect him. What enhances this dualism of articulation and intuition is the reference to «the condition of possibility of all creative processes», that antecedent unity, his relation between himself and his Creator: «I cannot *think* much of the school without *wishing* much to distinguish myself in them – that much wishing would make me discontented if I did not succeed; therefore it would be coveting,

---
82 *Ibid.*
83 *Id.*, p. 12.

for *then* we covet when we desire a thing so earnestly as to be dissatisfied if we fail in getting it. *I* am labouring at the means, but the *success* of those means is not in my hands; I am doing *my* part, but *God* chooseth the event and I know he will choose for the best. It therefore is not only my duty but my privilege to take no thought for the morrow... Do you therefore, dearest sister, wish for me to obtain that which is best for me, and for me to get high honours here; for then, whether I succeed or fail, I shall have the comfort of feeling assured that I have obtained *real* advantage and not apparent».[84]

Failure or success are valued both in relation to themselves and to the person concerned. Yet what is not missing is the presence of Him who gives life and meaning to that antecedent unity within the person which is the seat of identity. Events like these, interpreted through the model of polarity do not indicate a confused mind, but one which is quite conscious and comfortable with the diversity, since this is unified by a larger reality.

Another model of polarity that Walgrave adopts is that of «doubt and certitude».[85] He is of the opinion that in Newman there is the encounter both of the person who «is highly sensitive to difficulties and objections» and, on the other hand, «he has no doubt that man's mind, being made for truth, is capable to attain truth by the right exercise of his intellectual capacities».[86] Walgrave goes as far as to call Newman «a kind of an intellectual squint. He at once sees yes and no, *pro* and *contra*».[87]. As with the former model, even here the whole moves forward in a «fruitfully balanced way».[88] What is at stake here, though, is the risk of misunderstanding

---

84   Letter to Jemima Newman, in *LD* I, p. 85.
85   J.H. WALGRAVE,
J.H. Newman: His Personality, His Principles, His Fundamental Doctrines, p. 18.
86   *Id.*, p. 19.
87   *Ibid.*
88   *Ibid.*

Newman and of disqualifying his personality as lacking that necessary equilibrium he is supposed to have.[89]

The following reflection, also taken from the period before his 'BA' examination, exposes a personality with this «doubt and certitude» behaviour. He talks about being comfortable and calm, yet he also speaks of a heart being fearful. He looks at his soul as being «bright» yet «from a different point of view» all he can see is weakness, darkness and cold, only to return again to the first polarity of strength in faith together with light: «here at Oxford I am most comfortable. The quiet and stillness of every thing around me tends to calm and lull those emotions, which the near prospect of my grand examination and a heart too solicitous about fame and too fearful of failure are continually striving to excite... If I look at the mercies of God, my soul is bright; when I view myself from a different point of view, I wonder how I can dare to assert any growth in grace... I am weak, dark, and cold now, and then I trust I shall be strong in the faith, light, and fervent... It is my daily, and (I hope) heartfelt prayer, that I may not get any honours here, if they are to be the least cause of sin to me».[90]

Another example, also from the same period, confirms how easy it is to draw the conclusion that in Newman there exists a «lack of equilibrium». He himself is aware of it, in actual fact he calls it «hypocrisy» and «mockery», and, yet, it is this same awareness and the way he deals with it which provides the key to understand him: «yet with all the earnestness I assume, how little does my heart go with my words, or feel their extent. A very distinct thing it is to say so, when the trial is at a distance, and when the temptation comes in full force... I fear much more from failure, than I hope for success. Still may be I continue to pray,

---

[89] Walgrave is critical of Sobry. For the latter the tension is not productive of anything but rather indicative to a lack of balance. Walgrave on his part is keen to show that this tension can not only be described through the polar model but also holds the key for understanding Newman, see *ibid*.
[90] Letter to Francis William Newman, in *LD* I, p. 83; see also *AW* pp. 45-46.

'Let me get no honours here, if they are to be the slightest cause of sin to my soul'. But, while saying this, I often find that I am acting the part of a very hypocrite; I am buoyed with the secret idea, that by thus leaving the event in the hands of God, when I pray, He may be induced, as a reward for so proper a spirit, to grant me my desire. Thus my prayer is a mockery».[91]

These extracts provide not only an example of the existing polarities in Newman's mind, but they also show the productive tension that exists between them. Walgrave, strengthening the idea of an «antecedent unity», develops further this notion by saying that «the way Newman's mind moves between all kinds of difficulties may best be described by the term 'orientation' a prudent advance between opposites under the guiding light of the polar star».[92]

3. Oxford: Fellow and Tutor at Oriel

Newman attributes to this phase of his life some interesting discoveries on the level of thought that will later play an important role in his writings. Newman's election to the Oriel fellowship can only take place because of the system adopted for such posts by the College. Oriel was the first College: «to elect its Fellows from the University at large on their intellectual merits. This reform was the work of its great Provost, Eveleigh, who introduced a method of examination conducted upon the principle of ascertaining, not what a man had read, but what he was like. The result was remarkable».[93]

His election, on 12 April 1822,[94] is considered by Newman himself as «of all days the most memorable... He never wished

---

[91] Letter to Walter Mayers, in *LD* I, p. 87.
[92] J.H. WALGRAVE, *J.H. Newman: His Personality, His Principles, His Fundamental Doctrines*, p. 19.
[93] G. FABER, *Oxford Apostles. A Character Study of the Oxford Movement*. (Pelican Books, Harmondsworth – Middlesex 1954) p. 54; see also *AW* p. 65.
[94] *LD* I, pp. 127-131.

any thing better or higher than, in the words of the epitaph, 'to live and die a fellow of Oriel'».[95] This election means for him a whole new opening. At hindsight, Newman himself can rightfully say that the Oriel experience: «opened upon him a theological career... bringing him across those various influences personal and intellectual, and the teaching of those various schools of ecclesiastical thought whereby the religious sentiment in his mind, which had been his blessing from the time he left school, was gradually developed and formed and brought on to its legitimate issue».[96]

This is in a nutshell the meaning of Oriel. It is from here that he goes on to develop, amongst other things, the great ability to think for himself through Whately. Through Hawkins he discovers the principle of «tradition» with its «most fruitful consequences».[97] It is through his Oriel experience that he comes in contact with «liberalism», «that system of opinion (that) came before me at Oxford».[98] It is equally during this same period that he starts shredding off the remaining tenets of Evangelicalism, discovering the ideas of Butler and, above all, entering the realm of the Fathers.

3.1. Whately and Hawkins: Thinking and Tradition

Launched thus abruptly into a *milieu* so different from any to which he had hitherto been accustomed, Newman, overcome by shyness, enveloped himself in a cloak of unvarying silence, which, seeing the cordial welcome given him, caused his colleagues some misgiving.[99]

---

95 *AW* p. 63.
96 *Ibid.*
97 *Apol.* p. 9.
98 *Ibid.*
99 L. BOUYER, *Newman: His Life and Spirituality*, p. 59; «in the first place they had to deal with his extreme shyness. It disconcerted them to find that with all their best efforts they could not draw him out or get him to converse.

Whately, «the man of generous and warm heart»,[100] takes him by the hand. Newman's memory of Whately is firmly centred on how the latter helps the young fellow to open his mind, to teach him how to think and to use his reason. Whately, on his part, will soon discover the new fellow to be «the clearest-headed man he knew»,[101] and, later, will admit that he could only help Newman in his journey but he would never have succeeded, in any way, to condition his growth or direct his thought. He gives Newman the chance to grow but does not succeed in making Newman take the way he wants to.

For Newman, Whately's memory is very much in relation to the refinement of his own mind. He is encouraged to discover self-confidence in his ability as a thinker – «He had done his work towards me or nearly so, when he had taught me to see with my own eyes and to walk with my own feet»[102] – and that the idea of the Church became clearer: «what he did for me in point of religious opinion, was, first, to teach me the existence of the Church, as a substantive body or corporation; next to fix in me those anti-Erastian views of Church polity,[103] which were one of the prominent features of the Tractarian movement... I am not aware of any other religious opinion which I owe to Dr. Whately».[104]

Besides these views,[105] the importance of Whately's role on Newman's methodological approach and in pushing him further

---

He shrank into himself, when his duty was to meet their advances... his very admiration of his new associates made a sudden intimacy with them impossible to him... And then there was in addition that real isolation of thought and spiritual solitariness, which was the result of his Calvinistic beliefs», in *AW* p. 65.

100 *Apol.* p. 11.
101 *AW* p. 66.
102 *Apol.* p. 11.
103 The idea of the Church both as independent of State and its right to retain its property though separated from the State; see *id.*, p. 13.
104 *Id.*, pp. 12, 13.
105 «Much as I owe to Oriel, in the way of mental improvement, to none, as I think, do I owe so much as to you. I know who it was who first gave me heart to look about me after my election, and taught me to think correctly,

in his reflection, cannot be underestimated. It is through Whately that he comes in contact, in a clearly defined way, with the first element of the analogical argument of which he will further discover, a couple of years later, through Butler. Previous mention of the analogical approach confirms how in Newman there already existed some form of this argumentation. Surely, the contact with Whately proves beneficial in clarifying even more this model. «Newman like Whately, enjoys demonstrating that most of our certitudes rest ultimately on convergences of probabilities... It seems likely that though Newman's ultimate source for the argument for probability was Butler, his polemics came from Whately».[106]

Mr. Hawkins, a man of «a very high character» who «had an abiding sense of duty» is, in Newman's mind, «clear headed and independent in his opinions, candid in argument, tolerant of the view of others, honest as a religious inquirer».[107] It is on Hawkins that the young Newman «was thrown in a special way... he found in Mr. Hawkins a kind and able adviser».[108] As with Whately, Hawkins' contribution on Newman goes beyond the actual events which occasion it. Through Hawkins, Newman recognizes that the mild elements of Evangelicalism, that he

---

and (strange office for an instructor,) to rely upon myself. Nor can I forget, that it has been at your kind suggestion, that I have been since led to employ myself in the consideration of several subjects, which I cannot doubt have been very beneficial to my mind», in *LD* I, p. 307; «Whately's strongest subject was the formal logic of Aristotle, which he supported by English Aristotelians like Bishop Butler, and Francis Bacon. Significantly, he read little else. "My own learning", he wrote in his journal, "is of a very singular kind, being more purely elementary than anyone's I know. I am acquainted with the elements of most things, and that more accurately than many who are versed in them, but I know nothing thoroughly such studies as are intrinsically of an elementary character"», in M.R. O'CONNELL, *The Oxford Conspirators. A History of the Oxford Movement 1833-1845.* (University Press of America, Lanham/New York – London 1969) p. 71, quoting from A.D. CULLER, *The Imperial Intellect.* (New Haven 1955) p. 39.

106 T. VARGISH, *Newman: The Contemplation of Mind*, pp. 13, 14; see note n. 87.
107 *AW* p. 76.
108 *Id.*, p. 77.

still holds at the time, are slowly disappearing. It is during this period of friendship that Newman preaches what he calls his first sermon.[109] Hawkins immediately criticizes his approach where he «divided the Christians world into two classes, the one all darkness, the one all light, whereas, said Mr. Hawkins, it is impossible for us in fact to draw such a line of demarcation across any body of men, large or small, because [difference in] religious or moral excellence is a matter of degree. Men are not either saints or sinners; but they are not so good as they should be, and better than they might be, – more or less converted to God, as it may happen».[110]

The criticism by Hawkins can be best understood, first, by taking it from the point of view of contents. It helped Newman, in the long term, to steer clear of any Evangelical turn which he could have otherwise taken. Although this will not be the only cause to make him take his distance,[111] it proves to be a very important one, coming as it is from a person towards whom Newman feels a certain affinity on the level of thinking.

A second point of view is that which concerns how is Newman affected by Hawkins. In his *Autobiographical Memoir* he writes: «criticism such as this, which of course he did not deliver once for all, but as occasions offered, and which, when Newman dissented, he maintained and enforced, had a great though a gradual effect upon the latter».[112] This is all very enlightening when considered beyond the importance of the present stage and seen within the context of his whole life. This «gradual» aspect of

---

109 see *LD* I, p. 177.
110 *AW* p. 77; see also *Id.*, p. 201, and *LD* I, p. 179.
111 Newman also recognizes that Sumner's *Apostolical Preaching* «was successful in the event beyond anything else, in routing out evangelical doctrines for Mr. Newman's creed», in *AW* p. 77; «John Bird Sumner's *Apostolical Preaching considered in an Examination of St. Paul's Epistles,* 1815, was written for preachers, and in considering the actual preaching of the Apostles the whole teaching of the New Testament is shown to run counter to the Calvinistic doctrines of predestination, individual election, and efficacious grace», in *LD* I, p. 185.
112 *AW* p. 77.

any change which takes in Newman's life, tends to acquire certain value in understanding his mind process and the development of his ideas.

The meeting with Hawkins confirms the typical model of Newman's movement towards an idea examined previously – he proceeds by inclusion. He takes a stand, he lets himself be criticized, taking in all the criticism. Than he proceeds in a dialectical way: the idea is confronted by «dissent, maintenance and enforcement»,[113] the polarity movement. Finally, there is growth and enrichment: «I think I really desire the truth, and would embrace it, wherever I found it».[114]

Against this background, the words Newman dedicates to Hawkins in his *Apologia* can be fully appreciated: «he had been in many ways of great service to my mind. He was the first who taught me to weigh my words, and to be cautious in my statements. He led me to that mode of limiting and clearing my sense in discussion and in controversy, and of distinguishing between cognate ideas, and of obviating mistakes by anticipation, which to my surprise has been since considered, even in quarters friendly to me, to savour of the polemics of Rome. He is a man of exact mind himself».[115]

Besides this «gradual development» in his thinking, Newman also attributes to Hawkins «another great philosophical principle».[116] It is the doctrine on «Tradition» as «a main element in ascertaining and teaching the truths of Christianity».[117] This subject, being novel for Newman at the time, opens up for him an area which he himself will develop later on, with far reaching consequences. At this stage it is worth recording how Newman perceives this breakthrough and how he recalls it in his *Apologia*: «the sacred text was never intended to teach doctrine, but only

---
113 *Ibid.*
114 *Id.*, p. 78.
115 *Apol.* p. 8.
116 *AW* p. 78; see also L. Bouyer, *Newman: His Life and Spirituality*, pp. 63-65.
117 *AW* p. 78.

to prove it, and that, if we would learn doctrine, we must have recourse to the formularies of the Church; for instance to the Catechism and to the Creeds. He considers, that, after learning from the doctrines of Christianity, the inquirer must verify them by Scripture. This view most true in its outline, most fruitful in its consequences, opened upon me a large field of thought».[118]

Whately and Hawkins are two very important players in Newman's youth who have an impact on the growth which is taking place.[119] He recalls both with great admiration and, above all, respect. The fact that in both cases future events take a different turn from what one would have hoped for, does not in any way diminish the singular contribution they make towards the development of his intellectual journey. On Whately's death, Newman gives witness to the depth of the influence the former had on him and the affection that outlives the differences that followed: «the past is not dead to those, who, as the writer of these lines, owed much to him then, and who, amid the skirmishes of religious controversy, have loved him all along and to the end... Sad to say, it is our ordinary experience in life that men are cowards to those who make fight and bullies to those who yield. So was it not with a man, who, whatever were his faults, was in generosity, in boldness of speech, and in independence of mind, a prince... he would in private take the young, the timid and bashful, by the hand, raise their courage, open their minds, and make them think... It was his to preach the simple but momentous principles, that religion need not be afraid of argument, that faith can fearlessly appeal to right reason, that inquiry does but strengthen the foundations of revelation, and that the Church is founded on truth, and truth alone».[120]

---

118 *Apol.* pp. 9-10.
119 See M.R. O'Connell *The Oxford Conspirators. A History of the Oxford Movement 1833-1845*, pp. 116-117; see also a detailed study by Hollis which considers these two personalities in a broader Church of England contest, in C. Hollis, *Newman and the Modern World* (The Catholic Book Club, London 1967) pp. 27-33.
120 *AW* pp. 84-85.

3.2. Butler: Analogy and Probability

The influence of Whately and Hawkins is part of a larger picture which is slowly taking shape. Bouyer sums up their role in the following terms: «Newman began on the book at what seems like a providential moment. Whately had succeeded in giving back his freedom of conscience. Whately and Hawkins between them, leading him to abandon the Evangelical 'closed shop', brought him into view of some of the main features of Catholic tradition in a rejuvenated and refurbished form».[121]

The reading of Bishops Butler's *Analogy* is, for Newman, a source of ideas which, in the long term, will constitute an important imprint of his thinking. From Butler, Newman further strengthens his idea of «a visible Church, the oracle of truth and a pattern of sanctity, of the duties of external religion, and of the historical character of Revelation».[122] These ideas, connected with those discovered through Whately and Hawkins, are also in relation to two other religious principles which provide more food for Newman's thought.

The first is: «the very idea of an analogy between the separate works of God leads to the conclusion that the system which is of less importance is economically or sacramentally connected with the more momentous system, and of this conclusion the theory, to which I was inclined as a boy, viz. the unreality of material phenomena is an ultimate resolution».[123]

This principle features as one of the basic elements of that development that characterizes Newman's way of thinking. He is clear about the fact that «the starting point of Butler's whole philosophy, so clearly conveyed in a passage from Origen... imparts to his view of the world, and of life, the unity which it was seeking... 'He who believes the Scripture to have proceeded

---

121 L. BOUYER, *Newman: His Life and Spirituality*, p. 70.
122 *Apol.* p. 10.
123 *Ibid.*

from him who is the Author of Nature may well expect to find the same sort of difficulties in it as are found in the constitution of Nature'».[124]

This principle of «analogy», already found in the letter to the *Christian Observer*,[125] finds the right authority to highlight its importance for Newman. Through this principle Newman not only discovers more strength in his argument to overcome the dilemma of the contemporary presence of mystery and contradictions in religion, but through this method of thinking their very existence is the proof of the larger picture of revelation. This explains why Newman could never accept that any scientific theory (e.g. the Darwinian theory) was in any way a danger to revelation.

Then follows the second religious principle: «Butler's doctrine that Probability is the guide of life, led me, at least under the teaching to which a few years later I was introduced, to the question of the logical cogency of Faith, on which I have written so much».[126]

The importance of this second principle is evidenced from what Newman will publish later on in his life. It is not the aim of this study to enter into the whole area of «probability», its essential place in Newman's thought and its development. But it will suffice to highlight, through a reflection written to his mother, how at this early stage he is working towards the formation of its first elements: «listen to my theory. As each individual has certain instincts of right and wrong, antecedently to reasoning, on which he acts and rightly so, which perverse reasoning may supplant, which then can hardly be regained, but, if regained, will be regained from a different source, from reasoning not from nature, so, I think, has the world of men collectively. God gave them truths in His miraculous revelations, and other

---

124 L. BOUYER, *Newman: His Life and Spirituality*, p. 72.
125 *LD* I, pp. 102-104.
126 *Apol.* pp. 10-11.

truths, in the unsophisticated infancy of notions, scarcely less necessary and divine. These are transmitted as 'the wisdom of our ancestors', through men, many of whom cannot enter into them, or receive them themselves, still on, on, from age to age, not the less truths, because many of the generations, through which they are transmitted, are unable to prove them, but hold them either from honest and pious feeling (it may be) or from bigotry or from prejudice. That they are truths, it is most difficult to prove; for great men alone can prove great ideas and grasp them - Such a mind was Hooker's, such Butler's».[127]

3.3. The First Encounter with Liberalism

During his undergraduate years Newman is taken up by the Evangelical view of religion. Yet, there are other views and ideas which are challenging his mind. «At this time [1820] he seems to have been half conscious of some mental or moral change within him, which he fully recognized in the following year, when he took a retrospect of his undergraduate experiences».[128]

In a letter to Walter Mayers, written in January 1821, he shares these same feelings and fears: «I trust I may have always the same content and indifference to the world, which is at present the *prevailing* principle in my heart - yet I have great fears of backsliding».[129] The following lines, also written in 1821, shed more

---
127 *LD* II, pp. 130-131; the whole correspondence with his brother Charles which starts in December 1823 and went on till 1830, is also linked to the subject we are treating here. The choice to deal with it later is dependent on the fact that both this correspondence and some of the sermons written by Newman at the time are closely associated; see also *Apol.* p. 18: «The Christian Year made its appearance in 1827. It is not necessary, and scarlet becoming, to praise a book which has become one of the classics of the language... I think I am not wrong in saying, that the two main intellectual truths which it brought home to me, were the same two, which I had learned from Butler».
128 *AW* p. 45.
129 *LD* I, p. 99.

light on the real Newman: «In 1819 and the beginning of 1820 I hoped great things for myself, not liking to go into the Church, but to the Law. I attended the History Lectures (Professorial), hearing that the names were reported to the Minister».[130] He recalls these hopes as «dreams of a secular ambition, which were quite foreign to his frame of mind in 1817».[131]

All this helps to locate the real Newman as he entered the Oriel Common Room. His mind has the ability to be receptive and critical in relation to the different ideas he encounters. More is to come. The liberal tendencies of the time present themselves to Newman, only to become, some time later, the enemy that he has to deal with for the rest of his life.

The environment which is going to be his new life is made up of men who are enjoying great influence in Oxford at the time. The Oriel common room is the place «of keen hard talk... Its members were nicknamed 'the Noetics'... all of them men who began their lives, if they did not continue them, by putting reason before authority... To these 'Noetics' it must have seemed that the intellectual future of Oxford and of England was theirs».[132]

Newman detects the roots of this line of thinking and slowly becomes acquainted with it. All this is taking place when, at the same time, he is distancing himself from the Evangelical view of religion. The danger is that from one extreme he could easily end up into another: «The truth is, I was beginning to prefer intellectual excellence to moral; I was drifting in the direction of the Liberalism of the day».[133]

This shift in «excellence», promulgated by the liberals, is taking place in Newman's mind. The elements that constitute the basis for the liberal experience are the same that are directing Newman's inner experience in this particular juncture of his life,

---
130 *AW* p. 45.
131 *Ibid.*
132 G. FABER, *Oxford Apostles. A Character Study of the Oxford Movement* (Pelican Books, Harmondsworth - Middlesex 1954) pp. 54, 94.
133 *Apol.* p. 14.

that is «the broadminded Liberals played down the supernatural in religion. Natural goodness and respectability sufficed; little room was left for the intervention of God, and His grace and sacraments were disparaged in consequence. This was the kind of 'liberalism' to which Newman was drawn as his Evangelicalism evaporated».[134]

He recognizes in his *Apologia* a «certain disdain for Antiquity which had been growing on me now for several years. It showed itself in some flippant language against the Fathers in the Encyclopedia Metropolitana, about whom I knew little at the time».[135]

Yet, in all this, Newman's mind is not yet «locked» on a definite course. The two events which he considers to be the cause of awakening him from this «dream», at the end of 1827, are his illness and the death of his sister Mary.[136] These «two great blows» change his course from heading towards a definite liberal tendency.

In a letter to Joseph Blanco White, just few months after his sister's death, Newman reflects about the role of the «intellect» vis-à-vis the «right moral feeling». In this letter Newman starts taking his side against that liberal tendency which exalts the role of the intellect above anything else: «for *words* are not *feelings* - nor is intellect ηθοσ - Intellect seems to be but the attendant and servant of right moral feeling in this (sic) own weak and dark state of being - defending it when attacked, accounting for it, and explaining it in a poor way to others. - It supplies the medium of communication between mind and mind - yet only to a certain extent - and when we think we can detect honest principle, purity of heart and a single eye, it is irrational to delay the recognition of these real excellences till we have settled subordinate points, to exalt what are but means to an end, and make expressed

---

134 C.S. DESSAIN, *Newman*, p. 10; *AW* p. 83.
135 *Apol.* p. 14.
136 *LD* II, pp. 37, 47; see also *AW* pp. 212-213.

opinions and formal statements an objection to our *believing* in the existence of moral feelings in others which by the exercise of common sense we may actually see».[137]

This letter has no pretension to be a systematic analysis about the liberal idea. Meant simply to be a sharing of ideas with Blanco White, it succinctly hits at the root cause of the whole liberal movement: the supremacy of the intellect above moral feeling. In doing so, it shows the stand Newman is now taking within the Oriel common room.

The same is to be found in another letter belonging to the same period: «In all human works, it is our duty individually to discriminate between correct and incorrect opinions by our own judgment, informed - as it may be - by knowledge of scripture and by sound religious feeling».[138] What Newman writes later on in his *Apologia* as a definition of «liberalism», can already be traced to these letters and reflections.

In two of his letters, written in 1830, an explicit mention is made of liberalism and its main dangers. Arguing against any change in the Athanasian Creed, since some think that «certain parts offend certain minds», he asks if «there (is) not on the other hand an extreme danger of countenancing the false liberality of the age, which would fain have it believed that differences of *opinion* are of slight consequences?»[139] In a second letter he writes: «the tendency of the age is towards *liberalism* - i.e. a thinking established notions worth nothing - in this system of opinions a disregard of religion is included».[140] In both these letters, Newman, while referring to that area of immediate concern around which the issue is centred, exposes the root cause of the liberal idea: the «differences of opinion» and the «established notion (as) worth nothing».

---

137 *LD* II, p. 60.
138 *Id.*, p. 87.
139 *Id.*, p. 191; similar letter *id.*, p. 185, the word used is «the vain conceit of the age».
140 *Id.*, pp. 264-265

At this stage Newman is already well engaged with the liberals and the battle lines of both camps are drawn.

If the reflections of 1828 and 1830 are to be compared with what he writes in 1864, in his *Apologia*, the similarity is evident: «Liberalism then is the mistake of subjecting to human judgment those revealed doctrines which are in their nature beyond and independent of it, and of claiming to determine on intrinsic grounds the truth and value of propositions which rest for their reception simply on the external authority of the Divine Word».[141]

This detection of the dangerous consequences of liberalism on the idea of religion, unfortunately, is not common knowledge by those who hold liberalism dear. He himself is quite certain that the liberals «would have protested against their being supposed to place reason before faith, or knowledge before devotion; yet I do consider that they unconsciously encouraged and successfully introduced into Oxford a license of opinion which went far beyond them».[142]

Walgrave calls Newman's intuitiveness at this stage as that of a «psychological genius that was to expose them, to penetrate the recesses of their thought hidden even from them and to foresee the conclusions liberalism was later to draw and which lay already in germ, unperceived, in the principles of his friends».[143]

---

141 *Apol.* p. 288.
142 *Id.*, pp. 288-289; «they were well aware of their eminence. With full confidence in their intellectual prowess, they set out boldly to solve all problems solely by the light of a trained intellect... They attached greater importance to breadth of view and logical consistency than to the authority of the Church and doctrinal orthodoxy. Their standpoint was wholly rationalistic and superficial, and they detached such notions as sin and virtue from their religious context and their connection with conscience, to treat them in terms of autonomous reason and in a purely humanistic setting... In spite of this, the Noetics were Anglicans loyal to their Church and were motivated by the best intentions; but they failed to discern the impasse to which their movement was inevitably heading», in J.H. WALGRAVE, *Newman the Theologian*, pp. 32-33.
143 *Ibid.*; see T.C. HUMMEL, 'John Henry Newman and the Oriel Noetics', *Anglican Theological Review* 74 (1992) 203-215, this study offers an interesting and

3.4. The Devotion to the Fathers

The interest in the literature of the Fathers has different phases with varied importance attached to them. Studying his own reflections on the theme, four different periods of interest can be traced during which Newman was engaged with the Fathers.[144] The different stages are recognized by Newman himself and so is the importance each one of them holds in relation to the development of his thought.

The first interest in patristic literature goes back to the time of his first conversion. This contact with the Fathers «produced a deep impression» on Newman: «I read Joseph Milner's Church History, and was nothing short of enamoured of the long extracts from St. Augustine, St. Ambrose and the other Fathers which I found there. I read them as being the religion of the primitive Christians».[145] This interest continues until his fellowship at Oriel: «my testimony, then, is as follows. Even when I was a boy, my thoughts were turned to the early Church, and especially to the early Fathers, by the perusal of the Calvinist John Milner's Church History, and I have never lost, I never have suffered a suspension of the impression, deep and most pleasurable, which his sketches of St. Ambrose and St. Augustine left on my mind. From that time the vision of the Fathers was always, to my imagination, I may say, a paradise of delight to the contemplation of which I

---

detailed examination of the effects of the liberal ideas on the notion of doctrinal development and how Newman had to struggle to arrive at his theory of doctrinal development, overcoming the relativistic approach of the liberal tendency.

144 We take into consideration the Anglican period as the span where these four phases took place. In the following *Chapters* the role of the Fathers will be further .

145 *Apol.* pp. 6-7; «it seems, indeed, clear that Newman's interest in the Fathers was in a sense first of all a by-product of that interest in history which developed early and continued all his life, stimulated as it was bound to be, by a classical training which, in the nature of things, could not be divorced from history», in T. M. PARKER, 'The Rediscovery of the Fathers in the Seventeenth-Century Anglican Tradition', in *Rediscovery*, p. 38.

directed my thoughts from time to time, whenever I was free from the engagements proper to my time of life».[146]

During the second period of interest in the Fathers, more or less the period when «two great blows awakened (him) from his dream», that is end of 1827,[147] Newman approaches their writings in a more detailed way - «with attention and on system». Yet he himself acknowledges that his approach, and the aim it was meant to reach, were both conditioned by Protestant principles. Accepting the fact that in the end this approach ends up by producing nothing - «I laboured through the night and caught nothing» - Newman is still of the opinion that he owes his debt to some ideas which remain from this period, namely «a vivid perception of the divine institution, the prerogatives, and gifts of the Episcopate».[148]

These are the words that recall this period: «when years afterwards (1828) I first began to read their works with attention and on system, I busied myself much in analysing them, and in cataloguing their doctrines and principles; but, when I had thus proceeded very carefully and minutely for some space of time, I found on looking back on what I had done, that I had scarcely done anything at all... At the time I did not discover the reason of this result, though on the retrospect, it was plain enough: I had read them simply on Protestant ideas, analysed and catalogued them on Protestant principles of division and hunted for Protestant doctrines and usages in them... I knew not what to look for in them; I sought what was not there, I missed what was there».[149]

On considering these two periods, a question arises as to

---

146 *Diff*. I, pp. 370-371.
147 *Apol*. p. 14.148 *Diff*. I, pp. 371-372; *LD* V, p. 133: «thus I read Justin very careful in 1828 - and made most copious notes - but I conceive most of my time was thrown away. I was like a sailor landed at Athens or Grand Cairo, who stares about - does not know what to admire, what to examine - makes random remarks, and forgets all about it when he has gone».
149 *Diff*. I, p. 371; see also Newman's letter to T.W. Allies in 1842 as reported in C.S. DESSAIN, 'The Biblical Basis of Newman's Ecumenical Theology', in *Rediscovery*, p. 105, n. 1; «There is one remaining source of my opinions to be mentioned, and that far from the least important. In proportion as I

what kind of impression or effect did the Fathers really have on Newman's mind? Newman himself distinguishes two types of influence: the first one is an «impression, deep and most pleasurable» which was to «my imagination, I may say, a paradise of delight to the contemplation of which I directed my thoughts from time to time».[150]

The second effect is one of a philosophical nature: «the broad philosophy of Clement and Origen carried me away; the philosophy not the theological doctrine... Some portions of their teaching, magnificent in themselves, came like music to my inward ear, as if the response to ideas, which, with little external to encourage them, I had cherished so long. These were based on the mystical or sacramental principle, and spoke of the various Economies or Dispensations of the Eternal».[151]

These two aspects of the Fathers' role, the imaginative and the philosophical, explain what kind of influence they have on Newman's preaching. The core issue here is not centred around the Fathers as sources of historical events and quotations, although this was the case in his *Arians*, but rather the Fathers as exemplars of that *beau idéal* of Christianity with which Newman identifies himself both on the level of imagination and that of shared contemplation. On the level of philosophy, the Fathers also prove to be another source in confirming the sacramental principle, the principle that «the exterior world, physical and

---

moved out of the shadow of liberalism which had hung over my course, my early devotion of the Fathers returned; and in the Long Vacation of 1828 I set about to read them chronologically, beginning with St. Ignatius and St. Justin», in *Apol.* p. 25; «The ancient Fathers saved him from the danger that threatened him. An imaginative devotion to them and to their times had been the permanent effect upon him of reading at School an account of them and extracts from their works in Joseph Milner's Church History, and even when he now and then allowed himself as in 1825 in criticism of them, the first centuries were his *beau idéal* of Christianity», in *AW* p. 83.

150 *Diff.* I, pp. 370-371.
151 *Apol.* pp. 26-27.

historical, was but the manifestation to our senses of realities greater than itself».[152]

The other two periods during which he takes up the Fathers, are related to two particular publications which in his opinion proved «so fatal to the pretensions of the Anglican Church».[153]

In 1831 he studied again the Fathers while working on the history of Arianism. Yet even here, Newman did not really feel that there was any real breakthrough in their study. It is after this that he goes on studying the patristic works in relation to the controversies of the first centuries. This third stage, after the work on Arianism, he was «reading them for himself»: «after this I set myself to the study of them, with the view of pursuing the series of controversies connected with our Lord's Person; and to the examination of these controversies I devoted two summers, with the interval of several years between them (1835 and 1839). And now at length I was reading them for myself... In the former of the two summers above mentioned (1835), my reading was almost entirely confined to strictly doctrinal subjects, to the exclusion of history, and I believe it left me pretty much where I was on the question of the Catholic Church».[154]

It is in the summer of 1839, we call it the fourth phase, that he becomes engaged with the history of the Monophysite controversy, finding his faith in the Anglican principles disappear. «but in the latter of them ([summer]1839) it was principally occupied with the history of the Monophysite controversy, and the circumstances and transactions of the Council of Chalcedon, in the fifth century,

---

152 *Id.*, p. 27; «The Alexandrian Platonists taught Newman, or confirmed him in his suspicion, that one must see behind the attributes, through the disguises of the material world. They revealed to him the doctrine of the 'economy', that nature and history provide those who can read them with allegorical information on the spiritual world. Thus the more important function of consciousness seemed to Newman not to form simple ideas from basic sensory experience but to transcend the world of matter, the world of Lockean intelligence, by treating it as in itself a mere 'economy'», in T. VARGISH, *Newman: The Contemplation of Mind*, pp. 17-18.
153 *Diff.* I, p. 374.
154 *Id.*, p. 372.

and at once and irrevocably I found my faith in the tenableness of the fundamental principle of Anglicanism disappear, and a doubt of it implanted in my mind which never was eradicated».[155]

Conclusion

The reason behind this analysis is to unearth the wealth that lies in that relationship between the external events and their relationship with the heart that experiences them. Newman's early life is enriched by those events which are meaningful not much from a historical point of view but rather from the moral and intellectual effect they have him.

His conversion and the people who accompanied him create a life story with far-reaching effects. The discovery of the inner self is not a refuge disjointed from outside reality. It is a discovery that serves as a pre-condition of and for conscience. We can envisage Newman's discovery as a journey because this inwardness helps him move towards God and truth. This inwardness becomes an ambiance from where Newman is able to identify the force of a guide, conscience. Thus the moment he is discovering inwardness he is contemporarily discovering conscience as the force of truth that is calling for a personal and living response.

---

[155] *Id.*, pp. 372-373. The influence of the Fathers on Newman's thought is studied in the following articles: T.M. PARKER, 'The Rediscovery of the Fathers in the Seventeenth-Century Anglican Tradition', in *Rediscovery*, pp. 31-49, where he is convinced that «to speak of Newman's debt to the Anglican patristic tradition is therefore meaningful only, I would insist, if one realizes that this at most added, from about 1834 onwards, to a patristic tradition discovered for himself and already operative. In no way did it create it», p. 45; for a different opinion on the subject see article by G. ROWELL, 'Newman and the Anglican Tradition: Reflections on Tractarianism and the Seventeenth-Century Anglican Divines', *Louvain Studies* 15 (1990) 136-150; see also C.S. DESSAIN, 'The Biblical Basis of Newman's Ecumenical Theology', in *Rediscovery*, p. 105, n. 1, where the author refers to the role of the Fathers in a biblical context; see also J.H. WALGRAVE, *Newman the Theologian*, pp. 38-40 for a summary exposition of the Oxford Movement, from 1833-1845, from a Newman perspective related to his writings and to the role of the Fathers' teaching.

The phrase «myself and my Creator»[156] epitomizes the essence of this experience.

The quest for holiness becomes, also, a question of the whole personality: mind and soul. His journey of faith seems to move on not irrespective of what happens around him, but in relation to what happens around him. This trait, already so clear at this early phase of his life, remains with him right till the end.

It is at this moment that he starts focusing his own ideas about the proper disposition of the mind in relation to spiritual realities. His first steps in this most delicate area contain a sense of equilibrium. He succeeds in not sacrificing reason at the altar of religion. He is aware that there exists the risk of relegating the moral and let it be preceded by the intellectual.

Thus the importance of Oriel is derived from how a potential danger to Newman's future development, far from proving detrimental, turns out to be a most beneficial encounter. It was Oriel that helps him to take distance from Evangelicalism through liberalism, which proves quite tempting for any talented mind. It was Oriel which gives him confidence in his intellectual powers. And it is this same environment which offers him the possibility to prove the Oriel authorities right in choosing him as Fellow.

His encounters with Mayers, Whately and Hawkins, Butler and Milner, and their respective contributions, help him to acquire foundational principles that he develops later on in life.

Yet, the biggest challenge to this new Fellow of Oriel lies in the open fields of liberalism. Had Newman's mind been simply the sum total of intellectual achievements, the course of history would have been much different. Newman, though, proves to be equipped with an intuitive geniality that ends up being more powerful than any intellectual arrogance. The course of his story witnesses to the principles his life is built on. The dangers and the challenges that lie ahead prove only to be the test of its worth.

---

156 *Apol.* p. 4.

Thus, Walgrave's claim is substantiated: «a brief conflict arose between his worldly experience and his conscience, each striving to fix the direction his personality was to take. Now he was to choose deliberately between two orientations of life, two conceptions of the world; his was the grave responsibility of deciding which was to be victorious. This crisis brought home to him strongly the opposition between the liberal and the religious 'ethos'. Newman was never likely to decide in favour of reason divorced from the findings of conscience».[157]

---

157 J.H. WALGRAVE, *Newman the Theologian*, pp. 33-34.

CHAPTER 2
Advocacy of Conscience
1825-1832

A true understanding of John Henry Newman's concept of conscience, as presented in his sermons, cannot be limited to the published *Parochial And Plain Sermons*. The latter are the written expression of a process. Newman's idea of conscience goes beyond the sermons.

In Newman's case, it is not the purely theoretical thinking on conscience that we are faced with. His ideas on conscience presented in the sermons have a background to them – his own personal life – the disregard of which would not do justice to the understanding of the final written word.

Although Newman's statements on conscience, *per sé*, have every right and strength to stand on their own worth, without any back-up support, the study and examination of the wider arena of his personal life will give an added dimension to the whole.

The events which will be examined here have a dual role in relation to the reflections on conscience: firstly, they have an originating role in the development of the notion. They are the ones which anticipate, in a general way, the notions in the sermons. Secondly, they serve as the «humus», the background, which confirm the depth of the notion from a practical perspective.

Thus, his life outside the pulpit acquires a determining function in relation to what is preached from the same pulpit. His written words reflect those events that, in their turn, provide the raw material for the working of his convictions.

The method adopted is very much respectful of the chronological process that brought the sermons to light. The approach is concerned with the understanding of those contemporary primary sources where Newman expresses himself freely, fully and frequently. There is the chance to look into the whole area of his personality, his convictions and principles, his feelings and opinions, his personal struggles and public controversies, which offer to any Newman scholar the opportunity to approach, in an inclusive way, both the thinker and the preacher, who together «wrote» these reflections.

The in-depth research of these primary sources is a constant discovery of coherence between the *Parochial And Plain Sermons* and the *Letters and Diaries*. As one event after another are studied, comes to the fore an atmosphere of consistency that characterizes his personal life and his preaching. It is a journey of discovery, or rather of two contemporary, and deeply related, discoveries: the human being as mind and heart.

Being this the methodological trace that will take into consideration both sides of Newman's life, this *Chapter* will be mainly concerned with examining those moments of his life where the concept of conscience plays an important role.

1. Controversy with Charles – 1825

One of Newman's characteristics is his ability to maintain a huge correspondence. His letter writing, like his sermons, is very direct. Unlike his sermons, though, it is not formal. At times, things of no importance at all are as essential as the sharing of feelings and opinions. Through his letters he engages himself in controversies. These controversies, in their turn, enlighten the subject in question, its content, but they also shed light on the way

Newman deals with the subject in question, the methodological dimension.

The letters witness how much importance he attaches to dialogue in any controversy in which he finds himself engaged in. His letter writing is, in a certain sense, a conversation at a distance. It can be also qualified as the written expression of a mind in progress. It contains within it a sense of dynamism coming out from an alert mind which is engaged in a battle to uphold truth and principles.

Such first long controversy is that with his brother, Charles Robert Newman. It takes place over two different periods, the first one, mainly, in 1825 (although the first letter dates back to two years earlier) and the second in 1830. In respect to the chronological dimension, the two parts of the controversy will be dealt with in two different sections, in the proper line of events. This will help situate, in a more faithful way, the contents of the correspondence against the larger dimension of his life.

The letters that Newman wrote to his brother amount to seven. The first one was written in December 1823, while the other six were all written in 1825. Together with them, Newman, at a later stage, added a *Memorandum*, written in May 1874.[1] These letters contain and deal with the very first challenge Newman meets regarding religious belief in general.

The attack Charles opens is not one aimed at a particular tenet of faith, but it is rather against the whole idea of faith as being something contrary to reason. For Newman, the controversy with Charles would represent the initial traits of that future experience which he has to go through, mainly his struggle against liberalism. This challenge is an opportunity for Newman. It helps him clarify his own ideas and develop them into clear arguments.[2]

---

[1] *LD* I, pp. 169-70, 182-183, 212-215, 219-221, 224-228, 240-241, 246-248, 253-255.

[2] «These letters were understandably neglected. Yet they contain Newman's first systematic attempt to give an account of the grounds of Christian faith.; they are the result of a working out of his position rapidly under the pressure

1.1. Analogical Argument

In his first letter Newman starts his defence of the idea of faith using the analogical argument that he had already used in a previous letter to the *Christian Observer*.[3]

«Contradictions can no more be true in religion, than in astronomy or chemistry – and there is this most important distinction, to those who believe in revelation, between scientific and religious opinions, that, whereas errors in the former are unattended with danger to the person who maintains them, he who holdeth not "the faith", (I am not now determining what that faith is) such a one is said to be incapable of true moral excellence, and so exposed to the displeasure of God».[4]

This opening statement presents in synthesis the difficulty Charles is having about his own religious beliefs. The following remarks contain the thoughts Charles entertains, as perceived by Newman:

«In walking home this evening with Charles I took occasion to speak with him on the subject of religion... I shall put down a few of his remarks: – "The antecedent probability of eternal punishment is so great that it is absurd to believe it. The argument about the word αιωνιος is an absurdity; to be so nice as to make

---

of the urgency of his brother's need... They enable us to bring forward to the summer of 1825 the genesis in Newman's mind of a number of his most characteristic assumptions and habits of thought», in G.R. Evans, 'Newman's Letters to Charles', *The Downside Review* 100 (1982) 92; G.R. Evans' article is the only study so far produced concerning these letters.

3   It is important to point out to a short correspondence written to the *Christian Observer* in May 1821. The method Newman adopts in this letter is that of analogy: the main scope of this letter was to show that as in scientific matters we can confirm the existence of «contradictions and impossibilities», so, through analogy between mathematics and Christianity, we can also establish that the existence of such «contradictions and impossibilities» cannot be used as an argument against religion, but, if anything, as an argument for. Furthermore, for Newman, this analogy draws its own strength from the existence of a proper disposition of the mind, rightly cultivated, which helps one to approach the subject with «consistency and impartiality», in *LD* I, pp. 102-105.

4   *Id.*, pp. 169-170.

a doctrine depend on the meaning of a word! It is a point not to be thought about, and, if I must, how do I know even that the word is in the Bible, but by my eyes? but I suppose I choose to say that transcribers put the word in? Well, then, that leads me into a long argument which I do not choose to follow; so the shortest and the best way is not to inquire about it... Many presume on the aid of supernatural assistance, who have no such assistance. They weaken and soften their minds. All those arguments you produce about our being like prisoners, and thus bad judges of our guilt, and that we ought to feel love &c to God, &c &c seem to me absurd. People are not in earnest when they call themselves the vilest of sinners. In gratitude to God! I do not see we have so many calls for gratitude. Man is not so bad; your way of asking for grace is very roundabout; so much machinery; why not read the Bible, and employ reason at once? I acknowledge that the Bible is full of declarations that the frame of our minds must be changed"».[5]

As a first attempt to encounter Charles' line of thought, Newman believes that the analogical argument can sufficiently tackle his brother's difficulties. Yet, Newman immediately realizes that this will not go too far. In actual fact this argument does not feature again in his letters.

1.2. The Notion of Conscience

This situation forces Newman to search another form of meeting Charles' arguments. He tries to establish a point outside the discussion, by, first, introducing the notion of conscience. He promotes it as the experience through which attitudes are decided and the frame of mind is formed. This insertion here, although it does not give the impression of being fundamental to the whole

---

5   *AW* pp. 192-193; this is what Newman recorded in 1872.

argument in itself, is rather serving as an important shift: the basis of the discussion moves from the mere technical and scientific arena, conditioned by the contents, to that level which is related to both the intellect and the heart.

«The first point to press upon the conscience is, that we are playing with edged tools, if instead of endeavouring perseveringly to ascertain what the truth is, we consider the subject carelessly, captiously, or with indifference... This is not the frame of mind in which they can hope for success in any worldly pursuit, why then in that most difficult one of religious truth? ... In every one of us there is naturally a void, a restlessness, a hunger of the soul, a craving after some unknown and vague happiness, which we suppose seated in wealth, fame, knowledge, in fact any worldly good which we are not ourselves possessed of...».[6]

This is a fundamental leap for Newman's line of reasoning. It will further develop as a force, and an essential point of reference, in his future reflections on the reasonableness of religion. The sermons he wrote and the themes that guide his reflections give ample proof to this.

1.3. External and Internal Evidences

Building on the argument of conscience, Newman shares his conviction that the whole question of religion needs to be approached from the dimension of the person's inner convictions. From this point, the internal evidence, dependent as it is on that moral feeling within, external evidences are discovered for what they really are, their real worth. No type of *a-priori* objections can become a stumbling block, in a way that both evidences are disjointed one from the other.

«Yet how monstrous is it to attempt overturning a system by a-priori objections to its doctrines; while the great body of

---
6   *LD* I, p. 170.

external evidence on which it is founded remains untouched! – as if a man should endeavour to refute Newton, not by showing some flaw in his reasoning, but by expiating on the antecedent absurdity, the ridiculousness of supposing the earth go round the sun. Remember too the external evidences are built upon the obvious and general canons by which we judge of the truth or falsehood of every thing we hear; not on rules peculiar to religion, or modelled by it: here at least we do not argue "on Christian principles". The internal evidence depends a great deal on moral feeling».[7]

As will become clearer later on in the correspondence, Charles seems to have difficulty with the internal type of evidence. If the difficulty exists at the very initial stage where approach to Scripture begins, the origin of such state of mind is to be found in that *grand objection* of the mind to revelation.[8]

Through the proposed model of «evidences», related as it is on the notion of conscience, Newman opens up a whole new dimension to the discussion. He is wide-opening the door of the personality to include the dimensions of the intellect and the heart: the power of the rational and the disposition towards the divine. Moving along between the two, he can justify both the tension of the rational towards the divine, and the challenge the divine poses to the rational.

1.4. The Heart

Following this development, in the third letter, March 24th, Newman achieves two other important points. First, he explains the source of the rejection of Christianity as a «fault in the heart», where the dislike of Scripture is the guiding factor for further decisions. Second, reflecting on the arguments brought forward

---
7 *Id.*, p. 214.
8 *Id.*, p. 240

by his brother, he sees them not so much as reasons which cause unbelief but rather as reasons which try to justify unbelief.

The reference to the heart as the place where decisions are taken, is intimately related to the notion of conscience, while both complement each other. If the heart is the place where the person is constantly deciding, in favour or against the growth of his relationship with the Maker, than the role of conscience is to be understood as a force which enlightens and guides its decisions.

«I consider the rejection of Christianity to arise from a fault of the heart, not of the intellect; that unbelief arises, not from mere error of reasoning, but either from pride or from sensuality. It is important that at starting I should premise this, lest I should appear inconsistent, and to assert both that the Christian evidences are most convincing, and yet that they are not likely to convince those who reject them. A dislike of the contents of Scripture is at the bottom of unbelief; and since these contents must be rejected by fair means or foul, it is plain that in order to this the evidences must in some sort be attacked. But this is quite an afterthought; and, thus unbelievers (...) reverse the legitimate process of reasoning, and act in a manner which would be scouted as unfair were they examining Newton's Principia or Lavoisier's Chemistry».[9]

In this letter, Newman shows all his ability not much to convince through argument but rather to expose the illegitimacy of a wrongly adopted rational proceeding. His view of Christianity is not tied to intellectual structures which need to be justified so as to be able to justify in return. It is rather based on the notion that the rational power within the person is open to the divine and, at the same time, cannot be fully convinced of it through mere reason.

«Hence the most powerful arguments for Christianity do not convince, only silence; for there is at the bottom that secret

---

9   *Id.*, p. 219

antipathy for the doctrines of Christianity, which is quite out of reach of argument. I do not then assert that the Christian evidences are overpowering, but that they are unanswerable; nor do I expect so much to show Christianity true, as to prove it rational; nor to prove infidelity false, so much as irrational».[10]

It is within a dialectic tension between reason and faith that the experience of the divine unfolds. The equilibrium between the two is delicate; the balance is as indispensable as it is difficult. The end result is not intended to satisfy the reason, since it is well beyond it.

1.5. Pride and Prejudice

The tools Newman uses at this point are the «heart» and «conscience». He knows that the person has to be true to self at the very starting point of inquiry. Pride and prejudice, understood as corruption of the heart, cannot be admitted at this stage. Their role will be to denaturalize the process of the whole experience. Revelation is the encounter with the «something otherwise indiscoverable», the disclosure of what the person tends towards but never able to attain on his or her own. The risk is that the whole process proceeds in a way that wrong conclusions will of necessity be attained.

«I gave my opinion that you had taken up the subject under discussion quite at the wrong end: that instead of beginning with the external evidence you had most illogically plunged into the consideration of the contents of the Bible. This I hold to be a mode of proceeding dishonourable and unfair to yourself; and as the question it involves is on the very threshold of the inquiry, it is

---

10 *Ibid*; for a reflection on the relationship that exists between heart and conscience see O. DE BERRANGER, 'Des paradoxes au mystère chez J.H. Newman et H. de Lubac', *Revue des sciences philosophiques et théologiques* 78 (1994) 55, 59.

but proper you should defend your line of argument before you enter upon it... A revelation implies the disclosure of something before unknown: nay, if we consider the circumstances of the case, something otherwise indiscoverable. Now doubtless what is thus discovered may prove agreeable to our own experience, but as certainly it may turn out to be beyond its reach. We know how an enlarged view of a subject changes our ideas respecting it... a person who judged of the contents of the revelation by his own preconceived notions would infallibly have pronounced the revelation spurious».[11]

Newman is conscious of the fact that the consequences of his brother's line of thought are as dangerous as much as they can give the impression that the reasoning is valid. Once the argument is left to float on the wrong premise, there is no way of pointing out where the flow is wrong. It is at source where the fault is. And it is to that source that Newman is urging Charles to be clear about.

«We survey moral and religious subjects, through the glass of previous habits; and scarcely two persons use a glass of the same magnifying power. I venture confidently to say, that if the contents of a professed revelation on divine things are to be made the test of its genuineness, no revelation could be made us: for scarcely two persons can be got together, who will agree in their antecedent or self-originated ideas of God and his purposes towards man... I deprecate the practice of measuring those contents by any preconceived standard or morals or philosophy».[12]

Thus clear about the dangers of a prejudiced heart, Newman does not need to go any further in proving anything which is beyond the disposition of the heart. And it is on this point that he deepens his reflections within the letters. Being convinced that the seat of our relationship with God is the heart, therefore,

---
11   *LD* I, pp. 224-225.
12   *Id.*, p. 226.

it is there where wrongness of the decision originates. And, for Newman, the cause of that decision is «pride».

«Before I close this long letter, I will attempt to explain, though it is painful to do so, what I meant by implying that you were under the influence of pride. One proof, to my mind, of pride, is the circumstance so much insisted on above: your rejecting the credentials of Christianity because you dislike the contents. But the grand evidence your conduct supplies, is, your assuming that unassisted reason is competent to discover moral and religious truth. If this were the case, I confess it would be a great argument in limine against any revelation at all... Doubtless, you never entered into the spirit of Christianity: whose fundamental doctrine it is, that the mind cannot arrive at religious truth 1st without a revelation, 2nd without God's dispersing its prejudices in order to it's receiving that revelation. Had you felt not only the desirableness of religious truth, but also the inability to attain it of ourselves, you would not have been seduced into your present opinions. Nor, till you have recourse to the Author of Nature himself for direction, humbly, sincerely, perseveringly, can you expect to possess real knowledge and true peace».[13]

1.6. The Conscientious Inquirer

These words contain in a nutshell Newman's basic ideas about revelation and the power of the person to relate to it. We cannot fail to notice, though, how in this correspondence with Charles there is what we may call the development of a theory of religious belief.[14] While it was during this period that Newman «was beginning to prefer intellectual excellence to moral; I was drifting in the direction of the Liberalism of the day»,[15] he is, at

---
13   *Id.*, pp. 227-228.
14   See G.R. Evans, 'Newman's Letters to Charles', *The Downside Review* 100 (1982) 92.
15   *Apol.* p. 14.

the same time, gradually moving towards a concept of person seen not much as an agent with illimited powers, but rather as dependent on a «superior being», a dependency which is open to the divine.

The role of the rational powers is taken in its proper dimensions, not in absolute terms, but in relation to the Author of Nature. Thus for Newman, the honest inquirer, besides feeling, first, the desirability for the truth, also feels, secondly, the inability to fully attain it on his or her own; and in the acceptance of the latter lies the real test of the former.

The recourse to God, therefore, is a necessity in the order of human nature. The recognition of this necessity is, at the same time, the willingness of the human to interact with the divine. It is a topic which will feature in his letters, as well as in his sermons.[16]

In his later recollection of the controversy, in 1872, Newman recapitulates, in the following words, how he felt at the time:

«I repeated my strong conviction that no one could understand the Scriptures fruitfully, unless it were given him from above, however orthodox the creed &c. that I did not confine salvation to one sect – that in any communion whoever sought truth sincerely would not fail of heaven; that three things were incumbent on everyone, before he could pretend to judge of the Scripture doctrines, – to read the Bible constantly and attentively, to pray for grace to understand it incessantly, and to strive to live up to the dictates of conscience and what the mind acknowledges to be right».[17]

«Scripture», «grace» and «conscience» are the elements which feature prominently in Newman's mind after all those years. These same elements feature in his sermons given during the period of his letters to Charles.

---

16   *PS* VII. 15. *Mental Prayer*, *PS* I. 19. *Times of Private Prayer*, *PS* I. 20. *Forms of Private Prayer*.
17   *AW*, p. 193.

At the beginning of this study, the relation was pointed out, direct and indirect, between the sermons and the wider dimension of his life. The following two sermons contain almost identical vocabulary to the above controversy. Written after the letters, the expressive form is different, the ideas are the same.

1.7. Secret Faults

In the sermon *Secret Faults*,[18] Newman talks about self-knowledge as a means for discovering the relationship between the person and the Almighty. The discovery of our sinful nature is by no means an unbridgeable gap between the creature and the Maker. On the contrary, it is the moment in which the person is invited to take a decision, a personal decision of the heart. It is from this decision that the rest will follow.

«Now (I repeat) unless we have some just idea of our hearts and of sin, we can have no right idea of a Moral Governor, a Saviour or a Sanctifier, that is, in professing to believe in Them, we shall be using words without attaching distinct meaning to them... for it is in proportion as we search our hearts and understand our own nature, that we understand what is meant by an Infinite Governor and Judge... God speaks to us primarily in our hearts. Self-knowledge is the key to the precepts and doctrines of Scriptures».[19]

Charles' difficulty is tackled here in a spiritual way. While the knowledge, resulting from the heart, questions our whole being

---

18 *PS* I. 4, pp. 41-56, on 12th June 1825.
19 *Id.*, pp. 42-43; at a later stage, in the same sermon, Newman writes: «First of all, self-knowledge does not come as a matter of course; it implies an effort and a work. As well may we suppose, that the knowledge of the languages comes by nature, as that acquaintance with our own heart is natural. Now the very effort of steadily reflecting, is itself painful to many men; not to speak of the difficulty of reflecting correctly. To ask ourselves *why* we do this or that, to take account of the principles which govern us, and see whether we act for conscience' sake or from some lower inducement, is painful», pp. 49-50.

and doing, the yearning contained in it is never fully satisfied. The voyage of the heart is the journey towards eternity. As such it only asks for conscientiousness and earnestness.

«But let a man persevere in prayer and watchfulness to the day of his death, yet he will never get to the bottom of his heart. Though he know more and more of himself as he becomes more conscientious and earnest, still the full manifestation of the secrets there lodged, is reserved for another world».[20]

1.8. *Inward Witness to the Truth of the Gospel* [21]

In the sermon bearing this name, Newman treats, in a more detailed and organic way, the themes of his correspondence with Charles. It starts with defending the external evidence of Scripture which is similar to that in the letters, as «built upon the obvious and general canons by which we judge of the truth or falsehood of *every thing* we hear; not on rules peculiar to religion, or modelled by it».[22] This is mixed with a hint to the analogical argument.

«We may sometimes hear men say, "How do you know that the Bible is true? You are told so in Church; your parents believed it; but might they not be mistaken? and if so you are mistaken also". Now to this objection it may be answered, and very satisfactorily, "Is it then nothing toward convincing us of the truth of the Gospel, that those whom we loved best and reverence most believe it? Is it against reason to think that they are right, who have considered the matter most deeply? Do we not receive what they tell us in other matters, though we cannot prove the truth of their information; for instance, in matters of art and science;

---

20 *Id.*, p. 48.
21 *PS* VIII. 8, pp. 110-123, on 18th December 1825.
22 *LD* I, p. 214.

why then is it irrational to believe them in religion also? Have not the wisest and holiest of men been Christians? ... If we have no good reason for believing, at least we have no good reason for disbelieving».[23]

1.9. The Indications of Conscience

Newman, moving on to treat the person's yearning to arrive at the truth, combines the role of conscience to that of the heart. There exists harmony in their relationship. The decisions of the heart have necessarily to be sustained by the indications of conscience. The heart is the forum where the person is enlightened by that attitudinal respect towards conscience. Conscience is the guide which enlightens the path of the decisions of the heart. The role of Scripture is indicated by conscience as a source of light for the heart's journey.

«His own natural sense of right and wrong tells him that peevishness, sullenness, deceit and self-will, are tempers and principles of which he has cause to be ashamed, and he feels that these bad tempers and principles are in his heart. As he grows older, he will understand this more and more. Wishing, then, and striving to act up to the law of conscience, he will find that, with his utmost efforts, and after his most earnest prayers, he still falls short of what he knows to be right, and what he aims at. Conscience, however, being respected, will become a more powerful and enlightened guide than before; it will become more refined and hard to please; and he will understand and perceive more clearly the distance that exists between his own conduct and thoughts, and perfection. He will admire and take pleasure in the holy law of God, of which he reads in Scripture».[24]

---

23 *PS* VIII. 8, pp. 111-112.
24 *Id.*, p. 116.

The heart, then, as a seat of decision is considered not in its exclusive singularity but rather in its relation to the whole; it is the place where the person finds his or her own self and is responsible for it. The great decisions to be taken, concerning the «great vision of Truth external» to self, cannot be realized as part of self unless the self consents to them. This consent is not a single unrelated decision. It is rather the result of an attitude, the act of a trained heart.

«When, then, even an unlearned thus trained – from his own heart, from the action of his mind upon itself, from struggles with self, from an attempt to follow those impulses of his nature which he feels to be highest and noblest, from a vivid natural perception (...), from an innate, though supernatural perception of the great vision of Truth which is external to him (...) – I say, when a person thus trained from his own heart, reads the declarations and promises of the Gospel, are we to be told that he believes in them merely because he has been bid believe in them? Do we not see he has besides this a something in his own breast which bears a confirming testimony to their truth?»[25]

1.10. The Obedient Heart

The trained heart does not find obedience a difficult exercise. Being aided by the light of conscience, the heart finds itself naturally obliged to obey. The demands of belief, together with the urgings of conscience, find in the trained heart a natural inclination towards following this sense of right and wrong. Thus, in Newman's vision of belief, the heart, together with conscience and Scripture are related and act in unity one to the other.

«The Bible, then, seems to say, – God is not a hard master to require belief, without affording grounds for believing; only

---

25   *Id.*, pp. 117-118.

follow your own sense of right, and you will gain from that very obedience to your Maker, which natural conscience enjoins, a conviction of the truth and power of that Redeemer whom a supernatural message has revealed; do but examine your thoughts and doings; do but attempt what you know to be God's will, and you will most assuredly be led on into all the truth».[26]

At this point in the sermon, we notice again how Newman, reflecting about the dangers which lie ahead for the Christian who is trying to share with some one who is not thus tuned, has some remarks which are directly related to his controversy with his brother.

«When men think they know more than others, they often talk for the sake of talking, or to show their ability (as they think), their shrewdness and depth; and they speak lightly of the All-Holy God, to gratify their empty self-conceit and vanity. And often it answers no purpose to dispute with such persons; for not having been trained up to obey their conscience, to restrain their passions, and examine their hearts, they will assent to nothing you can say... and when they talk of religion they are like blind persons talking of colours. If you urge how great a gift it is to be at peace with God, or of the arduousness and yet desirableness of perfection, or the beauty of saintliness, or the dangerousness of the world, or the blessedness of self-control, or the glory of virginity, or the answers which God gives to prayers... They will laugh, they will scoff, at best they will wonder: any how what you may say is no evidence to them».[27]

2. Peel Affair

Before entering into the second part of the correspondence with Charles, there are two events which have meant a lot for Newman in their own time. The second one was even recalled by Newman himself later on in his life.

---

26 *Id.*, p. 120.
27 *Id.*, p. 121.

The Peel affair,[28] although it does not seem to have a direct bearing on the sermons, yet it plays an important role in helping Newman to sharpen his own sense of duty in relation to his principles. This, in a nutshell, is the effect the affair has on Newman. He feels it as a call, first and foremost, to examine himself before taking any position in favour or against an issue. «Every fresh opinion indeed we hear, is a call upon us to search *our own* opinions more rigidly and to examine their soundness».[29]

What is of interest here is to understand how Newman perceives his role and what are the impressions he conveys to his friends in his letters. Both his perceptions and the sharing of them, show a person who is becoming more concerned about the Church as a spiritual reality, in combat with a mentality influenced by indifference. «One of the signs of the Times (is that) of the incroachments of philosophism and indifferentism on the Church».[30]

These two elements, «philosophism and indifferentism», in their own way, form part of that struggle against liberalism which already features in these years. Newman is concerned at this time about the independence of the Church and Oxford, very much in line with the anti-erastian view of the Church which he had inherited earlier through the influence of Whately.[31]

---

28 «Mr. Peel, the representative of the University in Parliament, had declared in favour of the Catholic claims, had resigned his seat, and then, changing apparently his purpose, had offered himself for re-election. The Provost took his side, the four Tutors were against him. In the eyes of the latter, his re-election was far more than a question of politics and political expediency; it was a moral, an academical, an ecclesiastical, nay a religious question; at least it grew to be such with them. Their opponents were liberals, and the liberal side, little as some of those recognized it, who took their stand on it, was anti-Church, anti-Church side», in *AW*, p. 97; see also I. KER, *John Henry Newman*. (Oxford University Press, Oxford - New York 1988) pp. 32-33.
29 *LD* II, p. 31.
30 *Id.*, p. 120.
31 «What he (Whately) did for me in point of religious opinion, was, first, to teach me the existence of the Church, as a substantive body or corporation; next to fix in me those anti-Erastian views of Church polity, which were one of the most prominent features of the Tractarian Movement», in *Apol.*, p. 12; the anti-erastian views are presented by Newman as: «Church and State

«We have proved the independence of the Church and of Oxford. So rarely is either of the two in opposition to Government, that not once in fifty years can independent principle be shown; yet in these times, when its existence has generally been doubted, the moral power we shall gain by it cannot be overestimated... We endured all this, scarcely hoping for success, but determining as good Churchmen and true, to fight for the principle, not consenting to our own degradation... How much of the Church's credit depended on us residents! and how inexcusable we should have been, if by drawing back we had deprived our country friends of the opportunity of voting, and had thus in some sort betrayed them!»[32]

In seeing the danger and in trying to act against it, Newman highlights the motives underlying his attitude at the time. The same motives, respect for principles and for conscience, will surface later on in his life, always with the same coherence. He himself is aware that what he is going through is an opportunity intended to bear on the future.

«Mistaken we may have been, but never inconstant... Better be bigoted than time-serving... In these perilous times the influence of the Church depends on its Character. I look upon that opportunity as providential, and intended (probably) to bear upon times to come and events as yet undisclosed... In such cases we have no right to look to consequences. We must do our duty straightforward, and be faithful servants to the Church... Christianity is of faith, modesty, lowliness, subordination; but the spirit at world against it is one of latitudinarianism, indifferentism, republicanism, and schism, a spirit which tends to overthrow doctrine, as if the fruit of bigotry, and discipline as if the instrument of priestcraft. All parties seem to acknowledge that the stream of

---

should be independent of each other... that the Church may justly and by right retain its property, though separated from the State», in *id.*, p. 13.
[32] *LD* II, p. 125.

opinion is setting against the Church... I do not doubt it will live on in the most irreligious and atheistical times...»[33]

These letters contain the same line of thought that will be characteristic of Newman not only in the immediate future, his dealings within the college structure and the liberal controversy, but right through his life. While his character is being formed, the vision he has of the reality around him is not limited to, or taken up by, the events in themselves. On the contrary, we can witness a mind constantly engaged in reading the situation, being influenced by the search for truth and encouraged to live it out to the best of his ability.

3. Grave College Questions

The events related to his Oriel period are two: the first one being the dispute he has with Edward Hawkins on the tutorial system and the other is the way he perceives his role in view of the possibility of him becoming Dean.

Although chronologically these two events are divided by the second part of the controversy with Charles, yet they belong to the same class of issues and, in a certain way, they are related one to the other. Both of them are concerned about the undergraduates, whether it is the lecturing system or the appropriateness of the reception of the sacrament by the mass of them. Both of them touch principles to which Newman attaches great value.

3.1. The Tutorial System

Edward Hawkins becomes Provost of Oriel College mainly through the insistence of Newman himself. What follows after that

---

33 *Id.*, pp. 127-128, 129-130.

election, though, by no means reflects the same level of friendship and intimacy which existed before between the two men.[34]

The origin of the dispute starts before Hawkins was elected Provost. «The College quarrel... (which) was founded on religious principle, was brought into shape and to its issue in the course of the year which followed upon Mr. Peel's matter».[35] The principle which triggers the quarrel concerns the arrangement of the lectures in a way that the new proposals would be «more direct, more intelligible, more practical than heretofore, and more in accordance with their own idea of a Tutor's office and duties».[36]

This arrangement touches on «whether in their ordinary Lectures, as fixed in the Terminal Lecture Paper, the Tutors should each give the place of primary interest and care to his own special pupils, or to all the Undergraduates in lecture indiscriminately, his own and those of others».[37]

For Newman, the value of lecturing is not understood simply as imparting knowledge. For him the interaction between the lecturer and the student goes beyond the mere fact of conveying information. He sees the role of tutor from a religious, formative standpoint: «I have ever considered the Tutorship as a religious office, not unlike the Pastoral... I cannot conscientiously act on principles abandoning this view».[38] All this proves to be in contrast with what Hawkins is trying to introduce.

---

[34] «By 1829 their relation towards each other had become very different from what it was in 1824, when the latter [Newman] had been the unpretending and grateful disciple of the former [Hawkins]. Newman had been eager in Hawkins's behalf for years, and had sung his praises loudly, wherever he went. He had expected great things from is promotion to the Provostship... but he had various grievances in regard to Dr. Hawkins from the time that he became Provost, which made him very sore», in *AW*, p. 101.
[35] *Id.*, p. 98.
[36] *Id.*, p. 99.
[37] *Id.*, pp. 101-102.
[38] *LD* II, p. 307; see also *AW*, p. 103, about Newman's feeling that his educational engagements were a fulfilment of his ordination.

«My [Newman's] chief objection to the system you propose, is, that in my own case, as I know by experience, (whatever others may be able to effect) the mere lecturing required of me would be incompatible with due attention to that more useful private instruction, which has imparted to the office of Tutor the importance of a clerical occupation. This is to me an insuperable objection, not that a few words can do justice to it – but, without needless discussion, pray believe me to be in earnest in saying once for all, I cannot act on the principles of your system».[39]

This strong position taken by Newman witnesses to the importance he attaches to his role as tutor. This is also confirmed by Hawkins himself who seems to recognize the serious approach taken by Newman regarding his tutorial position, an approach based on principle and lived out with conscientious exactitude: «for I regard you not only as a conscientious man doing your best endeavours to discharge your official duties, but as entirely desirous of the good of your pupils and of Oriel College in all your views and intentions respecting our system of Tuition».[40]

Yet despite this recognition, Hawkins proves himself unable to understand fully the depth and the far reaching consequences of Newman conscientious beliefs. Not having fully grasped the meaning of Newman's resolve, Hawkins entertains the false idea that Newman will eventually change.

«You can scarcely be bound to desert a very useful and honourable post in consequence of your conviction that a better system might be adopted; not to speak of the possibility that your judgment may change and coincide by and by with that of others who have certainly had more experience in Tuition than yourself».[41]

This proves to be Newman's biggest difficulty in the dispute: being taken lightly; thinking that for him honourable posts are

---
39 *LD* II, p. 233.
40 *Id.*, p. 229.
41 *Id.*, p. 232.

Advocacy of Conscience

more important than duty; his views being completely passed over; he himself being fully misunderstood.[42] A reference to Newman found in a letter by Edward Copleston to Hawkins, the latter being the successor of the former as Provost of Oriel, evidences the way Newman is perceived, at the time, by those who do not share his views: «From what you say of Newman's religious views, I fear he is impracticable. His notion of dangers to Church and State I cannot understand».[43]

Newman's reaction in the end is to be that which proves more coherent with his views, even if the risk is that no more pupils will be given him for tuition. Hawkins clearly puts the choice in front of him.

«For if, which I trusted and would fain hope still need not be the case, you were conscientiously opposed to a gradual return to the old system of this College, than I certainly contemplated your voluntarily relinquishing an office to which you were appointed under a different understanding by the late Provost... I would rather have you reconsider them calmly, and reconsider especially the question whether [you] cannot with a safe conscience, [and] the purpose of doing great good in your generation, so far suspend your opinion of the defectiveness of the system established at Oriel as to act under it».[44]

Newman decides to follow his conscience. In the *Memorandum. The Oriel Tuition*, 9 July 1830, Newman writes: «it was a point of conscience with me not to give my time and exertions to the system he upheld».[45]

---

42 «What irritated Newman most was his (the Provost's) imputing Newman's conduct to irritation, and refusing or not being able to see that there was a grave principle in it earnestly held, and betraying a confident expectation that what was, he considered, mere temper in Newman, would soon pass away, and that he would eventually give in», in *AW*, p. 103.
43 *LD* II, p. 214.
44 *Id.*, p. 240.
45 *Id.*, p. 248.

3.2. The Obligation of Higher Duties

The other event is the reaction Newman has to the possibility of him being elected Dean. Although the fact did not materialize, it is enlightening to discover how Newman has his ideas clear about a particular issue which caused him problems even in his undergraduate years.

The issue at stake is whether the reception of the sacrament by the undergraduates should be forced on him to administer if he objects to it. We know the difficulty he had when in his first year in Oxford he was scandalized with the fact that after the whole college went to Communion on Trinity Sunday, on Trinity Monday, the gaudy day, a «grand drink bout would take place».[46]

«O how the Angels must lament over a whole Society throwing off the allegiance and service of their Maker, which they have pledged the day before at His Table, and showing themselves true sons of Belial. It is sickening to see what I might call the apostasies of the many... An habitual negligence of the awfulness of Holy Communion is introduced».[47]

This same issue would have come up again had he been elected Dean. In contemplating this conflict, he shares with his friend Henry Jenkins two distinct principles: first that the administering of the sacrament to the masses of undergraduates is considered as a matter of conscience; this being so, if he is bid to follow an order by the Provost, a higher rank than Dean, to administer, this would appear to be going against his conscience; therefore, he does not consider himself bound to obey.

«I have at present no formed opinion about administering it to the masses of the Undergraduates; but, if I have to make up my mind, I think it very likely I shall make it a point of conscience to act upon it. The question will be, whether the Provost will make it a point of conscience to bid me administer it to individuals to

---
46 I. KER, *John Henry Newman*, p. 10.
47 *LD* I, p. 66.

whom I object to administer it. If so, it is frank to say that I should not consider myself bound to obey him in a matter so solemn. I will also say that I am against the present rule of obliging undergraduates to receive the Sacrament».[48]

This issue makes Newman think out his position not much in relation to his Provost, but rather in relation to himself, to his conscience. This is considered by Newman to be the first real test regarding whom to follow and what to do in matters so delicate when conscience is involved. It will in a certain way introduce the whole discussion which will find its ultimate treatment in his *Letter to the Duke of Norfolk*.[49] In his own diaries which he himself reads later on in his life, there is the following written statement:

«N.B. It is curious that this controversy in 1832 should have turned on the point whether a subject's conscience was to give way to the word of a Superior, when the word was a command as well as a prohibition – which was the question which turned up in regard to what I lately wrote about Conscience in my Letter to the Duke of Norfolk. JHN August 25. 1875».[50]

The context within which Newman expresses his dissent is that where a higher authority is concerned. He is careful not to destroy human authority, or to relegate its validity and importance. He rather goes beyond the human authority and finds in the call from «higher duties» not much the reason for not obeying human authority but rather the obligation to follow the voice of conscience: «in other words I *do* grant, as a general principle, that the Dean must yield (to the Provost), but still exceptions may arise from obligation of higher duties».[51]

He remains determined not to be put into the post «unless I can have my own way».[52] The invitation to take part in the Mediterranean tour settles the whole question and the inevitable

---
48 *LD* III, p. 63.
49 *Diff.* II, pp. 246-261.
50 *LD* III, p. 64, n.1.
51 *Id.*, p. 64.
52 *Id.*, p. 83.

dispute with the Provost, Edward Hawkins. The whole event succeeds, however, to expose the strength of character that Newman is gradually developing, and his determination to live up to his principles: «but depend upon it, I am not to be debarred the use of my discretion... Under these circumstances, I do not feel any great delicacy in declaring that I mean to have my way if I am elected».[53]

4. Controversy with Charles: 1830

Briefly recalling Newman's path up to now, he has first tried the analogical argument, only to move on to adopt the argument of the heart as a place where decisions are made, decisions which can be prejudiced and proud. Within this second argument he brought in the theme of conscience.

The second part of the controversy with Charles contains only one letter from Newman. It is a long one about which he writes to his mother, saying that «my head, hand, and heart are all knocked up with the long composition I have sent Charles. I have sent him 24 closely written foolscap pages, all about nothing. He revived the controversy we had five years ago. I have sent him what is equal to nine sermons».[54]

The letter contains some interesting developments on the previous letters. The «nothing» Newman writes about might be the expectations he has about the outcome of the whole issue, rather than about the ideas which are contained within the letter.

After referring to the previous correspondence, Newman insists that the methodological approach which Charles has taken leads to his own confutation. He refers to it as «an unsound moral state of mind»[55] which has adopted a «method by which you seem to me

---

53 *Id.*, pp. 84-85.
54 *LD* II, p. 284.
55 *Id.*, p. 270.

to have been led into your present opinions. Accordingly I spoke of the necessity of postponing the consideration of the *contents* of the Scripture revelation to that of the external evidences».[56]

Newman feels that he is failing in convincing his brother «*where* the error of your past inquiries into the truth of Christianity really lay. It was mere friendly advice (...) a friendly interference to reconcile your mind to a procedure».[57]

Charles is reminded of a phrase from a letter sent by Newman, in the first part of the controversy, in which he (Charles) is accused of not being a fair judge:

«you did decide against Christianity FIRST from its doctrines... and THEN with this prejudice against it in your mind proceeded to examine the external evidence of which in consequence you were no fair judge. I have stated what I consider a fact; that your doubts of the truth of Christianity originated in a dislike of its doctrines. I wished therefore to draw near, and put my finger on the seat of the disease... The mischief has been done, but tho' prejudice may have had great effect in forming your opinions, it cannot sharpen your arguments or blunt mine. I am not allowed to convince you, I must now attempt to confute you».[58]

4.1. Certainty and Probability

This part of the correspondence contributes to the notion of the acceptance of a Moral Governor: «there are certain phenomena, which Christians assign to a certain *known* cause (the divine agency) – because of their *unaccountableness* in any other way, and their *resemblance* (both in means and end) to be [the] known works of that agency».[59]

---

56 *Ibid.*
57 *Ibid.*
58 *Ibid.*, see also *LD* I, pp. 246-247.
59 *LD* II, p. 279.

Newman uses this argument since it is the bone of contention between him and his brother. He is quite aware of the consequences if this notion of a moral governor is not taken into consideration. In actual fact, it gradually transpires, throughout this whole debate, that Charles has no reference outside the human sphere.

Through the introduction of the argument from probabilities, Newman tries to remove any justifying ground from under his brother's feet. It was, after all, Charles himself who introduced the argument first. It seems that Charles denied «the propriety of this reference». To which Newman asks, «surely then the Cause which you assign, should be a *more* probable one than that which we produce – but you have recourse to a (professedly) *unknown* cause, the powers of the human mind».[60]

At this stage Newman moves on swiftly and strongly. In a few lines he dismisses any trifling attitude which disguises the absence of any valid argument.

«You have recourse to a (professedly) unknown cause, the powers of the human mind. From your own admission then that the Cause is unknown, (whatever be the merits of the hypothesis) I have a right in a controversy to treat it with disrespect. It is as if, when I see some Gothic building, instead of assigning it to its natural builders, I should hypothesize how it might have been the work of the Esquimaux or some unknown tribe of the interior of Africa. It is trifling with a disputant, to treat him thus. I am ready to meet argument, but I cannot meet shadows. – If there were need of an hypothesis, then we must have done as well as we could – or perhaps have had recourse to the unknown powers of the mind because we had no known cause to assign for the phenomena».[61]

Newman goes right to the centre of the discussion and, while not refusing any counter-argument which can give a valid contribution to the whole, he is ever ready to point out to any

---

60 *Ibid.*
61 *Ibid.*

shortcoming. He is receptive of his brother's contribution, but before that he invites his brother to disprove the known cause: «As things are before going to *unknown* causes, we must remove the known; – disprove the being of a Moral Governor».[62]

The substitute to this Divine Agency that Charles is putting forward is, according to Newman, a pure assumption: «You *assumed* that, because we do not possess a scientific knowledge of the human mind, therefore our knowledge is not sufficient for the determination of a practical question».[63]

In the following section of the letter, Newman goes deeper into the whole area of certainties and probabilities. He builds his argument slowly and clearly. Here we can witness the build-up of the argument from probabilities. «*Certainty* in the business of life means a *conviction sufficient for practice*».[64] This is his belief, not his brothers'. «You seem to think that no evidence for an alleged fact is certain, which admits of the chance of the fact being otherwise – i.e. you would hold that demonstration alone is certain proof».[65]

Newman, can never accept this principle. He sees in it an attitude of enclosure of the human within self. When he looks at his own self, he sees the opposite. The openness of the human towards the divine, reflected in the heart as the forum where the person is aware of something beyond, leads him to disagree.

«I differ... Here again the world is against you – and you besides are the assailant – yet you coolly take it for granted that no evidence from probabilities amounts to a certainty sufficient for action, and leave me to refute your assumption. The world is against you – for every thing we do, is done on probabilities. Even when we trust our sense and memory, we rely on evidence, which, in your own words, "is not certain and may be false". No

---

62 *Ibid.*
63 *Ibid.*
64 *Id.*, p. 280.
65 *Ibid.*

facts are known, no practical matters conducted, on demonstrative proof, which is found in pure mathematics alone and subjects of a similar nature: – there is always a chance of error... A man who is roused by the cry of fire gets up and looks about him – he does not think it philosophical to close his ears even to the slight evidence of the fact which the alarm supplies; – no scepticism bottomed on his view of his ignorance of mental science arms him against the fear. Thus there is no inherent weakness in an argument from probabilities in a question of practice. The matter will not be mended, should the man deliberately go to sleep after the alarm – his abstract objections will not save him from being burnt».[66]

Finally, after repeating briefly the points of disagreement, Newman concludes his letter: «I have now done with controversy. Farewell, my dear Charles; you cannot hinder my praying for you. God has His own time for all things».[67]

4.2. *Josiah, a Pattern for the Ignorant* – *Memorandum*

The reflections within the sermons, that are intimately related to this controversy, need to be examined together with another reflection on revelation, *Memorandum on Revelation*,[68] which Newman writes during this same period.

While the sermon *Josiah, a Pattern for the Ignorant*[69] contains in it reflections which are directly related to the letter to Charles, the *Memorandum*, in Newman's own words, is an «exposition of my own opinions, which I thought C. [Charles] ignorant of, was intended for corporation with the above (his last letter to Charles) – but was omitted for want of time and space, and

---

66   *Ibid*.
67   *Id*., p. 281.
68   *Id*., pp. 281-283.
69   *PS* VIII. 7, pp. 91-109.

perhaps fortunately – for it would not profit him now, and may at some future day».[70]

The exposition of the two, the sermon and the memorandum, in a parallel fashion is justified since the contents follow an almost similar path. In the sermon Newman, takes the example of Josiah, who «had not the aid of a revealed volume, at least not of the Law; he was surrounded by the diversities of idol-worship, the sophistries of unbelief, the seductions of sinful pleasures. He had every temptation to go wrong».[71]

He starts, first, by recognizing the fact the every person, «even the poorest and the most ignorant, has knowledge enough to be religious».[72] It is not education which makes a person religious, nor is it a reason for not being one. Like Josiah, every person has something within which acts like a constraining force and this is to be found in a «tender heart»: «He had that, which all men have, heathen as well as Christians, till they pervert or blunt it. In the words of the text, "his heart was *tender*"; he acknowledged a constraining force in the Divine voice within him».[73]

In the *Memorandum* Newman uses the vocabulary of light to affirm the same divine presence in the heart: «light enough is given for practical religious purposes – enough to lead them to heaven, and to condemn them if they do not employ themselves in disciplining and changing their moral nature».[74] There lies the dignity of the person, in answering to the call within.

A second point on which the two reflections take similar path is the role of natural conscience as the main instrument recognized by the heart. Taking humanity as not having any aid whatsoever, Newman presents Josiah as the representative of the person who starts from himself to arrive at truth. This he does by letting the suggestions of natural conscience act as his guide.

---

70 *LD* II, p. 281.
71 *PS* VIII. 7, p. 95.
72 *Id.*, p. 96.
73 *Ibid*.
74 *LD* II, p. 282.

«[Josiah] at first, not having the Book of the Law to guide him, he took such measures as natural conscience suggested; he put away idolatry generally. Thus he set out, not knowing whither he went. But it is the rule of God's providence, that those who act up to their light, shall be rewarded with clearer light... He was seeking God in the way of His commandments, and God met him there».[75]

In the *Memorandum* the same thing is said adopting different terminology: «for all have a natural conscience, which at once exhorts them to virtue and by an instinctive vigor extracts from even the worst religious systems those better parts and real truths which relate to the being, providence, and moral governance of God».[76]

In both reflections Newman confirms that «natural conscience» is the common denominator of humanity. It is contemporarily an inner source of privilege and duty.

Third, this presence in the heart, presented as natural conscience, divine voice or inward sense, having been recognized as such, has a definite role in helping the person not only to hear but also to obey: «he heard and obeyed... this same inward sense of his, strengthened by practice, unhesitatingly chose out the true one, the worship of the God of Israel».[77]

What the heart points towards is not information, in the sense of knowledge. It rather evidences obedience to the law within it. Newman constantly explores this dimension in his reflections on conscience: the truth of what conscience conveys lies not much in its being intellectually recognized, but, rather, in the imperativeness of its requests. Obedience takes on this dual role: it accepts truth as encountered in the heart and it willingly decides to live it out, as a decision of faith.

---

[75] *PS* VIII. 7, p. 98.
[76] *LD* II, p. 282.
[77] *PS* VIII. 7, p. 96.

4.3. Faith or Conscientiousness

Newman continues to explore a different aspect of conscience: its very important relation to faith.

«In conclusion, my brethren, I would have you observe in what Josiah's chief excellence lay. This is the character given him when his name is first mentioned; "He did ... right in the sight of the Lord, and walked in all the ways of David his father, and turned not aside to the right hand or to the left" (2Kings 22,2). He kept narrow the middle way. Now what is this strict virtue called? it is called faith. It is no matter whether we call it faith or conscientiousness, they are in substance one and the same: where there is faith, there is conscientiousness – where there is conscientiousness, there is faith; they may be distinguished from each other in words, but they are not divided in fact. They belong to one, and but one, habit of mind – dutifulness; they show themselves in obedience, in the careful, anxious observance of God's will, however we learn it».[78]

«Faith and conscientiousness» are linked together. This most valid contribution springs out in an almost natural fashion, especially when we evaluate the experience of conscience in relation to the voice it conveys.

While Newman firmly believes conscience to be the voice of the divine, he is also aware of the fact that the person going through this experience can risk either not seeing the truth in itself, or not taking the truth with the deep meaning it holds.

This is Newman's fear in his correspondence with his brother. The latter failed to see that the recognition of the voice within the heart cannot be taken lightly. If it is treated lightly, the person is missing an opportunity to discover the beyond, the relationship with his Maker, ultimately the experience of faith.

The other option left is to remain enslaved within an intellectual vicious circle, a rational *cul-de-sac*. For Newman, respect to that

---
78   *Id.*, p. 107.

voice is a conscientious attitude. It is the gateway to our relationship with God. Knowing that it is in us, recognizing the sound of that inward sense, and obeying it, is equivalent to faith. All this shows itself in dutifulness, as a habit of mind with the consequent obedience as the way to live out that presence.

4.4. Temptation of Sight: Preconceived Notions

Both reflections end up stressing the same point: the temptation of reducing the invisible to the power of human proof. In the sermon, Newman refers to the temptation of sight and the seductions of the world. In the *Memorandum* he refers to the danger of subjecting revealed doctrines to the test of our own «preconceived notion or moral theories» – a clear reference to the method he tries to confute in dealing with his brother. It is not difficult to detect how this controversy is, in some way, connected with the larger challenge that the tenets of liberalism will present to Newman.

«Hence it is that St. Paul tells us that "the just shall live by faith" under every dispensation of God's mercy. And this is called faith, because it implies a reliance on the mere word of the unseen God overpowering the temptations of sight. Whether it be we read and accept His word in Scripture (as Christians do), or His word in our conscience, the law written on the heart (as is the case with heathens); in either case, it is by following it, in spite of the seductions of the world around us, that we please God».[79]

«And the evidence for revelation (tho' in its own nature not demonstrative but practical) is very various in its forms and sources – in so much so, that no kind of evidence perhaps is supposable, which is not afforded us – ... – and lastly, I fully allow that arguments may be brought against it from any known facts, (...) – but that, since it professes to reveal things unknown, we

---
79 *Id.*, pp. 107-108.

may not subject those revealed doctrines to the test of our own preconceived notions and arbitrary theories of morals».[80]

Concluding the parallel study of both sources, Newman compares this experience of discovery to a child[81] who is left home on his own. In freedom, the child is grows in being his own master; he discovers obedience not through imposition but through love and fear: «just so, to try a child's obedience and to teach him to rule himself, instead of confining him when we go from home, we might leave him at large with a caution, as he loves and fears us, not to go out of doors».[82]

4.5. *The Self-Wise Inquirer*

The effects of the correspondence with Charles are also to be traced in the sermons preached between September 1830 and January 1831.[83] Among these, the one which contains a most systematic approach to the theme of revelation in relation to conscience is *The Self-Wise Inquirer*. In this sermon Newman organizes his ideas about the sources of our notions and the role of reason in relation to conscience.

There are two distinguished types of notions: those which can be trusted and those which cannot. «We must trust our notions in one shape or another, and some notions which we form are right and true».[84] The discriminating element between the two types is that false notions are a result of «that *evil* trusting to ourselves, that sinful self-confidence, or self-conceit, which is called in the

---

80 *LD* II, pp. 282-283.
81 Childhood, and the dynamics of moral growth it implies, is a very frequent theme in Newman's reflections on conscience.
82 *LD* II, p. 282.
83 *PS* VIII. 9. *Jeremiah, a Lesson for the Disappointed*; *PS* VIII. 13. *Truth Hidden when not Sought after*; *PS* I. 17. *The Self-Wise Inquirer*; *PS* VIII. 14. *Obedience to God the Way to Faith in Christ*; *PS* II. 9. *St. Paul's Conversion Viewed in Reference to His Office*.
84 *PS* I. 17, p. 216.

text the "wisdom of the world" [1Cor. 3,18. 19], and is a chief cause of our going wrong in our religious inquiries».[85]

Thus, from this premise, Newman concludes how the source of the good notions which conveys truth is natural conscience.

«These are the notions which we may trust without blame; viz. such as come to us by way of our Conscience, for such come from God. I mean our certainty that there is a right and a wrong, that some things ought to be done, and other things not done; that we have duties, the neglect of which brings remorse; and further, that God is good, wise, powerful and righteous, and that we should try to obey Him. All these notions, and a multitude of others like these, come by natural conscience, i.e. they are impressed on all our minds from our earliest years without our trouble».[86]

This is the first important point in the sermon: natural conscience, as a source of wisdom, comes from God since it proclaims his attributes. This wisdom is discovered as part of self yet transcending it. The recognition of the role of conscience, natural conscience, therefore, stretches far beyond the laying down of explicit commands; it is primarily concerned with an awareness of the sense of right and wrong, and encourages the discovery of a relationship with God who is «good, wise and powerful». These two notions, a sense of good and wrong and a sense of God, «do not proceed from the mere exercise of our minds, though it is true they are strengthened and formed thereby. They proceed from God, whether within us or without us».[87]

This profound relationship of dependence between God and our notions, safeguards the person from pride since the ultimate word does not belong to the created but to the Creator. Obedience leads to more certainty, while transgressions bring with them a sense of sin and guilt. Notions, therefore, do not pretend to be the result of personal conquests, but, rather, they

---
85   *Ibid.*
86   *Ibid.*
87   *Id.*, pp. 216-217.

are considered as a deeper understanding of a relationship. If these notions, then, are essentially related to God, it is the depth of Him, the knowledge about the All-wise, that enlarges their quantity and quality.

«These notions which we obtain without our exertion will never make us proud or conceited, because they are ever attended with a sense of sin and guilt, from the remembrance that we have at times transgressed and injured them. To trust them is not the false wisdom of the world, or foolishness, because they come from the Allwise God. And far from leading a man into error, they will, if obeyed, of a certainty lead him to a firm belief in Scripture; in which he will find all those vague conjectures and imperfect notions about Truth, which his own heart taught him, abundantly sanctioned, completed, and illustrated».[88]

The notions which are not rooted in this relationship with God, have the tendency of causing pride since their origin is solely restricted to the person's own self, where God is absent. The truth which these notions convey is the fruit of the value of self rather than a «revelation» of God: «everyone is in danger of valuing himself for what he does; and hence truths (or fancied truths) which a man has obtained for himself after much thought and labour, such he is apt to make much of, and to rely upon».[89]

If, then, a person relies solely on the reasoning powers, there is no place for other sources of truth, like Scripture, as a source of God's revelation of Himself. Since he:

«fancies he can find out truth by himself, (and) disdains revelation. He who thinks he has found it out, is impatient of revelation. He fears it will interfere with his own imaginary discoveries, he is unwilling to consult it; and when it does interfere, then he is angry».[90]

---
88   *Id.*, p. 217.
89   *Ibid.*
90   *Id.*, p. 218.

All this trust in one's own powers ends up by causing an attitude of indifference towards revelation. Here, again, Newman recalls the same reference to the heart which he used in the first part of the correspondence with his brother. Concluding, Newman writes: «Confidence, then, in our own reasoning powers leads to (what St. Paul calls) foolishness, by causing in our hearts an indifference towards, or a distaste for Scripture information».[91]

In the second part of the sermon, Newman deals with the role of reason and that of conscience. He presents the potential conflict that can occur between the two, one against the other, outlining what is the nature of the outcome if this conflict is in favour of the «usurping empire of mere reason».[92] He reminds us that: «our reasoning powers are very weak in all inquiries into moral and religious truth. Clear-sighted as reason is on other subjects, and trustworthy as a guide, still in questions connected with our duty to God and man it is very unskilful and equivocating».[93]

This is a very important definition of reason. As will become clearer later on in his life, Newman has no intention whatsoever of downgrading the importance of reason. His whole life goes on to witness an importance attached to the role of reason and of intellectual endeavours that is second to none. Yet, he is convinced that in matters which touch the depth of our being, reason cannot claim to be the best of guides.[94] The pattern of the relationship between the person and the Maker, does not allow

---

91 *Ibid.*
92 *Id.*, p. 224.
93 *Id.*, pp. 219-220.
94 In the sermon *PS* I. 9. *The Religious Use of Excited Feelings*, in reference to conversion, Newman outlines the relationship between conscience and reason: «Conscience, and Reason in subjection to Conscience, *these* are those powerful instruments (under grace) which change a man. But you will observe, that though Conscience and Reason lead us to resolve on and to attempt a new life, they cannot at once make us *love* it. It is long practice and habit which make us love religion; and in the beginning, obedience, doubtless, is very grievous to habitual sinners. Here then is the use of those earnest, ardent feelings of which I just now spoke, and which attend on the first exercise of Conscience and Reason, - to take away from the *beginnings* of obedience its *grievousness*, to give us an impulse which may carry us over the first obstacles, and send us on our way rejoicing», p. 115.

for the exclusive use of reason as a source of notions, since the latter is limited in its nature and function when compared to the whole. It cannot fully reach those «same great truths which are authoritatively set forth by Conscience and Scripture; and if it be used in religious inquiries, without reference to these divinely-sanctioned informants, the probability is it will miss the Truth altogether».[95]

The tension between the two is the scene of this world; it is the experience of every person, beginning from childhood. Every person lives this struggle between reason and conscience. It seems to be humanity's lot, besides being, also, humanity's temptation.

«Trusting our own powers for arriving at religious truth, instead of taking what is divinely provided for us, whether in nature or revelation. This is the way of the world. In the world Reason is set against Conscience, and usurps its power; and hence men become "wise in their own conceits", and "leaning to their own understandings", "err from the truth"».[96]

Childhood is the period where the person is in contact with the inward guide, pure and unquestioned. It is a time of trust and transparent behaviour where the temper of faith helps this divine enlightenment. Even if conscience is transgressed, yet it is not done away with – its authoritative presence is not questioned. The difficulties start when we leave this phase. In the measure our intellect grows, so does the temptation towards unbelief and disobedience.

«But when our minds became more manly, and the world opened upon us, then in proportion to the intellectual gifts with which God had honoured us, came the temptation of unbelief

---

95 *PS* I. 17, p. 219.
96 *Ibid.*; in a later sermon, *PS* VIII. 5. *Curiosity a Temptation to Sin*, Newman furthers this thought in the following way: «at first our conscience tells us, in a plain straightforward way, what is right and what is wrong; but when we trifle with this warning, our reason becomes perverted, and comes in aid of our wishes, and deceives us to our ruin», p. 67.

and disobedience. Then came reason, led on by passion, to war against our better knowledge».[97]

Here, then, lies the source of the conflict as Newman perceives it. The introduction of the intellect, with its workings and notions, tends to take the place of those notions which come from «natural conscience or revelation». The conflict is one which has the potential of leading to the exclusion of religion completely. The outline of that conflict is presented in all its implications.

«A murmuring against that religious service which is perfect freedom, complaints that Christ's yoke is heavy, a rebellious rising against the authority of Conscience, and a proud arguing against the Truth, or at least an endurance of doubt and scoffing, and a light, unmeaning use of sceptical arguments and assertions, these are the beginnings of apostasy. Then come the affection of originality, the desire to appear manly and independent, and the fear of the ridicule of our acquaintance, all combining to make us first speak, and then really think evil of the supreme authority of religion. This gradual transgression of the first commandment of the Law is generally attended by a transgression of the fifth. In our childhood we loved both religion and our home; but as we learn to despise the voice of God, so do we first affect, and then feel, an indifference towards the opinions of our superiors and elders. Thus our minds become gradually hardened against the purest pleasures, both divine and human».[98]

This is the journey of unbelief. One does not set out to refute the notions, «which are to be trusted». One is rather carried away by the notions which he arrives at by his own ability. Once this attitude is set in motion, there is a «graduality» about its growth. Nothing happens suddenly. One thing calls for another, as in a chain reaction. The whole person becomes involved: affection for originality and fear of ridicule, affections and then feelings of contempt for the voice of God and indifference towards superiors.

---

97 *PS* I. 17, p. 220.
98 *Id.*, pp. 220-221.

«It is quite plain, that, having nothing of that faith which "overcomes the world", they must be overcome by it... Deadness to the voice of God, hardness of heart, is one of the very symptoms of unbelief».[99]

By way of conclusion, Newman proceeds to analyse how the self-centred believer justifies his own position. First, having taken reason as the measure of truth, the influence of conscience has necessarily to give way. If conscience is absent so is religion, the symbol of the divine presence. These latter sources are substituted by a rational approach which functions through the power of the intellect as its sole medium to move forward. In this picture, moral growth becomes the result of what reason approves and of what intellect helps to bring about. Virtue is the daughter of intellectual knowledge.

«Having thus cast down moral excellence from its true station, and set up the usurping empire of mere reason, next they place a value upon all truths exactly in proportion to the possibility of proving them by means of that mere reason. Hence, moral and religious truths are thought little of by them, because they fall under the province of Conscience far more than of the intellect. Religion sinks in their estimation, or becomes of no account; they begin to think all religions alike; and no wonder, for they are like men who have lost the faculty of discerning colours, and who never, by any exercise of reason, can make out the difference between white and black. As to the code of morals, they acknowledge it in a measure, that is, so far as its dicta can be proved by reasoning, by an appeal to sight, and to expedience, and without reference to a natural sense of right and wrong as the sanction of these informants. Thinking much of intellectual advancement, they are much bent on improving the world by making all men intellectual; and they labour to convince themselves, that as men grow in knowledge they will grow in virtue».[100]

---

99 *Id.*, pp. 222-223.
100 *Id.*, p. 224.

Although other references in the sermons belonging to this period would help us to enlarge this vision, we are of the opinion that in this sermon we have an organised presentation of all the essential elements.

The point with which Newman himself concludes the sermon is that about obedience to conscience and how acting in obedience to this light is the source of more light. It is worth recalling because this same theme is brought up again and again in the sermons which follow the one examined above.[101]

«May we ever bear in mind, that the "fear of the Lord is the beginning of wisdom" (Prov. 1,7); that obedience to our conscience, in all things, great and small, is the way to know the Truth; that pride hardens the heart, and sensuality debases it; and all those who live in pride and sensual indulgence, can no more comprehend the way of the Holy Spirit, or know the voice of Christ, than the devils who believe with a dead faith and tremble!»[102]

5. The Spirit of Liberalism

Unlike the case of the correspondence with Charles, there does not exist a corpus of letters written precisely with the intent of liberalism in mind. There are, instead, reflections in various letters addressed to different people. Apparently, they do not appear to contain the uniformity that Charles' letters have, yet a detailed study will show how when these letters are taken together they convey an ensemble of ideas with a unifying factor running through them.

In these letters there seems to be a momentum gathering form one reflection to the next, until they reach a climax around

---

[101] They are *PS* VIII. 14, pp. 202, 210, 214; *PS* II. 9, pp. 103-104, 106; *PS* I. 22, pp. 292-293.
[102] *PS* I. 17, p. 227.

April 1832, the ripples of which will continue to travel until the following September.

5.1. Benevolence

During the year 1832 Newman embarks on a more detailed approach of the liberal challenge. The preaching of the university sermon *On Justice as a Principle of Divine Governance*,[103] gives him the opportunity to formulate a frontal attack on the tenets of liberalism. He sends a letter to R. H. Froude,[104] together with the manuscript of the same sermon, in which he points out the main elements of the liberal theory.

«The main thesis is against Sir James MacIntosh, Knight, whose assertion is the following: that (imperative per se as is the voice of conscience) yet the test of its correctness is its tending to the general good. Accordingly he supposes benevolence, unmixed and absolute, to be the attribute of the Divine Governance, and the end of the general good – and that it is impossible ("a contradiction in terms") for anyone, who holds (as all must hold as soon as it is stated) the general good to be the most desirable conceivable end of the world's course, to love and revere, i.e. to have religious feelings towards, a being of mixed and imperfect benevolence. Accordingly, that the feeling of justice in the mind is but a divinely appointed expedient for promoting the general good – and so again that of purity».[105]

Against this approach, Newman first questions the «cheerfulness» which such a view leads to. «Nominally» it resembles the Christian cheerfulness but it is only «superficial», not being the result of «sowing in tears» but only a theory produced in untroubled times: «it is a fault naturally produced by quiet

---
103 *US* 6, pp. 99-119.
104 *LD* III, pp. 35-36.
105 *Id.*, p. 35.

times, when property is secure etc. It is essentially unpractical, as not taking the world *as it is*, but as a theory – hence it never will get general influence etc. Reduced to an intellectual basis, it is Socinianism and Theophilanthropism».[106]

Then, Newman moves on to expose its outline, the principles on which it is based: «benevolence *the* end of Divine Governance, that evil merely remedial, that sin venial, that repentance a self evident atonement, that benevolence is the moral sense, and that opinions do not influence character».[107] From this he moves further on to question the arguments on which this whole theory is founded. He divides the whole discourse on two affirmations: first, «benevolence is *not* the one main attribute of Divine Governance for... it is not the one moral instinct»;[108] and secondly, «if benevolence *were* the only instinct of our moral nature, nothing would follow about the Divine».[109]

In his university sermon, Newman expounds on these two principles by balancing to the element of benevolence that of justice, not only in relation to self but also to the divine. We limit ourselves to point out the answers he gives, which are founded on the notion of conscience. Regarding the first affirmation, he writes:

«Now first, it is surely not true that benevolence is the only, or the chief, principle of our moral nature. To say nothing of the notion of duty to an unseen Governor, implied in the very authoritativeness with which conscience dictates to us (a notion which suggests to the mind that there is, in truth, some object

---

106 *Ibid.*; Socinianism is full explained in *US* 6, p. 104: «The essential dogmas of Socinianism are such as these: that the rule of Divine government is one of benevolence, and nothing but benevolence; that the evil is but remedial and temporary; that sin is of a venial nature; that repentance is a sufficient atonement for it; that the moral sense is substantially but an instinct of benevolence; and that doctrinal opinions do not influence our character or prospects, nor deserve our serious attention».
107 *LD* III, p. 35.
108 *Ibid.*
109 *Id.*, p. 36.

more "desirable in its own nature" that "the general happiness" of mankind – viz. the approbation of our Maker)».[110]

Regarding the second he believes that:

«we are under a natural attraction to admire and adore the great sight, just as we are led on (to compare small things with great) to dwell rapturously upon some exquisite work of man's designing, the beautiful and the harmonious result of the highest and most accomplished genius. If we do not habitually thus search out and lovingly hang over the traces of God's justice, which are around us, it is because we are ourselves sinners; because, having a bad conscience, we have a personal interest in denying them, and a terror in having them forced upon us. In proportion as we grow in habits of obedience, far from our vision of the eternal justice of God vanishing from our minds, and being disowned by our feelings, as if it were but the useful misconception of a less advanced virtue, doubtless it increases, as fear is cast out».[111]

5.2. God's attributes

In more straightforward, expressive and condensed terms, Froude, having received Newman's manuscript, captures the whole in the following verses:

«"If benevolence is the only instinct of our Moral Nature still nothing follows about the divine". This is the contradictory of Sir J's (Macintosh) fundamental proposition – i.e. "that God has no attributes but what man approves". ... Might not something be said on the silliness of attempting to reduce all our Moral instincts to one, generally... All these fellows suppose that they have proved their point, as soon as they have proved that it is not palpably false – i.e. that their theory may be consistent with the

---
110 *US* 6, pp. 105-106.
111 *Id.*, p. 107.

main phenomena. This may be very well where the phenomena are as intricate as those of the heavens the hypothesis as simple as that of gravity, and the account as perfect as that of the Principia – but will scarcely do in another case – where the phenomena are almost as simple as the hypothesis, and the account requires itself to be accounted for».[112]

What follows after this correspondence and the preaching of the university sermon, is the ripple effect: reflections in his letters and also direct references to the liberal issue in his *Parochial And Plain Sermons*. In the period between April and July 1832, Newman gives the impression of quieting the whole affair. Few letters seem to contain direct reference to liberalism, yet what we find there is quite revealing.

In a letter the day after the preaching of the university sermon, Newman shares his idea about «the present reign of Whiggery», defining them as «neither fish, flesh, nor fowl – and have no resting place – their whole view is a supercilious theory – their policy is liberalism, and their basis Socinianism – they have no root in the heart».[113] Using more or less the same vocabulary of previous letters he rejects «that cold and scoffing theory, which says there is no great evil in the world, affects non-chalance, and says all religions are about the same, nothing can come of it – it is a shortlived dream».[114] These constant thoughts continue to occupy Newman's mind. The letters, while not dealing directly with the subject, nevertheless, they do contain phrases about liberalism.

What we can notice in his correspondence is an insight into the way Newman's mind continues to think and work on an idea, even though the latter does not seem to be holding centre stage in his letters. In July 1832, in a letter to F. Rogers, he writes: «is not this the very spirit of whiggery, opposition for its own sake,

---

112 *LD* III, p. 37.
113 *Id.*, p. 42.
114 *Ibid.*

striving against the truth because it happens to be commanded us, as if wisdom were less wise because it is powerful».[115] Thus, from August onwards we witness again a resurgence of interest in the form of two sermons[116] and a very important letter.[117]

5.3. *The Religion of the Day* [118]

In this sermon, Newman reflects, from a spiritual and moral point of view, on what are the implications of the liberal theory. He does not directly mention the theory, yet the study both of the vocabulary and the structure of the sermon are very similar to what we have discovered so far in his letters.

He calls the present difficulty in religion as «Satan's device» whose aim it is «to break our strength; to force us down to the earth, – to bind us there. The world is his instrument for this purpose; but he is too wise to set it in open opposition to the Word of God».[119] This is the scenario against which Newman presents the sermon.

First he explains how all those realities that have been influenced by revelation, are now being transferred outside its realm. The whole value system is completely shifted from under the influence of the word revealed:

«This is the religion natural to a civilized age, and well has Satan dressed and completed it into an idol of the Truth. As the reason is cultivated, the taste formed, the affections and sentiments refined, a general decency and grace will of course spread over the face of society, quite independently of the influence of Revelation. That beauty and delicacy of thought ... then extends to the conduct of life, to all we have, all we do, all we are. Our manners are

---
115 *Id.*, p. 72, on 25th July 1832.
116 *PS* I. 24. *The Religion of the Day*; *PS* I. 7. *Sins of Ignorance and Weakness*.
117 *LD* III, pp. 89-91, letter to Samuel Francis Wood on 4th September 1832.
118 *PS* I. 24.
119 *Id.*, pp. 310, 311.

courteous; we avoid giving pain or offence; our words become correct; our relative duties are carefully performed. Our sense of propriety shows itself even in our domestic arrangements, in the embellishments of our houses, in our amusements, and so also in our religious profession. Vice now becomes unseemly and hideous to the imagination, or, at is sometimes familiarly said, "out of taste"».[120]

Once this mind-set is promoted, the former influence of revealed religion becomes replaced by some other system. The measure with which we discover what is morally right or wrong, now has a new name, the sense of «elegance». Since this measure is not divinely revealed or divinely related, its effects have no claim on the conduct of the person. It is a fluid principle, adaptable to every situation: «elegance is gradually made the test and standard of virtue, which is no longer thought to possess an intrinsic claim on our hearts, or to exist, *further than* it leads to the quiet and comfort of others».[121]

With this newly adapted «test», the need for conscience is a contradiction. Conscience has no role to play since the person has nothing to be told or to be informed of: the self becomes the source and centre of the whole life experience.

«Conscience is no longer recognized as an independent arbiter of actions, its authority is explained away; partly it is superseded in the minds of men by the so-called moral sense, which is regarded merely as the love of the beautiful; partly by the rule of expediency, which is forthwith substituted for it in the details of conduct».[122]

This type of religiosity, or lack of it, necessarily leads to a vision where «everything is bright and cheerful. Religion is pleasant and easy; benevolence is the chief virtue; intolerance, bigotry, excess of zeal, are the first of sins».[123]

---

120 *Id.*, pp. 311-312.
121 *Id.*, p. 312.
122 *Ibid.*
123 *Ibid.*

This first part of the sermon, therefore, presents the picture to us of a religion which is «only partially evangelical, built upon worldly principle, yet pretending to be the Gospel, dropping one whole side of the Gospel, its austere character, and considering it enough to be benevolent, courteous, candid, correct in conduct, delicate». Newman identifies the origin of this «new framework... new character of mind» in the work of «the enemy of our souls» and is done in a way as «to resemble the Christian obedience as near as it may, its likeness all the time being accidental».[124]

The centrality of the heart, or the absence of it, resurfaces again in this sermon with the same importance that it appeared in the first letters to Charles. When the heart factor is not taken into consideration, the intellect needs to create parameters and find reference points where the place of the divine is appropriated and, consequently, substituted with something else.

In Newman's understanding, the heart experience, directly linked to the voice of conscience, necessarily leads to the contact with the word of God. The person who, on the contrary, chooses the role of the intellect, at the exclusion of the contribution of the heart, is especially attracted to «the form of doctrine, which I have called the religion of the day, (which) is especially adapted to please men of sceptical minds».[125] These are the ones «who have never been careful to obey their conscience, who cultivate the intellect without disciplining the heart, and who allow themselves to speculate freely about what religion *ought to be*, without going to the Scripture to discover what it really is».[126]

Here, for Newman, lies the central issue of the religion of the day: the cultivated mind, having discarded the experience of the heart, goes on to substitute true religion with something similar to it but essentially different; a religion accidentally related to God but intentionally relative to self. In the following quotation,

---

124 *Id.*, pp. 313-314.
125 *Id.*, p. 316.
126 *Id.*, pp. 316-317.

it is evident how for Newman religion is not a space signed by admiration but rather an invitation to enter into a relationship and dialogue. The distance between «myself and my Creator» vanishes the moment we discover God who speaks to us from within.

«They lay much stress on works on Natural Theology, and think that all religion is contained in these; whereas, in truth, there is no greater fallacy than to suppose such works to be in themselves in any true sense religious at all... how are we concerned with the sun, moon and stars? or with the laws of the universe? how will they teach us our duty? how will they speak to sinners? They do not speak to sinners at all... They "declare the glory of God", but not His will... We see nothing there of God's wrath, of which the conscience of a sinner loudly speaks. So there cannot be a more dangerous (though a common) device of Satan, than to carry us from our own secret thoughts, to make us forget our own hearts, which tell us of a God of justice and holiness, and to fix our attention merely on the God who made the heavens; who is our God indeed, but not God manifested to us sinners, but as He shineth forth to His Angels, and to His elect hereafter».[127]

Those who found their existence on the intellect at the exclusion of the heart, therefore, cannot quench the tension of self towards the divine. Since «they have no language within their heart responding to them: conscience has been silenced»,[128] they will have to provide a substitute which will only satisfy in a superficial way. And, adopting the same vocabulary of the previous letters, Newman repeats that «the only information they have received concerning God has been from Natural Theology, and that speaks only of benevolence and harmony; so they will not credit the plain word of Scripture».[129]

In the latter part of the sermon, Newman presents the biblical examples of Jonah and Christ: both are sleeping in the boat. That

---

127 *Id.*, p. 317.
128 *Id.*, p. 319.
129 *Ibid.*

«peace of mind, a quiet conscience, and a cheerful countenance»[130] which seem to characterize both states, the Christian religion and the religion of the world, have as much different causes as the sleep of Jonah and that of Christ.

«Jonah slept in the storm, – so did our Blessed Lord. The one slept in an evil security: the Other in the "peace of God which passeth all understanding". These two states cannot be confounded together, they are perfectly distinct; and as distinct is the calm of the man of the world from that of the Christian… Applying this to the present religion of the educated world, full as it is of security and cheerfulness, and decorum, and benevolence, I observe that these appearances may arise either from a great deal of religion, or from the absence of it; they may be the fruits of shallowness of mind and a blinded conscience, or of that faith which has peace with God through our Lord Jesus Christ».[131]

5.4. Knowledge and Improvement of Morality

In a letter written after the above sermon, Newman shares a reflection regarding the effect of knowledge and education on the moral life of the person. In recalling the role of the intellect and the experience of self within the heart, he sees in the acquisition of knowledge the danger of self-confidence and arrogance unless it is balanced with a real knowledge of the person.

«If men could be brought to know their weakness in proportion as they learned what is called their strength, then of course knowledge would not be dangerous – but this is impossible. This is the cause of self conceit and vanity generally – not that men fancy good in them which is not, but that they do not see the evil mixed with it and overbalancing it».[132]

---
130 *Id.*, p. 321.
131 *Ibid.*
132 *LD* III, p. 90.

As Newman's idea of the person is one which is centred on the heart, in this «moral structure» knowledge has a definite place in relation to the whole. What has previously been suggested regarding the role of reason, can be applied to knowledge. When the latter becomes a principle in itself, by itself, its tendency is to create self-conceit. This, in turn, leads to another practical mistake, that is, a vision is put forward where things can be put right by scientific knowledge rather than by the human will.

«Men see that those parts of the national system, (...) which really depend on personal and private virtue do not work well – and, not seeing [where] the deficiency lies, viz. in want of personal virtue, they imagine they can put things right by applying their scientific knowledge to the improvement of the existing system – Hence political economy is to supersede morality... our existing systems may be materially improved... but still, in spite of all this, I will state a principle, which seems to be most important and most neglected – that the difference between this and that system is as nothing compared with the effects of the human will upon them, that till the will be changed from evil to good, the difference of the results between two given systems will be imperceptible... But it is the fashion of the day to consider the human mind as a machine and to think that education will do any thing for it».[133]

Education considered as the power of the human mind, supreme and exclusive, is alien to the whole notion of the person discovered so far in Newman. This reference of the human will,[134] an aspect of moral agency, features in the following sermon, which closes the examination of the different sources for this first period before Newman starts his Mediterranean tour in December 1832.

---

133 *Id.*, pp. 90-91.
134 The role of the human will be further developed by Newman in his sermon *PS* V. 24. *The Power of the Will*, where the role of the will is intimately related with that of the heart.

5.5. *Sins of Ignorance and Weakness*[135]

In this sermon the references in relation to the liberal attitude recall some of the main elements that have surfaced all along this study, namely, heart, prayer and conscience. The sermon, taking the text from the letter to the Hebrews – «Let us draw near with a true heart in full assurance of faith, having our heart sprinkled from an evil conscience, and our bodies washed with pure water» (Heb. 10,22) – starts by considering the role of prayer as more than mere ritual demand. Newman presents prayer as that action which after recognizing the sinfulness of human nature, it follows to cleanse conscience from guilt.

«Among the reasons which may be assigned for the observance of prayer at stated times, there is one which is very obvious, and yet perhaps is not so carefully remembered and acted upon as it should be. I mean the necessity of sinners cleansing themselves from time to time of the ever-accumulating guilt which loads their consciences».[136]

This is very much in line with was said before in his previous sermons,[137] where prayer is that work of faith which is «bidden by conscience, and authorized by reason».[138] The role of prayer, then, is taken to be an act of the person flowing from faithfulness towards reason and conscience. It is an act of the will of the person, as a moral agent, to put into practice the saving power of Christ, helping him or her towards light.

«We cannot profit by the work of a Saviour, though He be the Blessed Son of God, so as to be saved thereby without our own working; for we are moral agents, we have a will of our own, and Christ must be formed in us, and turn us from darkness to light,

---

135 *PS* I. 7.
136 *Id.*, p. 83.
137 *PS* VII. 15. *Mental Prayer*; *PS* I. 19. *Times of Private Prayer*; *PS* I. 20. *Forms of Private Prayer*.
138 See also *PS* I. 19, p. 245 and *PS* VII. 15, pp. 204-205.

if God's gracious purpose, fulfilled upon the cross, is to be in our case more than a name, an abused wasted privilege».[139]

The free moral agency is not simply an experience of self enclosed in a relationship with self, as it would be in the liberal spirit. It is rather a recognition of the power of self in relation to God. It is within this framework, that the person, not only becomes aware of the sinfulness within, – «men can without trouble be brought to confess that they sin, i.e. that they commit sins. They know well enough that they are not perfect; nay, that they do nothing in the best manner»,[140] – but also be convinced of the need to be cleansed. This attitude of the heart does not leave space for pride, which leads the person in a state where he or she is «far gone in degradation, has lost even that false independence of mind which is often a substitute for real religion».[141]

Although sin is a shame, it contains within itself an invitation to go deeper into that knowledge of conscience which leads us nearer to God. «This is our shame; but I notice it here, not so much as a humbling thought, as with a view of pressing upon your consciences the necessity of appearing before God at stated seasons, in order to put aside the continually-renewed guilt of your nature».[142] Sin, therefore becomes the moment to go within and listen to the voice. «Let him have recourse to a more accurate search into his conscience; and ask himself whether he "draws nearer to God with a true heart"».[143]

Conclusion

Newman is a pilgrim on a journey of discovery, who, in his movement forward, is continually strengthening his basic beliefs

---

139 *PS* I. 7, p. 85.
140 *Id.*, p. 87.
141 *Ibid.*
142 *Id.*, p. 88.
143 *Id., p. 95.*

concerning the person. The convictions that come out are enriched and focused with every written reflection, with every event. There is consistency and growth in an inclusive way.

Another dimension of Newman's personality is that of his ability to read a situation, analyse its different composite elements, and through understanding, intelligence and also intuition, succeeds to highlight what is essential. The ability to detect the subtleties between true and false religion, to point out where correct and false reasoning is found, is a trait already found at the early stages of his life.

The years under examination here constitute the first period of his preaching ministry. In general, events are mainly of a causal nature, that is, they help, or cause, Newman to bring out what is best in him. The sharing and development of his ideas are, so far, mainly conditioned by the events which are taking place around him and in which he gets involved.

In the next *Chapter*, concerning the second period of Newman's anglican preaching ministry, the inverse tendency will take place. Notions will not develop as a result of events which take place around him, but notions and ideas will be the causes in directing and influencing events. The primacy will belong not to events over notions, but to notions and beliefs, principles and convictions, over events. The «Oxford Movement» is a case in point. What Newman sees intuitively, his «idea», is the foundational cause in bringing about this movement. The conversion to the Church of Rome will symbolize the natural outcome of a conviction, lived in conscience, which will reach its fullness of strength and meaning.

CHAPTER 3
Advocacy of Conscience
1833-1843

The second period of Newman's Anglican ministry starts with the tour of the Mediterranean.[1] Besides the historical and literary interest, this voyage proves beneficial in giving Newman a chance to look at his own personal experience from a distance. While recognizing this benefit in his letters, he still longs to be back in Oxford, in his Oriel rooms: «I am for many reasons very glad that I have come out here. I think travelling a good thing for a secluded man, not so much as showing him the world, as in realizing to him the limited sphere of his own powers».[2]

The tour cannot simply be considered as an event that divides, or unites, two periods. It has an effect on Newman in helping him to understand reality with broader mind. His going away is an occasion for him to think and reflect both on his own personal life and on the life of the Church, to which he feels so much attached. The tour does not change Newman in any dramatic way. It enlarges his vision, it brings him in contact with existing realities which from now on acquire a new meaning for him. It makes him aware that he can run the risk

---

[1] The Mediterranean tour started the day after he preached university sermon on Sunday, 2nd December 1832. It lasted until Tuesday, 9th July 1833; see I. KER, *John Henry Newman*. (Oxford University Press, Oxford - New York 1988) pp. 54-80.
[2] *LD* III, p. 194.

of being so near to where things are taking place, yet being so far by not realizing it.

«I think I have much deepened my conviction of the intellectual weakness which attaches to a mere reading man – his inability to grasp and understand and appropriate things which befal him in life – so that he seems powerless as a child while the action of life is passing and repassing, and tossed about and caught and transmitted on all sides of him».[3]

1. A Work to do

In the *Apologia*, Newman writes about his feelings while visiting Rome during the tour. Two realities are troubling him at the time: the course of the liberal idea, and, as a consequence of this, the deep-seated feeling that he has to do something about the Church. These two realities need to be essentially linked with each other. Since it is the love he has for the Church which guides his journey of faith, he is very much aware of the dangers the liberal mentality holds in relation to the understanding of faith. Liberalism for Newman means draining the experience of faith from that which characterizes it, that is the pre-eminence of the divine. The love for the Church is nothing more than belonging to that body where faith is lived as an experience between «myself and my Creator». Thus «the success of the Liberal cause... fretted me inwardly. I became fierce against its instruments and its manifestations».[4]

A second feeling, connected with the first, is that he is becoming more and more convinced that he has a «work» to do once he is back home: «when we took leave of Monsignore Wiseman, he had courteously expressed a wish that we might make a second

---

3   *Ibid.*
4   *Apol.*. p. 33.

visit to Rome; I said with great gravity, 'We have a work to do in England'. I went down at once to Sicily, and the presentiment grew stronger».[5]

In one of his letters to his mother just days before he is about to reach home, Newman writes that he feels «some unseen power, good or bad, was resisting my return… God is giving me a severe lesson of patience, and I trust I am not altogether wasting the opportunity of discipline. It is His will. I strive to think that, wherever I am, God is God, and I am I».[6]

These few lines contain what can be considered as a programme for Newman's action for the coming years. As his story unfolds, it becomes clear that, whether he is struggling against the liberal idea or preaching on the journey of faith, there is the constant prayer and reminder that doing the will of God is his main aim during these turbulent years.

What will be later known as the «Oxford Movement», has to be traced back to what Newman experiences before the tour and, more importantly, to how Newman feels immediately after it. «Especially when I was left by myself, the thought came upon me that deliverance is wrought, not by the many but by the few, not by bodies but by persons».[7]

What follows in the line of events will only confirm how Newman's contribution cannot be explained in terms of a reaction. Newman moves forward sustained by a vision and it is from inside that vision, that he is enlightened and strengthened. The following pages deal with this vision and where does that energy, eventually, leads him.

---

5   *Ibid.*«My servant, who had acted as my nurse, asked what ailed me. I could only answer him, 'I have a work to do in England'», in *id.*, p. 35.
6   *LD* IV, p. 3.
7   *Apol.* p. 34.

1.1. Primitive Christianity

The Church is for Newman a reality where the human and the divine meet. It is within the Church, through the sacrament of Baptism, that the person is admitted into the visible body of Christ. Thus the human reality and the divine come together in the Church.

«No harm can come of the distinction of the Church into Visible and Invisible, while we view it as, on the whole, but one in different aspects; as Visible, because consisting (for instance) of clergy and laity – as Invisible, because resting for its life and strength upon unseen influences and gifts from heaven».[8]

With this idea of the Church in mind, Newman is aware of the consequences the liberal idea has in highlighting the rational at the expense of the divine.[9] The only way to overcome this challenge, is to go back to the source, primitive Christianity, to understand how the ecclesial experience developed and to measure how far, or how near, the experience of the Church now is to the Church then. This, essentially, meant rediscovering the Fathers, with whom he had already established a familiar rapport before, while studying the life of the first centuries of the Church.

At this stage, what Newman brings to the Anglican Communion is the emerging conviction that *sola Scriptura* is not sufficiently strong to stand the attack of the liberal idea. He is gradually becoming aware of the fact that the *sola Scriptura*[10] needs roots, that is the backing of the tradition, which give to the message both life and energy.

---

[8] *PS* III. 16, p. 222.
[9] «The High Church Oxford Movement began in 1833, under the aegis of John Keble, John Henry Newman and Richard Hurrell Froude, in a conservative reaction against the radical forces, political and religious, which even then seemed to threaten the Church of England's destruction», in S. GILLEY, 'The Ecclesiology of the Oxford Movement: a Reconsideration', in P. VAISS (ed.), *Newman: From Oxford to the People*. (Gracewing, Herefordshire 1996) pp. 60-61.
[10] *Id.*, p. 64.

«Men may say what they will about going by Scripture not tradition – but nature is stronger than systems. The piety and services of the Primitive Christians add to their authority an influence which is practically irresistible, with those i.e. who are trained in right feelings and habits. And I think this was intended by the Author of all truth – And none but Primitive Christianity can bring this about, or other ages, if they have the high spirit, yet have not (of course,) the authority of the first age. As to Scripture being practically sufficient for making the Christian, it seems to me a mere dream – nor do I find it anywhere said so in Scripture – nor can I infer logically that what is confessedly the sole oracle of doctrine, is therefore also of practice and discipline».[11]

1.2. The Fathers as Precedents

The Fathers start featuring again in Newman's reading immediately after his return to England: «for myself, I am poking into the Fathers with a hope of rummaging forth passages of history which may prepare the *imaginations* of men for a changed state of things, and also be precedents for our conduct in difficult circumstances».[12]

Their appearance is directly related to the need of being informed about the Church of the first centuries. This need, though, is not primarily connected with Newman's later publication on development. It is rather concerned with the importance these centuries hold in relation to the actual state of the Church of England.

The same applies to the «Oxford Movement». In the beginning, the willingness to discover the Fathers is more in line with the need of a force and a guide. As the idea of the Church becomes more

---
11 *LD* III, p. 127.
12 *LD* IV, p. 24.

and more clear through the contact with the Fathers,[13] so does the strength of the «Oxford Movement» gather its momentum.[14]

In 1835, this interest in the Fathers starts producing some clear ideas in Newman's mind. Before presenting them, it is worth recalling the method Newman is adopting in reading the Fathers. He himself has come to realise that unless one has an object for his reading, the risk is that of wasting energy on study without really collecting anything. He takes advantage of the fact that he has already worked on the Fathers for his *Arians* and of having been in contact with them in 1828. Yet, he is also conscious of the fact that the way he is approaching them now is completely different and more fruitful.

«For myself, I am prosecuting my reading of the Fathers, which is very slow work. There is so much to digest, that it is quite dispiriting to find how little I get through; though I suppose one moves on imperceptibly... It is so difficult to read without an object. I may also add so unprofitable – but I rather mean this – that nothing at all is done, if a man begins to read the Fathers without a previous knowledge of controversies which are built upon them. Till then their writings are blank paper – controversy is like the heat administered to sympathetic ink. Thus I read Justin very careful in 1828 – and made most copious notes – but I conceive most of my time was thrown away. I was like a sailor landed at Athens or Grand Cairo, who stares about – does not know what to admire, what to examine – makes random remarks, and forgets all about it when he has gone».[15]

---

13 «We all know that the Oxford Movement began precisely with the discovery and the very strong affirmation of the specific nature of the Church, the Body of Christ, the Spouse of Christ, in this world but not of this world... A call to strengthen their (faithful) deep roots in the life of the Church as it has been essentially since the time of the Apostles», in N. LOSSKY, 'The Oxford Movement and the Revival of Patristic Theology', in P. VAISS, (ed.), *From Oxford to People*, p. 79.

14 «Both these elements – an appeal to the Fathers as interpreters of Scripture, and a sacramentalism of nature and the world, into which the sacraments of the Church fitted easily – were to be fundamental to the mind of the Oxford Movement», in O. CHADWICK, *The Mind of the Oxford Movement*, p. 18.

15 *LD* V, p. 133.

The synthesis that is slowly forming is based on three basic ideas: the Church, Scripture and Tradition. The essential reality of the Church consists in the experience of faith as presented in Scripture; Tradition is the witness to this experience. In a letter to Froude, written in great haste, Newman shares his opinions on these ideas.

«I incline to say the Creed is the faith necessary to salvation as well as to Church communion – and to maintain that Scripture, according to the Fathers, is the authentic record and document of this faith… I am surprised more and more to see how entirely they fall into Hawkins' theory even in set words, that Scripture proves, and the Church teaches… It seems that when a heresy rose, they said at once 'That is not according to the Church's teaching –' i.e. they decided it by the praejudicium (N.B. prescription) of authority – Again when they met together in Council, they brought the witness of Tradition as a matter of fact – but, when they discussed the matter in council, cleared their views etc etc. proved their point, they always went to Scripture alone. They never said 'It must be so and so – because St Cyprian says this – St Clement explains in his 3rd book of the Paedagogus etc –' and with reason – for the Fathers are a witness only as one voice not in individual instances, or much less isolated passages – but every word of Scripture is inspired and available.

I am writing so fast, I cannot think what I am saying – but though I have not yet the clearest and most defined views, or a καταληψισ (grasp) as the Stoics called it, I think it is not a mares nest».[16]

With the knowledge that he is following the route of the Fathers, Newman is convinced of the fact that he is following the right path:[17] «You see when one knows one has all the Fathers round

---

16   *Id.*, p. 126.
17   «I can answer but throw myself on the general Church, and avow (as I do) that if any one will show me an opinion of mine which the primitive Church condemned I will renounce it – any which it did not insist on, I will not insist on it», in *id.*, p. 100.

one, let be that little mishaps and mistakes may befall, yet on the whole one feels secure and comfortable».[18]

An essential dimension, at this point, lies in the fact that the search for truth is not purely understood and sought on the level of knowledge. Discovering the truth is not mainly confirming one's own ideas in relation to another set of ideas. In Newman there exists an attitudinal tension towards truth that is based on his relationship with the Almighty. His whole personality, intelligence and will, the mind and the heart, tend to form a pattern of living where the will of God becomes life.

1.3. Precedents and Trial

The realm of the Fathers, with its historical value, is a reassurance to Newman that, whatever action to be taken or path to be followed, all he needs to do is to refer to their authority. On them he wants to trace his own path. Through times of trial and challenges, when having a guide becomes indispensable, Newman knows where to look for help.

«I feel more and more the blunders one makes from acting on one's own partial view of a subject, having neither that comprehensive knowledge nor precedents for acting which history gives us. – I am resolved, if I can help, not to move a step without some authority to back me, direct or by fair inference... we are led to hope that, after a crisis, the Church has a fair prospect of raising her head again, and reigning as in her youth».[19]

While still in Rome, during the tour, Newman prepares himself for the hard times that lie ahead – «evil is before us. Clouds seem to gather round the Church. No one can tell what his lot will be».[20] On his return, in two separate letters to Keble, he writes, first,

---

18   *LD* VI, p. 13.
19   *LD* III, pp. 249-250.
20   *Id.*, p. 292.

about the need to «ascertain our position, get up precedents, and know our duty»;[21] secondly he is «convinced about the propriety of preaching and otherwise preparing one's flock for some trial of their Church Principles».[22]

He sees the times ahead as ones where what is at stake is the survival of the Church.[23] His approach is consistent with his beliefs: he is more concerned about the truth that needs to be discovered and proclaimed, rather than with the results which, humanly speaking, can condition one's approach.[24] On his return, Newman is already propagating the idea of a society to handle precisely this duty. The eventual «Oxford Movement», which issues out of it, embodies Newman's thinking at this stage:[25] «my first notion of the Society was this, 'a mere name, which may give us pretext for agitating'... I cannot but hope on the whole, that this Society will be a first step towards bringing men of like minds together».[26]

Understanding the role of the Fathers as light bearers, Newman applies this image to the meaning of the society. He sees it as an act of duty towards a Church which is running the risk of being robbed of its real nature: «we must not be shuffled out of our faith; we have a duty to perform, lest others be seduced also... Who can doubt, with these facts before him, that the movement at Oxford is but the *advanced guard* of a black host, and that it desires to achieve the first of a series of changes?».[27]

---

21 *LD* IV, p. 21.
22 *Id.*, p. 22.
23 «It would give me a real pleasure to find myself with you: and these are times when one's feelings and principles are tried so at every turn, that it is particularly needful to see one's friends often, to be sure how one is going on», in *id.*, p. 33.
24 «I am sure the Apostles did not sit still; and agitation is the order of the day. I do not at all fear for the result, were we thrown on the people», in *ibid.*
25 «Newman gave the Movement leadership, and coherence, and influence, the form of a party. He was the decisive kind, he made opponents and disciples. He gave them a beauty of language in sacramental apprehension, a concern for forms of worship and for the ascetic modes of holiness, a love of the Fathers and their thought», in O. CHADWICK, *The Mind of the Oxford Movement*, p. 46.
26 *LD* IV, pp. 51-52.
27 *LD* V, p. 51.

1.4. The Clergy

The fact that Newman is himself a clergyman gives considerable weight to his views regarding the state of the clerical class of his time. His position at Oxford lends even more authority to his views. He is aware of the effects the coming years of trials will have considering the quality of their formation. Newman qualifies the present situation of the clergy as «deficient in ecclesiastical *knowledge*».[28] This state of affairs calls for something to be done.

After his return from the tour, he identifies the «rousing» of the clergy as an important aim of the society. What the «Oxford Movement» will achieve in a direct way through learning, will have as one of its objectives that of animating the clerical class, making it more aware of the need «to unite on this simple principle – with a view to stir up our brethren to consider the state of the Church, and especially to the practical belief and preaching of the Apostolic Succession».[29]

The state of this clerical deficiency develops into two correlated problems. First, from the clerical standpoint, those who are the ones called to offer their help at this time of crisis are unable to give it. Secondly, from a broader perspective, and for Newman a greater cause for suffering, the liberal attitude is making progress not much out of its own steam but more from the lack of effective presence the same clergy are called to have. The following quotation, from a letter to his auntie, laments about these two sides of the same situation.

«But I have far graver objects in view. I mean, one must expect a flood of scepticism on the most important subjects to pour over the land, and we are so unprepared, it is quite frightful to think of it. The most religious-minded men are ready to give up important doctrinal truths because they do not understand their value. A cry is raised that the Creeds are unnecessarily minute,

---

28 *LD* IV, p. 24.
29 *Id.*, p. 29.

and even those who would defend, through ignorance cannot...
What is most painful is that the clergy are so utterly ignorant on
the subject. We have no theological education, and instead of
profiting by the example of past times, we attempt to decide the
most intricate questions, whether of doctrine or conduct, by our
own blind and erring reason».[30]

1.5. The Church Visible and Invisible

The ecclesiology within Newman is evidently proclaimed by the events of his life. What follows is not much a dogmatic presentation of the ecclesiological theories to be found in Newman, it is rather an exposition of how the ideas he shares about the Church, present him as a person who convincingly feels part of a living reality. This understanding is the soul of his action; these beliefs are for him first principles that direct his life.

In the first years of this second period, a detailed idea of Newman's understanding of the Church can be discovered through a parallel study between his letters and his sermons. In the year 1833, in one of his controversies, published on *The Record*, there are some important principles on the notion of the Church which will develop in the following years.

Newman understands the Church as presented in the parable of the wheat and the tares. The characteristic of the Church as invisible does not exclude the human aspect, its being also visible. They are two aspects of the same reality.

«At the same time when I speak of a pure Church, I would not be supposed to imply the expectation that the time will ever come when all the members of a Church will be members of Christ's invisible kingdom; no rules can do this, of course; and we know,

---

30 *LD* V, pp. 120-121.

on our Lord's own authority, that the tares will ever be mixed with the wheat while the present state of things lasts».[31]

The existence of the wheat and the tares, not being a static reality, expresses the visible experience of the Church which is in constant tension towards the invisible type. This energy and this movement need to be well understood if one wants to get a real meaning of history[32] and a healthy reading of the present reality.

«Now my notion of our blessed Lord's design as to the visible Church is this; that, besides its being the bosom of the Church invisible (i.e. as having the dispensation of the sacraments), it was intended as a type of it, and a means towards forming it – a means, by preaching and teaching; and a type or figure, as holding up conspicuously before the ungodly world, the rules of God's governance, the gospel system, and the final separation of sinners from the elect».[33]

The same theme is developed in his preaching. Reference to two sermons, besides confirming the internal relationship between his preaching and his personal reflection, goes a long way to show how for Newman the reality of the Church is not dependent on any human or political calculation. The first sermon, *The Visible Church an Encouragement to Faith*[34] centres on the faithful and their relationship with the world. The Church is a source of support and encouragement. It touches the practical side of the living of faith as an experience clearly based on the idea that «in the Visible Church the Church Invisible is gradually moulded and matured. It is formed slowly and variously by the Blessed Spirit of God, in the instance of this man and that, who belong to the general body».[35]

---

31 *LD* IV, p. 63.
32 «This is why it is a Christian's characteristic to look back on former times. The man of this world lives in the present, or speculates about the future; but faith rests upon the past and is content. It makes the past the mirror of the future», in *PS* III. 17, pp. 244-245.
33 *LD* IV, pp. 63-64.
34 *PS* III. 17, pp. 236-253.

«Hence, in their spheres, whether high or low, the faithful few are witnesses; they are witnesses for God and Christ, in their lives, and by their protestations, without judging others, or exalting themselves... still, on the whole, they are witnesses, a light witnesses against darkness by the contrast – giving good and receiving back evil; receiving back on themselves the contempt, the ridicule, and the opposition of the world, mixed, indeed, with some praise and reverence, reverence which does not last long, but soon becomes fear and hatred».[36]

In the second sermon, *The Church Visible and Invisible*,[37] Newman presents what he believes the Church really is: «the word Church, applied to the body of Christians in this world, means but one thing in Scripture, a visible body invested with invisible privileges».[38] Along with this explanation he deals with two issues. The first one is «that bad men are in the Visible Church».[39] The second is that «there are good men external to the Visible Church, therefore there is a second Church called the Invisible».[40]

To the first statement, Newman uses the paradigm of the dead branch of a tree. The death of the branch is not the death of the tree. The branch receives life from the tree but can never inflict death to it.

«Let us return to the instance of a tree, already used. Is a dead branch part or not part of a tree? You may decide this way or that, but you will never say, because the branch is dead, that therefore the tree has no sap. It is a dead branch of a living tree, not a branch of a dead tree. In like manner, irreligious men are dead members of the one Visible Church, which is living and true, not members of a Church which is dead. Because they are dead, it does not follow that the Visible Church to which they belong is dead also».[41]

---

35 *Id.*, pp. 240-241.
36 *Id.*, p. 242.
37 *PS* III. 16, pp. 220-235.
38 *Id.*, p. 221.
39 *Id.*, p. 227.
40 *Id.*, p. 230.
41 *Id.*, p. 228.

The second statement, that there are good persons external to the «Visible Church», calls for the true meaning of baptism and what the regenerated make out of it. Here, Newman clearly explains how the Church cannot be considered lightly, she is the minister. Yet, this does not exclude the goodness that exists outside it. The whole reasoning has a direct bearing on the understanding of the natural conscience and the call that it contains within.

«If a man has not been baptized, be he ever so correct and exemplary in his conduct, this does not prove that he has received regeneration, which is the peculiar and invisible gift of the Church. What is Regeneration? It is the gift of the new and spiritual nature; but men have, through God's blessing, obeyed and pleased Him without it... Therefore when you bring me the case of religious Dissenters, I rejoice at hearing of them. If they know no better, God, we trust, will accept them as He did the Shunnamite... and His appointment, I say, is this – that the Church Visible should be the minister, and baptism the instrument of Regeneration. But I have said not a word to imply that a man, if he knows no better, may not be exemplary in his generation without it».[42]

In these two sermons, then, the basic idea is twofold. First, that the present experience of Church holds more that what it actually shows. The visible is sustained and animated by that which is beyond it. Second, the attitude towards the Church has to find its roots within the heart of the person where the decision is made for God. The Church is the body made up of those who decide to live this gift of regeneration.

This understanding of the Church is enriched when considered against the background of history where the danger of the «human system, acting on us, can make us read Scripture so

---

42 *Id.*, pp. 230-231.

perversely».[43] As a consequence Newman asks, «what must we think, my brethren, of the general spirit of this day, which looks upon the Church as but a civil institution, a creation and portion of the State?»[44]

1.6. Church and State

Newman's vision of the Church has an effect on his understanding of its structures. In his sermons he treats this subject in relation to that «general spirit of this day» which can reduce the Church to a purely human institution. In his letters he comes across as being very much aware of the danger that human structures tend to become end in themselves rather than means for a higher and more spiritual aim.

The state of the union between Church and State, in Newman's mind, is a source of corruption.[45] What he first insists on, though, is not the urgency to undo that union. He rather envisages as more urgent the need to make the clergy more conscious of their call and responsibility: «not that I would advocate a separation of Church and State, unless the Nation does more tyrannical things against us; but I do feel I should be glad if it were done and over, much as the Nation would lose by it – for I fear the Church is being corrupted by the union».[46]

His spiritual views of the Church, visible and invisible, strengthen his convictions that the anomaly of the present state

---

43 Id., p. 232.
44 Id., p. 234.
45 The following is a note from a letter to Pusey: «Is it not very clear that the English Church subsists *in the State*, and has no internal consistency (in matter of fact, I do not say in theory) to keep it together? is bound into one by the imposition of articles and the inducement of State protection, not by the ηθοσ and a common faith? If so, can we regret very much that a deceit should be detected? surely not, though we might think we had no right ourselves to disturb what we found established», in LD V, p. 214.
46 LD IV, p. 33; «We protest against doing anything directly to separate Church and State, while we think it necessary steadily to contemplate the contingency of such an event», in *id.*, p. 28.

of things has to come to a halt. «The Church is certainly in a wretched state, but not a gloomy one to those who regard every symptom of dissolution as a ground of hope. Not that I would do any thing towards the undoing».[47] Newman is positive that what he can see happening after that, is something good for the Church. He is not sure exactly how, yet he is standing on the ground of hope.

«But, after all, I see a system behind the existing one, a system indeed which will take time and suffering to bring us to adopt, but still a firm foundation. Those who live by the breath of state patronage, who think the clergy must be gentlemen, and the Church must rest on the great, not the multitude, of course are desponding. Woe to the profane hands who rob us of privilege or possession, but they can do us no harm. In the meantime, should (by any strange accident) the course of events fall back into its old channel, I will not be a disturber of the Church, though it is difficult to see how this return can be».[48]

In a very long letter to the editor of *The British Magazine*,[49] Newman writes about the same subject of the dependence of the Church on the State. Taking «centralization» as the central theme, he develops a reflection on the state of the Church of England.

The starting point is that in the world of politics the idea of «centralization» is slowly being accepted as a «requisite for the well-being of a state».[50] This does not obscure the fact that this principle is accepted with great difficulty since it has been «a characteristic of the British constitution hitherto, whether rightly or wrongly, to view the principle with jealousy, as hostile in its tendency to the liberty of the subject».[51]

Newman points out that this idea of centralization has created a shift of importance from the notion of «nation» to that of

---

47 *Id.*, p. 227.
48 *Ibid.*
49 *Id.*, pp. 339-342.
50 *Id.*, p. 340.
51 *Ibid.*

«government», seeing in the former the idea of «people» and in the latter the idea of «political organization». «In other words, it has hitherto been the English policy to make the *nation* the principal, and the *government* but an adjunct to it; it is now coming into fashion to merge the nation in the government».[52]

This subtle distinction is the central piece of the argument. Because of it, Newman asks what will the consequences be on the Church. If the process will initially start from the structures that express its being, it will only end up by affecting the pastoral identity, that is, the foundation of its call.

Newman, therefore, shifts his attention on the Church. Since the Christian «is bound by his profession, to watch the course of the world, from its necessary bearing upon the interests of the church... how does this bear upon the church?».[53] In brief, he explains, first, the character of the Church as a system which «is pre-eminently of a centralizing character».[54]

Secondly, he points to the fact that «the genius of the English nation, jealous of centralizations, has actually broken up this ecclesiastical system, though of Divine origin; that is, broken it as regards the practical conduct of it».[55]

Thirdly, Newman invites his readers to reflect on how the Church is going to find itself, «having abandoned that centralizing character, which the state is adopting instead».[56] He shares his

---

52 *Ibid.*
53 *Id.*, pp. 340-341.
54 *Id.*, p. 341.
55 «Mr. Hallam somewhere observes, that, were the bishops to be swept away, the country at large would hardly feel the change; and it has sometimes been said, with a remarkable naivete, by the laxer description of clergy, that «the great excellence of a bishop is his *not interfering* with the parochial ministers ecclesiastically subjected to him.» The legal sanction given to Church property, the family connections of the clergy, the system of lay patronage, the independent habits created by a country life, the utter abandonment of the principle of celibacy, have long made the clergy *members of the state*, – a civil order, slightly bound one to another, compared with the local ties which make each, in his own sphere, the religious member or chaplain of the parochial family, which is headed by the squire, and descends to the tradesman and the agricultural labourer», in *ibid*.
56 *Ibid.*

views on the prospects: the end result being one that he himself would have difficulty in accepting.

Newman sees the government as attempting «to organize the clergy, all over the kingdom, into one manageable body, and will form the bishops, or certain of them, into a commission, in a bureau of public instruction... I wish to direct the minds of the readers to the *tendency* of present political changes».[57]

This letter puts together, in a systematic way, what is to be found in other reflections that he shares with his friends, before and afterwards.[58] Its importance lies in the methodic exposition of his convictions, which are not developing in the empty space of idealism. The contents of the other letters confirm even more the qualities of a person who is fully aware of the call and the conditions in which that call has to be lived in.

His love for the Church is expressed in terms of a sense of duty. While he recognizes the role of the «Monarchy and Aristocracy» as secular instruments of power, yet:

«our first duty is the defence of the Church. We have stood by Monarchy and Aristocracy till they have refused to stand by themselves».[59] It is his love for the Church which determines the rest: «we shall do nothing against the Monarchy – we intend to be quiet subjects and obedient – but loyalty is almost an impossibility now. Our political affections are now centred in the Church».[60]

This affection for the Church, dependent on the search for truth, is a guiding force that goes beyond human calculations. Truth is, in itself, a good enough reason: «if we succeed, you will see the consequences: if we fail, we shall at least have the satisfaction of transmitting the sparks of truth, still living, to a happier age».[61]

---

57 *Id.*, p. 342.
58 *Id.*, pp. 44-45; *LD* V, pp. 213-215, 301-305.
59 *LD* IV, p. 44.
60 *Id.*, p. 45.
61 *Ibid.*; «Now suppose one had been born 30 years sooner, I think one should have kept quite quiet. But the times will not allow of this. They force us to speak our opinion – and I cannot so economize as not to speak in *substance*

Another evident quality is his determination. Newman is certain of the opposition he will have to face in keeping his stand: «doubtless I have made up my mind, as every one must, who tries to stand against the torrent, to be misunderstood and called names».[62] In one of his letters to Pusey he considers the position he is in, and also that of the «Oxford Movement», «as if Providence were clearing the μεταιχμιον (space between two armies) and forcing men to choose their side».[63]

Together with this conviction that the road taken is the right one, he is also conscious of the fact that a view is slowly opening up itself before him. The sense of development and growth becomes an essential part of the journey towards the truth. He constantly refers to this journey during which there is a gradual discovery of a view in front of him. The clearer the view gets, the more strength it gathers. The different events start forming a relationship one with the other. In the following reflection, from the same letter to Pusey, Newman shares his belief that proclaiming the truth about the Church is a process of loss and sorrow.

«Let us preach and teach, and develop our views into system, and in all likelihood we may be instruments in the preservation of the Church; and, if it loses in extent, if it is separated from the State, if it has certain parties torn from it, all this is most grievous, but still the better sort will be brought into clearer and more complete Christianity and the Church will be purer. As patriots we may well sorrow, but I suppose the Church ought to be dearer to us than country – and if the latter loses, the former will gain».[64]

One cannot fail to notice the internal relationship between his convictions, about the spiritual reality of the Church, and his actions. In this respect, one can witness how in Newman the

---

what I think. Again, outward circumstances are changing, the State is deserting us – we have a *reason* for being bolder», in *LD* V, p. 302.
62 *LD* IV, p. 315.
63 *LD* V, p. 214.
64 *Id.*, p. 215.

framework of his spiritual convictions embraces both the area of thinking and that of acting. One of the characteristics of this organic view of reality is that there seem to be no demarcation line between his action and his spirituality. There is a sense not only of complementarity between the two, but almost of complete fusion.

Secondly, Newman is not interested in any political change for its own sake. In that which concerns the Church, no sacrifice is big enough if this is geared towards the safeguard of its real identity. This emphasis results of paramount importance and nothing and nobody takes precedence over it.

Thirdly, both in his letters and his sermons, one is reminded how Newman understands the sense of time. Regarding the Church, he is not after any definite deadline. Time shapes history and history takes its own time. What is essential is that what needs to be done is actually done. For Newman, what needs to be done is the will of God. This view is very much influenced by an understanding of history which is not purely temporal. The discovery of the Church as a force in time, becomes an expression of the supernatural aspect of history. The spiritual dimension of the Church is in itself a fundamental discovery aided by his reading of the Fathers.

Thus, historical knowledge is, so to say, beyond the level of information and more on the level of growth, a growth into the awareness of the Church as a spiritual reality rooted in time. The knowledge of the past is essential in its function of enlightening the faith vision of the present moment, while guiding the believer in the future.

Finally, the understanding of the Church enlightens the role that conscience plays. The latter needs to be understood against this background of the search for truth – spiritual, ecclesial, historical, and political. A search for truth that impels the person to follow it wherever it leads. Conscience, in this context, is not limited to an action which has to be done in the here and now, only in connection with an isolated event. It is rather the moving force, hidden and almost unaccounted for, yet present and effective, towards the discovery of truth considered as a journey.

2. Truth – According to Light

The course that Newman is intent in following has as its destination the discovery of truth, in itself the latter becomes a source of energy and assurance. Both in his correspondence, and eventually also in his sermons, one is constantly reminded of this urge that has a double effect on his life. The first one is that of growth in the conviction of the cause. The second is the increase in the energy and determination to live the process it demands. These two sides of the same reality alternate in their effect on the theme of truth, until Newman reaches a point where the overwhelming force of the truth and the determination to live it will demand from him that act of leaving everything. The conversion to Catholicism acquires the force of an act of conscience, the consequence of both the knowledge of truth and the willingness and determination to live it: the primacy of convictions which direct events.

In the first months after his return from the tour, Newman is already conscious of the fact that this whole task of rediscovering the roots of the Church is an uphill struggle.

«We are as men climbing a rock, who tear clothes and flesh, and slip now and then, and yet make progress (so be it!) – and are careless that bystanders criticize, so that their cause gains while they lose... I trust I speak sincerely in saying, I am willing to be said I go too far, so that I push on the cause of truth some little way. Surely it is energy gives edge to any undertaking, and energy is ever incautious and exaggerated – I do not say this to excuse such defects, or as conscious as having them myself, but as a consolation and explanation to those who love me but are sorry at some things I do... nor can I wish any one a happier lot than to be himself unfortunate yet to urge on a triumphant cause... Let it be the lot of those I love to live in the hearts of one or two in each succeeding generation, or to be altogether forgotten, while they have helped forward the Truth».[65]

Another dimension which Newman writes about is that truth is a cause which needs time and energy to grow towards its full stature and, therefore, become accepted. In all this he sees himself as an instrument.

«So on the whole I think we are at this moment creatures of the Church feeling thro' the country. We may indeed stop in our course *altogether*, but we cannot moderate or control our course. We may, even if we proceed, burst like bubbles – but go on we must, if we do any thing; go on, to an end or to a development of truths which the world just now has forgotten».[66]

On his birthday, in 1836, he thanks his mother and sisters for the best wishes they sent him, sharing with them sentiments which express his deepest beliefs.

«Thanks too, and thank also my Mother and Harriett for their congratulations upon this day. They will be deserved, if God gives me the grace to fulfil the purposes for which He has led me on hitherto in a wonderful way. I think I am conscious to myself that, whatever are my faults, I wish to live and die to His glory – to surrender wholly to Him as His instrument to whatever work at whatever personal sacrifice – though I cannot duly realize my own words when I say so».[67]

Added to his convictions that truth is an uphill struggle, Newman does not see the force of truth in relation to its acceptance by the general opinion. He perceives truth in its objectivity, as standing on its own worth, without adding or loosing any of that strength when accepted or refused. In a letter to the Editor of *The British Magazine*, which was never published, he asks himself

---

[65] *LD* IV, pp. 116-117.
[66] *Id.*, p. 158; «I have great confidence in the Truth – Veritas prævalebit – where Truth is, it may be obscured, but it must make way – and its doing so is but a *matter of time*», in *LD* V, p. 349.
[67] *Id.*, p. 240.

the question: «You ask me 'what is the use of my taking the uncompromising part in Church matters, which you have heard me profess?' you say 'I am clearly in the minority'».[68]

This same subject is also mentioned in another letter, this time to his brother Francis William, where Newman agrees with him «that majorities are no way of getting at the truth, but voting is a way of peace in matters of secondary importance».[69] In the former letter he goes on to give an explanation why he believes that truth intrinsically demands assent, independent of how the human course of things turns out to be.

«I am not at all sure that I am in a minority; but, if I were, what has this to do with the right or wrong of the matter? What would have become of Christianity if the majority were to have settled its destiny? My opinions being singular neither proves their incorrectness nor augurs their failure. What is it to those who wish to follow the Truth, whether their cause succeeds in their actual lifetime or not? We are labouring for that which is eternal, for that which must succeed at length; we are exerting ourselves for our posterity of the 5th or 10th generation, for 500 years hence not for the year 1834. Let this be our deliberate sentiment; we are fighting the battle of 2334».[70]

It is precisely because of this attitude that Newman is conscious that certain dangers do exist for the Church. He is conscious that the environment he lives in will not be able to react in favour of truth in the moment of trial. During the different crises he goes through in these years, he points out to this missing link, the force of objective truth, which explains why people believe in truth but not to the point of being able to act on it and for it. «The truth is, we are in a peculiar situation in Oxford... We are morbidly tender – afraid to stand up for the Truth – willing rather to offend against it rather than to offend man».[71]

---

68 *LD* IV, p. 166.
69 *Id.*, p. 330.
70 *Id.*, p. 166, an intended letter to the Editor of *The British Magazine* but which never appeared.
71 *LD* V, p. 194.

3. The Indwelling of the Holy Spirit

From a detailed study of the sermons, we discover that, at a certain point in his preaching ministry, the theme of the indwelling of the Holy Spirit appears more frequently.[72] It is interesting to discover how the role of the Holy Spirit develops within the sermons and with its effect in the letters. This will favour the connection between the presence of the Holy Spirit and the role of conscience.

What is striking in both the sermons and the letters, is that although both seem to take a different road one from the other, yet, from a detailed analysis, there is a synthesis based on the belief that preaching about and living faith are two sides of the same coin. His preaching is completed in his letters and his letters find in the sermons their own hidden foundations.

3.1. The Indwelling Spirit

During the months of November and December 1834, Newman writes the sermon *The Indwelling Spirit*.[73] In it he brings forth, first, the Trinitarian aspect, where God is revealed by both the Son and the Spirit – «God the Son has graciously vouchsafed to reveal the Father to His creatures from without; God the Holy

---

[72] V.F. BLEHL, presenting sermon no. 198, preached on Whitsunday, 7th June 1829, explains that «although in the course of the sermons Newman frequently mentions the Holy Spirit especially in relation to justification and regeneration, it is generally in passing. Here he deals with the role of the Holy Spirit at some length in the latter part of the sermon, and, as Sheridan (...) has pointed out, there is one passage, beginning 'Now the agent producing in our hearts this spiritual state' which looks forward both to those later sermons and the *Lectures on Justification*, in which he treats explicitly of the Indwelling of the Holy Spirit. The latter will be Newman's final solution to the question of justification and sanctification», in V.F. BLEHL (ed.), *John Henry Newman: Volume II: Sermons on Biblical History, Sin and Justification, the Christian Way of Life, and Biblical Theology*. (Clarendon, Oxford 1993) p. 187; V.F. BLEHL quotes from T. SHERIDAN, *Newman on Justification*. (New York, 1967) p. 201.

[73] *PS* II. 19.

Ghost, by inward communications».[74] – and, secondly, the specific role of the Spirit both in creation and in history.

«The condescension of the Blessed Spirit is as incomprehensible as that of the Son. He has ever been the secret presence of God within Creation: a source of life amid chaos, bringing out into form and order what was at first shapeless and void, and the voice of Truth in the hearts of all rational beings, tuning them into harmony with the intimations of God's Law, which were externally made to them. Hence He is especially called the 'life-giving' Spirit; being (as it were) the Soul of the universal nature, the Strength of man and beast, the Guide of faith, the Witness against sin, the inward light of patriarchs and prophets, the Grace abiding in the Christian soul, and the Lord and Ruler of the Church».[75]

The Holy Spirit, is the continuation of the redemptive mission of Christ, as lived within the Church. His action is the continuation of that of Christ, as revealer of the Father. Christ «still is with us, not in mere gifts, but by the substitution of His Spirit for Himself, and that, both in the Church and in the souls of individual Christians».[76] Newman enfolds this mission of the Holy Spirit by starting from the doctrinal dimensions – Trinity, Creation, Redemption, Church – only to lead the hearer to that praxis that this doctrine intentionally calls for.

This practical aspect that the sermon calls for is, essentially, the pervasive presence of the Holy Spirit within the soul. As the Spirit is a source and a force, in Creation as much as in Redemption, so is His presence within the soul. It cannot be otherwise.

«The Holy Ghost, I have said, dwells in body and soul, as in a temple… He is all-knowing and omnipresent, He is able to search into all our thoughts and penetrate into every motive of the heart. Therefore, He pervades us (if it may be so said) as

---

74 *Id.*, p. 217.
75 *Id.*, p. 218.
76 *Id.*, p. 221.

light pervades a building, or as a sweet perfume the folds of some honourable robe; so that, in Scripture language, we are said to be in Him, and He in us. It is plain that such an inhabitation brings the Christian into a state altogether new and marvellous, far above the possession of mere gifts, exalts him inconceivably in the scale of beings, and gives him a place and an office which he had not before».[77]

In the above quotation, one can feel the strength of Newman's message: while gently leading the hearer through the tenets of faith, he is able to create a simple passage between doctrine and life. The use of the metaphors, the knowledge of Scripture and the familiarity with the mind's reasonings, all collaborate to give strength to the message which goes directly to the heart and helps the willing believer to realize the greatness of his or her call.

3.2. Spiritual Influences in the Heart

Just few weeks after this sermon, Newman, in a letter, returns on the same theme adding more reflections to it. The first is that the role of the Holy Spirit is one which, primarily, acts through nature rather than initially changes our human attributes.

«If I must express broadly my view of spiritual influences on the heart and will etc. I should say, that they were vouchsafed according to the constitution of man's nature – i.e. so as not to change it from its ordinary workings, but to make use of these. The Holy Spirit addresses us thro' our reason, affections, conscience, passions, natural-affections, tastes, associations etc but (generally and usually) only thro' them; He does not come immediately to change us, but through these».[78]

---

77   *Id.*, p. 222.
78   *LD* V, pp. 14-5.

Advocacy of Conscience

This mode of presence and action touches a very fundamental principle in Newman's understanding of the life of faith. As is the case in the workings of the natural mind, which develops and changes slowly from one stage to another, so is the case of the spiritual mind. Graduality is the mode and the rule, rather than the exception.

«Again whatever happens to the mind naturally, that may happen in grace – as the natural mind generally changes slowly, so does the mind of the spirit; as sudden conversions happen in nature (e.g. the spendthrift suddenly becoming a miser,) so they may in grace.

Such is the rule, the ordinary mode (I conceive) of God's dealings with us».[79]

The second reflection, contained in this letter, concerns the nature of the presence of the Holy Spirit in the person. What follows is an emphatic expression of Newman's idea regarding the indwelling of the Spirit. The strength of the language is tied to the fact that it is a letter, not a sermon. Newman is firmly grounded in the belief that the role of the Spirit is to sanctify: He is present in creation, bringing form and order, He is the voice of truth, bringing harmony between the person and God. What Newman adds to this view is that under the gospel, through the action of the Holy Spirit, regeneration and adoption take place.

«But you say that we are bid look out for the Holy Spirit to change us etc. Now I may perhaps imply more than I mean, but let me ask where we are told this of the sanctifying Spirit? The great gift of Christianity is not primarily the sanctifying Spirit, but only inclusively and by consequence... the peculiarity of the gospel is the Spirit of regeneration or adoption. Herein is the difference (I suppose) of St. James's epistle and St. Paul's – the former dwells more on sanctification, the latter on the regenerated state. Now I conceive as far as sanctification goes, the work of the Spirit is, as I have described it overleaf; He acts through the properties of

---

[79] *Id.*, p. 15.

the mind; nor do I know what authority we have for speaking of Him as the ultimate Agent, and not our own free will (to speak more strongly than I like.) In this sense salvation depends on ourselves, on our willing or not, i.e. prompted, enlightened, aided, carried on, perfected by the influences of grace».[80]

This regeneration is «the great gift of grace, marvellous beyond words, exceeding in bounty, and freely given to those whom God has chosen in Christ and brings to baptism».[81] At this point, it is worth recalling how the notion of the Church is enriched against this background: through baptism, becoming member of the body of Christ, the Christian becomes the temple of the Holy Spirit, he or she is adopted through the presence of the Spirit within: «in the first place it has (so to say) a physical, or (as we term it) a mystical influence on the soul, uniting it to Christ – it distinguishes the Christian from all unregenerate men, and it is *of course* attended by larger measures of sanctification so as to raise the soul in holiness».[82]

Finally, this gift works on the human will through co-operation and in a gradual manner. As is frequently found in his sermons, Newman is very much aware that the journey of the heart is a process, a long and slow one. For him it is a «truth that our hearts must be changed for heaven and can but be slowly changed».[83]

3.3. The Gift of the Spirit: Contemplation and Action

The presence of the Spirit within the person needs to be contemplated and acted on. The recognition that God the Holy Spirit is within the heart, which is the effect of contemplation, convinces the person to act accordingly.

---

80   *Id.*, pp. 15-16.
81   *Id.*, p. 16.
82   *Ibid.*
83   *Ibid.*

Advocacy of Conscience

«Let us adore the Sacred Presence within us with all fear, and rejoice 'with trembling'. Let us offer up our best gifts in sacrifice to Him who, instead of abhorring, has taken up His abode in these sinful hearts of ours... All we know is, that as we persevere in them, the inward light grows brighter and brighter, and God manifests Himself in us in a way the world knows not of. In this, then, consists our whole duty, first in contemplating Almighty God as in Heaven, so in our hearts and souls; and next, while we contemplate Him, in acting towards and for Him in the works of every day; in viewing by faith His glory without and within us, and acknowledging it by our obedience».[84]

The relationship with this presence is a process of enablement. This process, so natural in the child, develops as an act of willingness in the adult. For Newman this can only take place if the implicit trust of the child grows into a relationship of love between the person and God.

«God comes to us as a Law, before He comes as a Lawgiver; that is, He sets up His throne within us, and enables us to obey Him, before we have learned to reflect on our own sensations, and to know the voice of God... Love then is the motion within us of the new spirit, the holy and renewed heart which God the Holy Ghost gives us; and, as being such, we see how it may exist in infants, who obey the inward law without knowing it, by a sort of natural service, as plants and trees fulfil the functions of their own nature; a service which is most acceptable to God, as being moral and spiritual, though not intellectual».[85]

If, then, the presence of the Spirit is to be contemplated and acted on in a process of enablement, the mark of «a true Christian, then, may almost be defined as one who has a ruling sense of God's presence within him».[86] At this point, arises a

---
[84] PS III. 18, p. 269.
[85] PS IV. 21, pp. 312-313; this reflection reminds us of the principle that Newman himself tried to establish with his brother Charles when he insisted on the disposition of the heart as essential to approaching God.
[86] PS V. 16, p. 225.

very important aspect which relates directly to the reality of conscience. The following quotation from the same sermon brings together some familiar vocabulary about the notion of conscience which are typical of Newman. It is urgent to insist that it is within the contest of the Holy Spirit's action that these words are proclaimed, an aspect which, unfortunately, is almost totally absent in the mind of those who usually take these words only to prove a point of their own.

«A true Christian, or one who is in a state of acceptance with God, is he, who, in such sense, has faith in Him, as to live in the thought that He is present with him, – present not externally, not in nature merely, or in providence, but in his innermost heart, or in his conscience. A man is justified whose conscience is illuminated by God, so that he habitually realizes that all his thoughts, all the first springs of his moral life, all his motives and his wishes, are open to Almighty God... He alone admits Christ into the shrine of his heart; whereas others wish in some way or other, to be by themselves, to have a home, a chamber, a tribunal, a throne, a self where God is not, – a home within them which is not a temple, a chamber which is not a confessional, a tribunal without a judge, a throne without a king; – that self may be king and judge; and that the Creator may rather be dealt with and approached as though a second party, instead of His being that true and better self, of which self itself should be but an instrument and minister».[87]

3.4. The Law of Conscience

The next two sermons[88] offer a very valuable insight into the understanding of conscience in relation to the Spirit. They were preached in January 1840, a week one from the other. Here Newman talks about the theme of righteousness.

---

87   *Id.*, p. 226.
88   PS V. 11. *The Law of the Spirit*; PS V. 10. *Righteousness not of Us but in Us*.

The first sermon presents the theme of the «Law» through which a person becomes acceptable to God. Adam, before the fall, had «the Law (which) was his inward life, and Almighty God dealt with him accordingly, – He called, accounted, dealt with him as righteous, because he was righteous».[89] The fall had caused a change in the pattern of this relationship: «He then forfeited the presence of the Holy Spirit; he no longer fulfilled the Law; he lost his righteousness, and he knew he had lost it».[90]

The essential change after the fall does not consist in the absence of the law, but rather in the fact that the law within became the law without: «not utterly without the Law, yet not with it; with the Law not within him, but before him, – not any longer in his heart, as the pillar of a cloud... but departing from him».[91] This change meant that «what had been a law of innocence, became a law of conscience; what was freedom, became bondage; what was peace, became dread and misery».[92]

The message of the second sermon is centred about the role of the Spirit. He is given to us to complete the saving act of «Christ who came to save us, by bringing us back to righteousness».[93]

«But the Spirit came to finish in us, what Christ had finished in Himself, but left unfinished as regards us... As a light placed in a room pours out its rays on all sides, so the presence of the Holy Ghost imbues us with life, strength, holiness, love, acceptableness, righteousness. God looks on us in mercy, because He sees in us 'the mind of the Spirit', for whoso has this mind has holiness and righteousness within him. Henceforth all his thoughts, words, and works, as done in the Spirit, are acceptable, pleasing, just before God; and whatever remaining infirmity there be in him, that the presence of the Spirit hides. That divine influence, which

---

89 *PS* V. 11, p. 146.
90 *Ibid.*
91 *Ibid.*
92 *Id.*, p. 147.
93 *Id.*, p. 148.

has the fullness of Christ's grace to purify us, has also the power of Christ's blood to justify».[94]

These two sermons touch on an aspect of the notion of the law not simply in relation to the distance that the fall created but rather to the possibilities that still exist, through Christ and the presence of the Spirit, for the sinner to bridge that gap. By way of enriching this aspect, we refer to an unpublished sermon,[95] of the same period, in which Newman presents the notion of conscience in a close link with that of the Spirit. He takes the situation where the Christian is perplexed and is obliged to act without having any other guidance. In these circumstances «it seems then that Christians have a light within them, which discriminates between truth and error».[96] He goes on to say «that we should use as our guide the light of grace within us».[97]

This guidance is referred to as «the blessed gift of the Spirit (…) given to each Christian individually and personally, for his illumination and guidance»[98] which helps him to discriminate between the truth and falsehood of religious doctrines. Conscience forms part of this whole reality: «We may consult the light within us, the instinctive sense of truth, duty and conscience, and under certain limitations may fairly or rather ought religiously follow its guidance».[99] What follows then is a series of rules on how to apply this principle.

Besides this valuable reflection from the sermon, we also have a note by Placid Murray who undertook the study and the critical presentation of these sermons: «this sermon on inward holiness as a guide to test the holiness, and consequently the truth, of

---

94 *PS* V. 10, p. 138.
95 P. MURRAY, (ed.), *John Henry Newman: Sermons 1824-1834. Volume I: Sermons on the Liturgy and Sacraments and on Christ the Mediator*. (Clarendon, Oxford 1991) pp. 241-250; this sermon, bearing the title *Holiness of a Doctrine the Test of its Truth* was preached three times: 10th November 1839; 24th October 1841, 28th May 1843.
96 *Id.*, p. 242.
97 *Id.*, p. 243.
98 *Id.*, p. 241.
99 *Id.*, p. 244.

doctrines about which the believer may be perplexed, anticipates by three decades Newman's 'Illative Sense' of the *G.A.* He has not yet hit on the philosophical phrase, but the workings of the illative (religious) sense are grasped clearly by him in 1839».[100]

The note by Murray is a signpost to a whole area of development on the notion of conscience that occupies the best part of the Catholic Newman. The treatment given to conscience in the *Grammar of Assent*, being a development of the themes of «light within», «instinctive sense of truth» and «duty», has to find in these sermons, and, one needs to add, in his contemporary correspondence, the ground of meaning. The aim of this analytical study, although it has a definite object in mind, that of coming to terms with Newman of the *Parochial and Plain Sermons*, can only reach its ultimate goal when the whole of Newman's spiritual and intellectual output is completely studied. Insights by people like Placid Murray confirm this view.

4. Spiritual and Intellectual Controversies

The biggest challenge that most engages Newman's energy is surely that coming from liberalism which «is the mistake of subjecting to human judgement those revealed doctrines which are in their nature beyond and independent of it».[101] Through the different events that take place at this stage, namely the demands of the dissenters and, later, the election of Renn Dickson Hampden as Regius Professor of divinity, Newman is even more convinced that the rationalistic approach needs to be counter attacked. He is also becoming conscious of two things: first, that «for what we know, Liberalism, Rationalism, is the foe at our doors»,[102] second, that evangelicalism leads to dissent.[103]

---
100 *Id.*, p. 241, n. 1.
101 *Apol.* p. 288.
102 *LD* VII, p. 450.
103 See *id.*, p. 169.

4.1.   Evangelicalism

Reference to evangelicalism at this stage, very much in line with what has been examined earlier, is found in a series of letters to and from a certain James Stephen.[104] This correspondence started when the latter shared his opinions on Newman's sermons with Samuel Wilberforce, Newman's conviction being that evangelicalism has reduced faith not much to belief but to feeling. The underlying elements of evangelicalism which concern Newman, help us to complement his vision of faith which he founds on the human response to God's word: «to depend implicitly upon it and obey it – asking no questions, not searching the limit or the mode in which it is true – only embracing and mastering it as vital and real, not verbal merely».[105]

The evangelical way is rather characterized by «rudeness, irreverence, and almost profaneness; the profaneness of making a most sacred doctrine a subject of vehement declamation, or instrument of exciting the feelings, or topic for vague, general, reiterate statements in technical language».[106]

Referring to Butler, Newman considers the latter as an example of a believer who has overcome this danger which leads to the liberal spirit. Butler «caught the idea which had actually been the rule of the Primitive Church, of teaching the more Sacred Truths ordinarily by rites and ceremonies».[107] Butler represents a temper of faith similar to the first Christians who received «the Gospel literally on their knees, and in a temper altogether different from that critical and argumentative spirit which sitting and listening engender».[108]

---

104   *LD* V, pp. 21, 31-33, 41-48.
105   *Id.*, p. 45.
106   *Ibid.*
107   *Id.*, p. 46.
108   *Ibid.*

4.2. R. D. Hampden: The Theory of Rationalism

The election of Renn Dickson Hampden means for Newman another advance towards that liberalism which is shaking the whole religious edifice. His idea of Hampden lies the following lines: «there is no doctrine, however sacred, which he (Dr. Hampden) does not scoff at – and in his Moral Philosophy he adopts the lowest and most grovelling utilitarianism as the basis of Morals – he considers it is a sacred duty to live to this world – and that religion by itself injuriously absorbs the mind».[109]

This is what worries Newman: if this is the doctrine of him who is at the helm of the divinity, then «the present state of things is miserable indeed... Considering Oxford is the only stronghold of Truth in the Country, the guilt of these men, though they know not what they do, is great indeed».[110]

The *Report of the Corpus Committee*, «evidently of Pusey's composition»,[111] presents the whole issue related to Hampden in clear terms. Its aim is not to put guilt on those responsible for this situation, but rather to point out the core issue: «the present controversy is not so much concerned with an individual or a book, or even an ordinary system of false doctrine, as with a *Principle*».[112]

It goes on to speak about the «*Philosophy of Rationalism*» and the «*Theory of Rationalism*»:

«this principle is the Philosophy of Rationalism, or the assumption that uncontrolled human reason, in its present degraded form, is the primary Interpreter of God's Word... It is the Theory of Rationalism, (as set forth systematically in the Bampton Lectures of 1832, and still more recently asserted in Lectures addressed to Students,) which is to be considered the root of all the errors of Dr. Hampden's system».[113]

---

109 *Id.*, p. 251.
110 *Ibid*; see also T.C. HUMMEL, 'John Henry Newman and the Oriel Noetics', in *Anglican Theological Review* 74 (1992) 205-206.
111 *LD* V, p. 264, n. 1.
112 *Id.*, p. 264.
113 *Ibid.*

The *Letter of the Corpus Committee*, of which «internal evidence suggests that the letter was at least largely of Newman's composition»,[114] is signed amongst others by Newman himself, of course, and Pusey. First, it presents the: «University of Oxford, as charged with the maintenance of all sound doctrine... a duty (...) naturally imposed by its situation in the country, and expressly enjoined by the Statutes – to prevent any principles, detrimental to the Christian Faith».[115]

Then goes on to point out that the main aim of coming out against Hampden, is not to be interpreted on a personal level, but rather needs to be considered against a wider background where the idea of philosophical and theoretical rationalism is «foreign and injurious to the Gospel».[116]

Concluding the considerations that give scope to this letter, the authors are convinced that: «to refuse, at this moment, to come forward, and maintain the fundamental safeguards of the Church, is to abandon that Church in its crisis, and to abdicate our noblest function of holding before the country the light of truth, when truth most require our support».[117]

4.3. R.H. Froude: Metaphysical and Practical

While the Hampden affair is going on, Newman suffers the loss of Richard Hurrell Froude. The meaning of this loss can only be measured by the sense of debt Newman feels towards his most dear friend.

«It is mysterious that anyone so remarkably and variously gifted, and with talents so fitted for these times, should be removed. I never on the whole fell in with so gifted a person – in variety and perfection of gifts I think he far exceeded even Keble – for myself,

---

114 *Id.*, p. 287, n. 1.
115 *Id.*, p. 287.
116 *Id.*, p. 288.
117 *Id.*, p. 289.

I cannot describe what I owe to him as regards the intellectual principles [[i.e. philosophy. J H N]] of religion and morals».[118]

Froude has a particular effect on Newman. Froude represents for him the synthesis of the inquisitive mind and the available heart. Whether it concerns the dangers of evangelicalism or the excessive importance given to rationalism, Newman sees in Froude the perfect combination and balance.

Newman's willingness to publish his papers springs forth from the idea that «these 'Thoughts' will show people what is the real use of such memoranda, and what is the true character of them, not to ascertain our spiritual state in God's sight, but by way of improving ourselves, discovering our faults etc.» And in a more personal way, he adds, « They show *how* a person may indulge *metaphysical* speculations to the utmost extent and yet be *practical*. It might be a good lesson to various Cambridge men and others».[119]

Froude's example for Newman goes deeper than memories. Froude symbolizes «a bold rider, as on horseback, so also in his speculation… (he) had that strong hold of first principles, and that keen perception of their value».[120] It is because of this latter sense, that Newman perceives in him the person who would not let himself be carried by the wave of rationalism. In him «the strong temptation (is) fairly met and overcome. We see his mind only breaking out into more original and beautiful discoveries, from that very repression which seemed at first likely to be the utter prohibition of his powers».[121]

Froude becomes for Newman the type who succeeds to enter into the realm of further discoveries, without the necessity of succumbing to the innovative temptations of rationalistic tendencies. In Froude the boldness not to give in, instead of

---
118 *Id.*, p. 249.
119 *LD* VI, p. 87.
120 *Apol.* p. 38.
121 *LD* VI, p. 87.

becoming a barrier to further development, develops into the channel towards a greater reward.

«By sacrificing the prospect of originality he has become in the event more original. His profound Church views... have sometimes seemed to me as a sort of gracious reward for his denying himself that vulgar originality which is rationalistic».[122]

5. Francis W. Newman

As happened before with his brother Charles Robert, Newman this time enters into another interesting correspondence with his other brother, Francis William. Needless to say, the letters are very much a reflection of what Newman himself is going through at this time. In actual fact the themes on which these letters focus on are the «Church», «Latitudinarianism», «Private Judgment» and the «Christian ethos». This last theme, in some way, reconnects the whole correspondence with that of Charles, where Newman insists that the moral disposition of the heart is crucial towards the acceptance or refusal of Christianity.[123]

The letters are written in two different periods. There is one letter, having the Church as its theme, written in 1835,[124] the rest are all written in 1840.[125]

---

122 *Ibid.*
123 «I consider the rejection of Christianity to arise from a fault of the *heart*, not of the *intellect*; that unbelief arises, not from mere error of reasoning, but either from pride or from sensuality. It is important that at starting I should premise this, lest I should appear inconsistent, and to assert *both* that the Christian evidences are most convincing, *and yet* that they are not likely to convince those who reject them», in *LD* I, p. 219.
124 *LD* V, pp. 166-167.
125 *LD* VII, pp. 301-302; 309; 319; 412-414; 436-442.

5.1. The Church

In dealing with the theme of the Church in his letter to Francis, Newman immediately disqualifies an individualistic approach towards Christianity, since it is in itself a contradiction of the notion of the Church.

«On what ground of reason or Scripture do you say that every one may gain the true doctrines of the gospel for himself from the Bible? Where is illumination promised an individual for this purpose? Where is it any where hinted that the aid of teachers is to be superseded? Where that the universal testimony of the Church is not a principle of belief as sure and satisfactory as the word of Scripture?».[126]

Newman considers this attitude as «the πρωτον φευδοσ (primary fallacy) of your notions».[127] And this, for two reasons: first, because it is going against the «witness of the whole Church»[128] and, second, because it is influenced by a sense of self-sufficiency which has an unknown destination.

In actual fact, Newman teases Francis asking whether he is approaching the same method previously adopted by their brother Charles. Although, he points out to him, a fundamental «difference, that you will admit a being of God», adding, «though this, I verily think, would be an inconsistency in you – but, admitting it, what else at least will you retain?»[129]

The inconsistency lies in the fact that, while Francis does not have any difficulty in accepting Scripture as coming from God, yet he finds problem with the universal teaching of the Church. In the final note to the letter, Newman explains to him that what Scripture is comes to us from the reality of the Church as a witness to it and not as a collection of opinions.

---

126 *LD* V, p. 166.
127 *Ibid.*
128 *Ibid.*
129 *Id.*, pp. 166-167.

«Observe I am not urging the testimony of the Church, as if the opinion of a number of persons of the meaning of Scripture, but as an independent source of truth, viz an historical testimony to a fact viz the Apostles' having taught such and such doctrines».[130]

This reflection, which has a dogmatic tone about it, is further confirmed in its value when it is considered in connection with Newman's understanding of faith as a living reality. In Newman, the dogmatic dimension does not stand on its own, but only as the basis and soul of the vision of faith, the latter being a living experience.

The following letters, will only confirm how this dialectic between the dogmatic and the moral are brought together to form a unified reality.

5.2. Latitudinarianism

In his letter to Newman, Francis presents the dilemma infront of which he is finding himself: either to demand «agreement in a creed» or to judge persons «by their sincerity, their reverential spirit, and practical benevolence and purity».[131] Francis excludes the first because it «is in my clear judgment too opposed to the whole spirit of Christianity, and too odious in itself, to be justified by any quoting of texts».[132]

The reason because of which he accepts the second is that:

«I am persuaded, that far deeper in the heart than all which is theologically prominent, there lies an inner element of the moral and spiritual, which is infinitely precious in God's sight, and if we are wise, may suffice to make us love each other when it [is] duly cherished and estimated; and though I must ever fear collisions, while your demands are so large, and my power

---

130 *Id.*, p. 167.
131 *LD* VII, p. 319.
132 *LD* VII, p. 319.

Advocacy of Conscience

of granting so small, I am very far indeed from deprecating that we should meet».[133]

Newman's answer does not contain a defence of his own position. In his usual style of controversy, his main aim is not that of showing where the contents of the arguments are wrong. He goes deeper and beyond the written thoughts. His aim is to point out to the foundations from which the opponents' arguments seem to get their strength.

Here, there is Newman at his best. He has come a long way towards a synthesis regarding the life of faith which includes both the theological, philosophical and historical dimensions. His notions on faith and reason, as a result of his struggle against the liberal/rationalistic tendency, have deepened their roots in him. His idea of the Church has grown beyond the purely limited dimensions of space and time, to grasp and embrace, merit of the Fathers, the value of the spiritual experience in its historical expression.

Newman takes his brother's letter as an expression of a state of mind that will cause problems to the Christian faith. The principles on which his brother assumes an attitude of openness, are none else than those adopted by the liberals.

«I think your reasonings are irresistible, granting certain latent principles which you all along assume. And since I anticipate that these will be generally assumed by the coming age, as they are in great measure already, I am prepared for almost a downfall of Christianity for a time. Moreover do not let me hurt you if I say that in the plain and undeniable irrationality of the religion of the Church, on the assumption of the principles alluded to, I see a vivid exemplification of what the Apostle meant when he said that the worldly wisdom knew not God, and spoke of the preaching of the Cross as foolishness».[134]

---

133 *Ibid.*
134 *Id.*, p. 412.

Once this point has been made, Newman unfolds his thoughts. He sees that «the more scepticism abounds, the more is a way made for the revival of a strong ecclesiastical authority; Christianity arose in the beginning, when the popular religions had lost their hold upon the mind».[135]

Recalling the same theme of *University Sermons*, 10 and 11, about the nature of certainty in faith, he believes that a «faint reason may be a valid reason».[136] The «probability» in the realm of faith is the result of reasons «which make it more probable, ever so little, that the Catholic Creed is true than that it is false».[137]

At this point, Newman brings forward the argument of which he reminded his brother Charles in the first controversy. The weight of probability is not simply dependent on its own. It rather needs a corresponding attitude within the heart of the person. «I conceive that if a man rejects such a mere preponderance of probability, this is a proof that he has no great desire to attain the truth in the matter in hand; and his fault becomes a moral one».[138]

5.3. The Ethos of the Christian and the Dissenter

This moral aspect, the whole question of the orientation of the heart, is taken on again in the last letter to Francis. In answer to his brother's statement, that «the dry external argument is inadequate as a demonstration of Christianity»,[139] Newman again points his finger to the centre of the controversy.

«It throws back our difference upon ethical grounds when argument ceases. I have been for so many years preaching University Sermons, as I have had opportunity, on this one subject, that men judge in religion, and are meant to judge by

---
135 *Ibid.*
136 *Id.*, p. 414.
137 *Ibid.*
138 *Ibid.*
139 *Id.*, p. 438.

antecedent probability much more than by external evidences, and that their view of antecedent probability depends upon their particular state of mind».[140]

In one way this correspondence reawakens the same sentiments Newman shared with his brother Charles. But this time, because of experience and study, he is clearer in his terminology. While in the first controversy, he was still familiarising himself with a method and its contents, this time he is able to formulate an answer that encapsulates the different aspects of his life of faith.

«Accordingly I think that a Churchman is (abstractedly speaking) a man of certain ηθοσ – and a Dissenter of another – And in like manner that, abstractedly, the Church has a tendency to produce in individuals a Church ηθοσ, and Dissent a Dissenting ηθοσ».[141]

Just few weeks after this letter, end of November 1840, we find an echo of this correspondence in his sermons. He refers to these same attitudes in two parochial sermons. In the first sermon, alluding to the way God deals with us, Newman brings forth the difference that exists between the experience of God, on one side, and the intrinsic difficulty to speak about it in the same certain terms through which it is felt.[142]

«God does not speak to us through the occurrences of life, that you can persuade others that He speaks. He does not act upon such explicit laws, they you can speak of them with certainty. He gives us sufficient tokens of himself to raise our minds in awe towards Him... God gives us enough to make us inquire and hope; not enough to make us insist and argue».[143]

In another sermon, a week later,[144] he refers to the ethos of the Christian who looks at faith not from the angle of evidences approved by reason, but from an attitude based on the love of things to be believed.

---

140 *Ibid.*
141 *Ibid.*
142 See *PS* VI. 17. *Waiting for Christ.*
143 *Id.*, p. 250.
144 *PS* VI. 18. *Subjection of the Reason and Feelings to the Revealed Word.*

«What is faith itself but an acceptance of things unseen, from the love of them, beyond the determination of calculation and experience? Faith outstrips argument... This, then, is what is meant by faith going against reason, that it cares not for the measure of probabilities; it does not ask whether a thing is more or less likely; but if there is a fair and clear likelihood what God's will is, it acts upon it.... Faith, then, does not regard degrees of evidence».[145]

6. Lights of the Uncomfortable Vista

The period after summer 1839 is the time when Newman feels that something is shaking him from the foundations. While reading the Monophysite and Donatists controversies, an article written by Dr. Wiseman, dealing with the same period, compares it to the present state of Christendom. The conclusion that worries Newman is that «he (Wiseman) maintains first that the present *look* of Christendom is such, that St Austin or St Basil coming among us would say at once '*That* is the Catholic Church – and *those* are the heretics –' meaning Rome and us respectively – and next that the said Fathers and all the Fathers teach that that '*look*' of things was ever meant to be a providential note, in order to *save* argument».[146]

Newman's reaction indicates that he is conscious that something new is slowly unfolding in front of him: «there is an uncomfortable vista opened which was closed before. I am writing upon *first* feelings».[147]

---

145 *Id.*, pp. 258-259.
146 *LD* VII, p. 241.
147 *Id.*, p. 155.

6.1. The Return to the Fathers

By the end of 1838, Newman, in a letter to Keble, expresses his desire to dedicate more time to the reading of the Fathers: «to read and otherwise employ myself on the Fathers, without venturing anything of my own, is what would give me most peace of *conscience*».[148] Writing to Bowden some months later, he confesses that he is «busy with the theology of the 5th century at present, preparatory (I trust) to my finishing my edition of Dionysius of Alexandria – and editing (for the Library of the Fathers) Theodoret, Leo and Cyril».[149]

Without fully acknowledging the implications of it all, Newman is on his way to enter the most delicate period of his life.

From a historical point of view, he discovers two things: first, «at Chalcedon – the great power of the Pope (as great as he claims now almost)», second, «the marvellous interference of the civil power, as great almost as in our kings».[150]

From a theological point of view, he is becoming more aware that the Father's age is one of light: «it was well enough for theologians to go on arguing, refuting and oversetting each other in the dark – I mean by extracts – and appeals to what their audience had not read – but this is an age of light».[151]

The conclusion that he is slowly arriving at through his reading of the Fathers is that they can easily be identified with Romanism for the doctrines and temper they teach. Also, he is conscious of the fact that, having gone so far, the Church he belongs to needs to undergo a fundamental change that is beyond himself.

---

148 *LD* VI, p. 353.
149 *LD* VII, p. 102; «I am able this long vacation to return to my own line of reading which has been suspended since the long vacation of /35 – the controversies of the first centuries. I hope to master the Nestorian and Eutychian controversies in the course of the Vacation», in *id.*, p. 106; see also *id.*, p. 110.
150 *Id.*, p. 105.
151 *Id.*, p. 121.

«I cannot deny that from the first the Fathers do teach doctrines and a temper of mind which we commonly identify with Romanism... Our Church is not at one with itself – there is not denying it. We have a heretical spirit in us. Whether it can be cast out, without 'tearing' and destroying the Church itself, is quite beyond me... I do really trust, if it may be said without presumption, that we are brought forward for a purpose, and we may leave the matter to Him who directs all things well. One thing seems plain, if it did not before, that temporal prospects we (personally) have none».[152]

6.2. Truth and Light

The return to the Fathers rekindles in him the roots of his beliefs regarding the cause of truth. As in the beginning of this second period, immediately after the tour, Newman's concern for the truth has two sides to it. It is simultaneously both the willingness to grow in the conviction of the cause and the determination to live the demands it makes on the believer.

This study so far has confirmed how Newman, in the varied situations he finds himself in, lives these two dimensions. They are the expression and example of coherence between beliefs and actions.

This time round, he is face to face with a choice that he never before expected to encounter. The fact that he frequently acknowledges that in Romanism there are things which should be incorporated in the Anglican Communion,[153] by no means detracts his love and dedication for the Church he is happy

---

152 *Id.*, pp. 183-184.
153 «Really, you must not suppose that I do not feel the force and influence of those parts of the Roman Catholic system, which have struck you. To express vividly what I mean, I would say, 'I would be a Romanist, if I could. I wish I could be a Romanist'. But I cannot – there is that mixture of error in it, which (though unseen of course by many many pious Christians who have

to belong to. The dilemma he is in now translates itself into a challenge: putting into practice his determination to follow truth wherever it leads him.

For the first time since his study of theology, «a vista has been opened before me, to the end of which I do not see».[154] He himself is slowly acknowledging that the road he has taken to strengthen the Church of England, besides creating a distance from the evangelical form, is also unable to find its ultimate goal within the same Church he would like to add strength to. This dilemma becomes more evident in his letters at this time when he starts talking about the most likely destination of those who are following the Tractarian line.

«I fear too that some persons will turn Roman Catholics, up and down the country; indeed how is this possibly to be helped as things are? they will be right in their major and wrong only in their minor – right in their principle, wrong in their fact – they seek the true Church, but do not recognize the Church in us».[155]

The truth that the Primitive Church is the type against which Newman verifies further developments, is also bringing home to him the harsh reality that this Church is represented in the Roman Communion rather than the Anglican.

«I fear I must allow that, whether I will or no, I am disposing them (my hearers) towards Rome. First, because Rome is the only representative of the Primitive Church besides ourselves; in proportion then as they are loosened from the one they will go to the other. Next because many doctrines which I hold have far greater, or their only scope, in the Roman system – e.g. the principle of reserve, or the consequences of post-baptismal sin».[156]

---

been brought up in it), effectually cuts off the chance of my acquiescing in it. I admire the lofty character, the beauty, the sweetness and tenderness of its services and discipline – I acknowledge them divine in a certain sense, i.e. remnants of that old system which the Apostles founded», in *LD* IV, p. 367.154   *LD* VII, p. 161.
155 *Id.*, p. 240.
156 *Id.*, p. 417.

In the same letter, to John Keble, there is a sentence that reveals the spiritual dilemma Newman finds himself in.

«People tell me on the other hand that I am, whether my sermons or otherwise, exerting at St Mary's a beneficial influence on our prospective clergy; but what if I take to myself the credit of seeing further than they, and having in the course of the last year discovered that what they approve so much is very likely indeed to end in Romanism?».[157]

The reality of this dilemma becomes even harsher when it is considered in relation to the commitment Newman took in the years after 1835. Then, he committed himself to express his opinions against popery in a more pronounced way. Now it seems that, the more he expressed his convictions against Rome, the more the latter seemed to be catching up on him. In succeeding to give an image of himself as anti-papist, he is now realizing that that has solved only one side of the problem, but has utterly failed to influence the outcome of his own beliefs in the long term: «it must be added that this very circumstance that I have committed myself against Rome, has the effect of setting to sleep men's suspicions about me, which is painful now that I begin to have suspicions about myself».[158]

Together with the anxiety that Newman is feeling, there is a constant element within his correspondence that the honest inquirer respects truth and accepts to follow the light that is given him.

---

157 *Ibid.*
158 *Id.*, p. 418; «You and the Oxford Tracts will be one day charged with rank Popery. Would it not be *worldly wise* to put out in the Series one number containing a few sweeping assertions obviously inconsistent with the truth of such a charge?», in *LD* IV, p. 304; «I took your hint about Popery immediately, and wrote the Tract called Via Media which appeared the beginning of this month – tho' I am diffident whether it will answer your aim. I am quite prepared for the charges of both Popery and Pelagianism», in *LD* IV, p. 321; «Your anti-popery Tracts should soon be out. If but *one* apostolical should unfortunately fall into that system, it would be a fearful blow to us all», in *LD* V, p. 237, note 2.

The following phrases from his letters at the time testify to this constant belief and expose this sense of expectation: «there either is something in what Dr W (Wiseman) says, or there is not. If not, all will reject it – if there is, all will accept it, i.e. at length»;[159] «I am more and more convinced that the business of all of us is to be honest and court no one – and to leave the course of things to itself, or rather to higher guidance»;[160] «grace alone surely can guide our argumentative power into truth, and grace is not attained in such anxious and difficult enquiries as those which are in question between us without fasting and prayer».[161]

In a very important letter, which was never sent to its addressee, Newman again expresses this deep conviction that light has to be followed, no matter where it leads. This determination, also to be found in his sermons, accepts the challenge and the difficulty that such an eventual call would make on him.

«And if at any future time, I have any view opened to me, I will try not to turn from it, but will pursue it wherever it may lead. I am not aware of having any hindrance, whether from fear of clamour, or regard for consistency, or even love of friends, which could keep me from joining the Church of Rome, were I persuaded I ought to do so».[162]

The force of truth and the invitation to follow its light, bring home to his mind certain fears and questions. John Keble, to whom Newman turns for advice and comfort, at this very delicate period, expresses in a couple of phrases the anatomy of the problem, pointing to Newman the source of true peace.

«But I suppose no honest man, having been instrumental in setting a great power in motion, can help feeling anxious and responsible, as to whether it move in the right or wrong direction. Yet surely in this as in all other matters we ought not to feel

---

159 *LD* VII, p. 156.
160 *Id.*, p. 330.
161 *Id.*, pp. 406-407.
162 *Id.*, p. 180.

ourselves charged with the event, if only we have watched our intentions or proceedings well».[163]

6.3. *Divine Calls*

During this trying period, Newman writes and delivers the sermon on *Divine Calls*.[164] The knowledge of what is going on in Newman's mind and heart makes the reading of this sermon an extremely revealing one.

The outline of this sermon is based on the Scripture model of the call: the call demands obedience, and this obedience is followed by darkness: «such are the instances of Divine calls in Scripture, and their characteristic is this; to require instant obedience, and next to call us we know not to what; to call us on in darkness. Faith alone can obey them».[165]

When a person feels the call of Christ, «there is nothing miraculous or extraordinary in His dealing with us. He works through our natural faculties and circumstances of life».[166] Whichever instrument of communication Christ operates to reach us, «whether He commands by a visible presence, or by a voice, or by our consciences, it matters not»,[167] what matters is that it is a command and as such asks for obedience.

In a very personal way, Newman talks about these divine calls, which «are commonly from the nature of the case, sudden now, and as indefinite and obscure in their consequences as in former times. The accidents and events of life are, as is obvious, one special way in which the calls I speak of come to us; and they, as we all know, are in their very nature, and as the word accident implies, sudden and unexpected».[168]

---

163 *Id.*, p. 432.
164 *PS* VIII. 2.
165 *Id.*, p. 22.
166 *Id.*, p. 24.
167 *Id.*, pp. 24-25.
168 *Id.*, p. 25.

These circumstances, through which the call is transmitted, are animated by tension towards the discovery of truth. Receiving the call and accepting it, is not a process which is imposed from outside, but rather a process which is influenced by this search. Newman talks about truth as of two kinds. First, there is the truth which leads us from one stage to another, through decisions which need to be taken and through calls to be obeyed. Second, there is the Truth, which God alone knows it, and this is the Perfect Truth towards which He is leading us.

«Many a man is conscious to himself of having undergone inwardly great changes of view as to what truth is and what happiness. Nor, again, am I speaking of changes so great, that a man reverses his former opinions and conduct. He may be able to see that there is a connexion between the two; that his former has led to his latter; and yet he may feel that after all they differ in kind; that he has got into a new world of thought, and measures things and persons by a different rule... Only one is the truth and the perfect truth; and which that is, none know but those who are in possession of it, if even they. But God knows which it is; and towards that one and only Truth He is leading us forward».[169]

All this is a process that involves the whole person, his heart and mind. The test of the willingness of the search for the truth lies not only in growing in its knowledge but more so in following its path. If that truth is God's, the call to follow it involves a «greater renunciation of the world, and exacts a sacrifice of our hopes and fears».[170]

In such a state is Newman when he preaches this sermon. His love for the Church, his openness to the action of the Holy Spirit, his decision to follow Christ's call, all make him realize that when these thoughts are «properly entertained, (they) have no tendency to puff us up; for if the prospect is noble, yet the risk is

---

169 *Id.*, pp. 26-27.
170 *Id.*, p. 31.

more fearful. While we pursue high excellences, we walk among precipices, and a fall is easy».[171]

Conclusion

The dominant dimension that characterizes this period is the reality of the Church. The experience of the latter presents him with questions the answers of which he searches for in the wells of history. Through the Fathers, he strengthens the basic belief that the Church is more than a mere institution: he witnesses an experience where the divine enters into a privileged relationship with humanity.

Equipped with this understanding, Newman dedicates all his energy to safeguard the ecclesial experience from being left to the mercy of the currents of the day, be they political or philosophical.

This, for Newman, becomes a matter of fundamental importance: an experience of conscience, which is taking the form of a journey towards the discovery of truth.

Added to the ecclesial dimension, the theme of the «indwelling of the Holy Spirit» is more than purely theological knowledge: it is «the promise of the indwelling of the Holy Spirit in the soul, and through him, of the Father and the Son, (as) the culminating point of the Christian revelation».[172]

All this makes up the experience of conscience, as a privileged place, where «God takes possession of man and is present in him».[173]

If the search for truth is a heroic task, following the light that that truth presents is a demanding and difficult call. The call to

---
171 *Ibid.*
172 C.S. Dessain, 'The Biblical Basis of Newman's Ecumenical Theology', in *Rediscovery*, p. 102.
173 Ibid.

live out the demands discovered within the shrine of conscience, invites Newman to advance forward courageously in the search for truth, and to follow it wherever it leads him.

It is the unfolding of this journey that makes Newman a great personality, whose writings are primarily witnessed in his actions, while his actions can be read in his writings.

CHAPTER 4

The reason behind the sermon

The correspondence during this period contains much of what Newman thought of his sermons, together with the feed back received from his correspondents.

In coming to terms with the «why?» and the «how?» of the sermons, the opportunity is offered to better appreciate the «what?», the contents, of the sermons. In his *Letters and Diaries* there is abundant material to help identify what exactly Newman wanted his sermons to be. The knowledge of the mind behind the written word and the experience of the person behind the pulpit, are both essential to discover what effect Newman intended his sermons to have.

Equipped with these ideas, the examination of the sermons proceeds in full respect of the parameters within which he himself moves. Thus the danger is avoided of inventing interpretative models, which are out of tune with his own intentions. The sermons are the end part of a personal process. The guidelines for writing the sermons and the acknowledgement of the process that accompanies them, both ask to be respected and accepted in their entirety if any benefit is to come forth from the examination the sermons.

1. Correspondence before 1834

We are fortunate enough to have Newman's own ideas both during the composition of the sermons and during the publication of the same. He started writing sermons in 1824. The first volume was published in the year 1834.[1] During this ten-year period, Newman himself shared his own ideas with a small circle of relatives and friends. After 1834, his letters are longer and more numerous. The people to whom he writes are not only, or always, his admirers. While the correspondence gives a varied picture of Newman's own sentiments and reasons, at the same time, it deals with the challenges and different opinions of the correspondents with whom he was sharing his ideas. The examination of the letters will unearth both his attitudes and reactions, and those of his addressees.

In the first years of his preaching ministry, the letters already convey a sense of conviction about the aims and scopes of preaching. In line with the methodology previously adopted, the letters will be studied in a chronological manner, thus letting the single reflections come forth as when they were written. The advantage of this method helps to locate not only what Newman thought about his preaching ministry and at what period, but also, more importantly, how the organic development of his ideas took place.

1.1. Truth and Holiness: Scope of Sermons

The doctrine of Christ crucified and a conduct which is consistent with this belief, are themes that in his first two letters directly deal with the sermons. These letters, written a month one from the other, are addressed to his mother.[2] At this early stage,

---
1 *LD* IV, p. 203.
2 *LD* I, pp. 181, 189.

July – August 1824, Newman already succeeds to identify two dimensions of the Christian faith, doctrine and life. It is more a discovery of unity rather than distinction. He is convinced from the start that only a synthesis between the two can lead to the veracity of the claim that one is Christian.

«The Sermons I send you were not intended for composition: you will find them full of inaccuracies. I am aware they contain truths, which are unpalatable to the generality of the mind - but the doctrine of Christ crucified is the only spring of real virtue and piety, and the only foundation of peace and comfort».[3]

«I shall certainly always strive in every pulpit so to preach the Christian doctrine, as at the same time to warn people that it is quite idle to pretend to faith and holiness, unless they show forth their inward principles by a pure disinterested, upright line of conduct».[4]

In line with this synthesis, Newman writes another reflection in his *early journals*, just a couple of weeks after the aforementioned letters. He writes about the «great end» of preaching: «holiness» which constitutes the main aim for which the preacher employs all his energies.[5]

«Those who make comfort the great subject of their preaching seem to mistake the end of their ministry. Holiness is the great end. There must be a struggle and a trial here. Comfort is a cordial, but no one drinks cordials from morning to night».[6]

In the above three reflections, written in the first year of his preaching ministry,[7] there lies a clear idea of the end of preaching and of the preacher's aims regarding this responsibility. Newman also acknowledges that, from a personal point of view, these

---

3   *Id.*, p. 181.
4   *Id.*, p. 189.
5   See article by J.E. LINNAN, 'The Search for Absolute Holiness: A Study of Newman's Evangelical Period', *The Ampleforth Journal* 73 (1968) 161-74, where the theme of holiness is treated in relation to the effect that evangelicalism had on Newman's first sermons at St. Clement.
6   *AW* p. 172, 16.09.1824, also in *LD* I, p. 191.
7   Newman started writing and preaching his sermons in June 1824, see *LD* I, p. 177.

expectations encourage him to organize his own intellectual energies and put them at the service of his ministry: «The necessity of composing sermons has obliged me to systematize and complete my ideas on many subjects».[8]

After almost two years into his preaching ministry, Newman receives his first feedback, from his mother. In it she speaks about «comfort and delight». It is the «comfort» of a mother who rejoices in seeing her son being able to «enlighten, correct, support and strengthen» others on their way of faith. It is a first affirmation of his principles from somebody whose advice he treasures dearly. Others will, later on, follow the acknowledgement expressed by his mother.

«I assure you your Sermons are a real comfort and delight to me. They are what I think Sermons ought to be to enlighten, to correct, to support, and to strengthen. It is, my dear, a great gift to see so clearly the truths of religion - still more to be able to impart the knowledge to others. You will, I am sure, duly appreciate the treasure, and make it valuable to many besides yourself».[9]

1.2. Danger of Vanity and Love of Literary Pursuit

One of the traits of Newman's overall personality is his ability to see beyond the visibility of the events. As his life goes on, it becomes clearer how he grows in this intuitive intelligence. The letters confirm that, already at this early stage of his life, he is conscious of the danger of falling into the trap either of inflating self or of abusing a religious responsibility in favour of a secular office. He foresees this danger in the first months when he started writing sermons, and becomes more and more aware of it as time goes by. With this in mind, he confides this apprehension to his sister Harriett:

---

8 *AW* p. 204.
9 *LD* I, p. 277.

«I feel pleased you like my Sermons - I am sure I need not caution you against taking any thing I say on trust. Do not be run away with by any opinions of mine. I have seen cause to change my mind in some respects, and I may change again. I see I know very little about any thing, though I often think I know a great deal... There is always the danger of the love of literary pursuits assuming too prominent a place in the thoughts of a College Tutor, or his viewing his situation merely as a secular office, a means of a future provision when he leaves College».[10]

This consciousness of self and the responsibility he is faced with, combined with the knowledge of the dangers surrounding such a life as his, makes Newman more keen on fulfilling his call in the same coherent way that he tries to present the Christian calling. It is a typical example of how Newman strives to share in his preaching what is coming out of a very personal journey. The word, written and preached, is the same word contemplated and lived. It is this coherence, not only within the contents of thought in itself, but, more importantly, the connection between this and his willingness to live what he contemplates, that he himself expresses as consistency, which becomes the hallmark of his life.

1.3. Intellect Servant of Moral Sense

In another letter, Newman writes that «I ever find in the case of sermon writing, that the stimulus of an object and proposed hearer is necessary to enable to write at all with satisfaction or

---

10 *Id.*, pp. 280-281; «these advantages of composing sermons are greatly counterbalanced by the empty vanity of the mind to which they have given rise. Many gownsmen frequent the Church - several of our Colleges sometimes go, and all this puffs me up. My parish occupies my time so much, that I have little opportunity for devotion or private study of the Scriptures, and, though they come before me in writing sermons, and I am constantly praying in my walks, business etc, yet I am by no means satisfied with myself. Of late too I have neglected stated self examination. It would be a great comfort to me to give up my pupils - and a great one, if I were not to have, at least for some time, the public tutorship at Oriel», in *AW* pp. 204-205; see also *LD* I, p. 211.

comfort to myself».[11] It is not the comfort of self-centredness or, to use another term, popularity, based on the sharing of impressive modes of preaching. It is rather the comfort, which issues out of an experience of the real, shared both by the preacher and the hearer.

Another complementary aspect of this commitment in the preaching ministry is evidenced later on in the same letter where Newman expresses his views on the role of the intellect in relation to the «right moral feeling».[12]

The importance of this reflection lies not only in the fact that it touches a particular line of thought, where intellect is subordinate to moral sense, but that it forms part of a reflection on sermon writing itself. The importance of the intellect's role is related to its being subordinate to the moral sense.

«Intellect seems to be but the attendant and servant of right moral feeling in this (sic) own weak and dark state of being - defending it when attacked, accounting for it, and explaining it in a poor way to others. - It supplies a medium of communication between mind and mind - yet only to a certain extent - and when we think we can detect honest principle, purity of heart and a single eye, it is irrational to delay the recognition of these real excellences till we have settled subordinate points, to exalt what are but means to an end, and make expressed opinions and formal statements an objection to our believing in the existence of moral feelings in others which by the exercise of common sense

---

11 *LD* II, p. 59.
12 'Feeling' here is not to be understood on the same line as 'taste' or 'opinion' which is only relative to the state a person is in. This would be the liberal interpretation of 'feeling'. As becomes clearer in the letter quoted at this point and in later reflections, 'feeling' here is that 'voice' of our moral nature, a moral sense, deeply rooted within the person and in direct relation with the experience of conscience. Although the vocabulary varies at this initial stage, we need to keep in mind that, in presenting the variety of terms that exists, there is a consistency in the way Newman understands the moral aspect of our nature. The different words used in this respect is more related to the fact that this is still an initial period, and thus this should not be the source of any confusion in this regard.

we may actually see.- I have Froude's authority for lowering the intellectual powers into handmaids of our moral nature».[13]

This profound reflection is indicative of the methodological approach that Newman adopts in his sermons at this very first hour. The primacy does not belong to the intellectual arena. While it is taken into consideration, yet it does not hold the balance of power. The way of the Christian is concerned with «real excellences» that cannot depend on what in the end is only a «handmaid of our moral nature».

1.4.   Divine guidance

Few months later, Newman returns again on the subject of preaching. In one of the letters the reference is direct, while in the other the reference is based on the need of discriminating between correct and incorrect opinions. The two letters, in their own way, complement the point about the role of the intellect. They insist on the need of divine guidance and heavenly illumination, on one side, and the duty to have one's judgment informed by «scripture and sound religious feeling», on the other.

«I think, as to the object, manner etc of preaching - I cannot say any thing better to you, than, what you already feel abundantly, the need of divine guidance, and the promise made especially to ministers of heavenly illumination».[14]

«In all human works, it is our duty individually to discriminate between correct and incorrect opinions by our own judgment, informed - as it may be - by knowledge of scripture and by sound religious feeling; - to take nothing for granted, but with reliance on the promised grace, to try every spirit, whether it is from God».[15]

---
13   *LD* II, p. 60.
14   *Id.*, p. 84.
15   *Id.*, p. 87.

1.5. Preparation, Study and Calm

Whatever Newman undertakes, there is a hallmark about the way he executes his tasks: seriousness. Surely, writing is the area where he excels. His own correspondence confirms that sermon writing is considered by him to be a very important ministry. Blanco White, in two different letters to Newman, recognizes this trait of seriousness in Newman, and, through some suggestions, tries to encourage him to take a slightly different approach. This he tries to do using a little dose of praise.

«I know how difficult it is to persuade a mind like yours to write without preparation. But I should strongly advise you to venture upon the strength of your household stuff - on the reading and reflection of many years. Write without much concern; you are sure to write well... tell us your mind on paper.[16]

«You want an outlet for your mind and heart, which are running over, where there is no call for their riches. Tell the world at large what you feel and think; talk with the people of England through my journal, and let me have the benefit of their delight.

I am writing in a great hurry, and yet I cannot help inclining to Poetry, in my style; such is the effect of your article. Adieu, my Oxford Plato».[17]

Newman's own guidelines on sermon writing cannot take into consideration Blanco White's proposals. The sermons are considered by Newman as vehicles of moral truths, which truths are «gained by patient study, by calm reflection, silently as the dew falls».[18] In a way, Newman's indirect answer to White's invitations, slightly late but just as pertinent, is short and to the point: «I never would undertake to write lightly on any subject which admits of being treated thoroughly. I think it is the fault of the day».[19]

---

16   *Id.*, p. 99.
17   *Id.*, p. 105.
18   *Id.*, p. 131.
19   *Id.*, p. 306.

1.6. Unwritten Memory

Due to this deep and respectful attitude, Newman understands his ministry not simply as limited to the actual proclamation of the word, but, even more so, as the communication of an experience through the preached word. In keeping in mind that Newman has both this intuitive capacity of seeing beyond the visible and the conviction that time is the space for the supernatural, the sermons enter into that category of experiences which transcend visibility, time and space.

The sermons, although they come to us under the form of an oral instruction, yet they have succeeded to rise above the time they were written in. They are not simply appreciated for what they were then. It is not admiration that they elicit. Newman's sermons created then, as they still do now, an environment with an aftermath. That aftermath is affecting us in our own time, as much as it affected his hearers when they heard the same sermons in his time.

These sermons succeed to create an environment which has a lasting effect in the memory of the hearers. In one of his letters he explains this ripple effect in the following words.

«Men live after their death - or, still more, they live not in their writings or their chronicled history but in that αγραφοσ μνημη (unwritten memory) exhibited in a school of pupils who trace their moral parentage to them. As moral truth is discovered, not by reasoning, but [by] habituation, so it is recommended not by books b[ut by] oral instruction».[20]

2. Correspondence after 1834

References to the sermons tend to become more frequent after 1834, the year the first volume of sermons is published. The ideas

---
20 *Id.*, p. 255.

contained in his correspondence are, more or less, on the same lines as those previously expressed. There is a more detailed reflection on the preaching ministry. A particular aspect that is dealt with more deeply in these letters is a difference which Newman himself is aware of: the difference that exists between the preaching of the evangelical school and his mode of preaching. Another element, which is to be found at this stage, is the role of the Holy Spirit which from this time onwards features frequently in his sermons.

2.1. Ministers as Protesters

The very first letter in which Newman talks about his first published volume of sermons, expresses, in a certain sense, his *raison d'être* as a preacher. After expressing his thankfulness for the remarks that come his way, towards which he is always open – «that there is much to criticize in them I am quite sure - else they were inspired - and that they do not execute in the best or always the right way, objects and principle which are themselves right» – he does not fail to highlight that what he is embarked on is not a personal concern but rather a ministry which has effect on people and on history. He recognizes his role not simply as one who is there to hand out a message, but rather as one whose understanding of preaching is not disjointed from the age. Newman is convinced that the latter has an influence both on the preacher and the hearer. The honesty of the preacher in front of the message to be delivered goes hand in hand with the knowledge that his word will out of necessity meet resistance. This is the context in which the preacher finds himself.

«Again I am persuaded that often, when one accommodates the age, one hurts posterity... Again the Church and its Minister are by very profession protest against the peculiar errors of every age, as it comes – so that one must not be surprised to find a great argument in various sorts of objectors against this or that point one advances, which is not therefore proved to be wrong».[21]

2.2. The Heart and the Holy Spirit

In a second long letter addressed to the same person, Samuel Wilberforce, Newman enters into the details of his convictions as regards his ministry. What one cannot fail to notice in this letter is the width of the perspective Newman has about preaching.

In the following long quote, it is important to note, first, how Newman presents the action of the Holy Spirit within the person. The «constitution of man's nature» is the «locus» where the Holy Spirit operates. His presence is not primarily concerned with changing human nature. The notion that the Spirit presupposes that nature and works through it, is delivered in very practical language.

Secondly, that this whole action of the Holy Spirit on nature seems to be a natural coming together of the both realities, the divine and the human. As things take their course in nature so do they in grace.

Thirdly, this experience is characterized by a «slow change», graduality.

There is a sort of a lesson that needs to be derived for the benefit of preaching. In other words, if God's dealing with us has definite traits, our preaching ministry has simply to follow the same pattern, since it is aimed at serving the same Lord.

«If I must express broadly my view of spiritual influences on the heart and will etc. I should say, that they were vouchsafed according to the constitution of man's nature – i.e. so as not to change it from its ordinary workings, but to make use of these. The Holy Spirit addresses us thro' our reason, affections, conscience,

---

21 *LD* IV, pp. 354-355.

passions, natural-affections, tastes, associations etc but (generally and usually) only thro' them; He does not come immediately to change us, but through these. Again whatever happens to the mind naturally, that may happen in grace – as the natural mind generally changes slowly, so does the mind of the spirit; as sudden conversions happen in nature (e.g. the spendthrift suddenly becoming a miser,) so they may in grace.

Such is the rule, the ordinary mode (I conceive) of God's dealings with us. And such ordinary mode it is our duty to proclaim. We have little to do with exceptions in preaching His will – the great outlines of His providence must be set forth, the rule of His grace».[22]

The second part of the same letter is a reflection on the direct function of the Holy Spirit under the dispensation of the gospel. It is important to point out to the fact that the understanding of the Spirit has its own effect on the methodology of the sermons.

Newman's approach to the tenets of theology is not limited to the proclamation of the same. It goes beyond the fact, rather the duty, of delivering the theological contents. The sermons are as much concerned about the contents as they are about the way those contents elicit a response from the hearer. In the sermons we feel that there is a perspective which caters for both aspects. This approach differs greatly from the stand adopted by those who fail, or who refuse, to see any connection between the two.

For Newman the Spirit has a dual role: that of sanctification and that of regeneration or adoption. The first role has always been present well before Christianity. It is the second function which is the peculiarity of the gospel.

«Now I may perhaps imply more than I mean, but let me ask where we are told this of the sanctifying Spirit? The great gift of Christianity is not primarily the sanctifying Spirit, but only inclusively and by consequence. The sanctifying Spirit was given previously to Christianity, (only of course more fully under it)

---

[22] *LD* V, pp. 14-15.

– Cornelius was moved by the sanctifying Spirit when he sent for Peter, and before when he did alms and prayed – but he was not regenerated; the peculiarity of the gospel is the Spirit of regeneration or adoption».[23]

This distinction is as useful as much as it is indispensable to understand the subtlety with which Newman claims the importance of his approach. He sees his preaching as a medium through which the hearer is called to discover this adoption. In its own way, it is the Spirit, working through the whole person, who facilitates the beauty of this discovery. The following reflection reconnects the whole idea.

«Now I conceive as far as sanctification goes, the work of the Spirit is, as I have described it overleaf; He acts through the properties of the mind; nor do I know what authority we have for speaking of Him as the ultimate Agent, and not our own free will (to speak more strongly than I like.) In this sense salvation depends on ourselves, on our willing or not, i.e. prompted, enlightened, aided, carried on, perfected by the influences of grace... It is the indwelling of the Holy Spirit in the soul as in a Temple – the Spirit of adoption. In the first place it has (so to say) a physical, or (as we term it) a mystical influence on the soul, uniting it to Christ... when a Christian first has grieved the Holy Spirit then fallen into sin, though not fallen away altogether... he is brought back by no illapse of the Spirit (which regeneration always is) but by His influences co-operating with the human will, i.e. gradually... I say 'for what we know' – and I put this for my comfort against the awful and eternal truth that our hearts must be changed for heaven and can but be slowly changed ... In truth we arrive at truth by approximations».[24]

If, then, there exists the invitation to discover this call for regeneration, the hearer needs to be aroused to the actual duty that lies before him or her. The insistence on the practical aspect

---
23 *Id.*, p. 15.
24 *Id.*, pp. 15-16.

of faith issues from this attitude and ends up by being one of the traits that guide Newman in his sermons. There is no salvation, no justification, in the abstract as much as there is no sinning in the abstract.

«We want the claims of duty and the details of obedience set before us strongly... Therefore, I maintain, it is necessary to bring out the details of the Christian life, as a matter of fact, before the world. Men will confess they are sinful in the abstract. Spoken to in the abstract they do not know whether they are spiritual or not».[25]

2.3. The Evangelicals

The following reflections help distinguish between Newman's idea of the preaching ministry as opposed to that of the Evangelicals. The Evangelicals understand their preaching more on the level of emotion – «melting the hearer». Newman, on the contrary, sees it less as a means of conversion and more as a means through which the way can be prepared the way for Him who is «persuasion itself».

«Preaching is not the means of conversion – but a subsidiary, as rousing, convincing, interesting, and altogether preparing the way... The Church with the Sacraments etc, and the life of good men seem to me the great persuasives of the Gospel, as being visible witnesses and substitutes for Him who is Persuasion itself. Yet surely He in His day had so little success, that even the Church His representative, much more a mere preacher, may well acquiesce in failure».[26]

In direct dependence with the same, Newman can never approve the Evangelical method of preaching which reduces the

---

25 *Id.*, p. 22.
26 *Id.*, p. 32.

mysteries of religion as instruments when this is done towards a so-called bigger aim, which is that of the excitement of feelings.

«Yet what I shrink from is their rudeness, irreverence, and almost profaneness; the profaneness of making a most sacred doctrine a subject of vehement declamation, or instrument of exciting the feelings, or topic for vague, general, reiterate statements in technical language».[27]

2.4. Ancient and Modern (Evangelical) School

The whole issue about the method of preaching features again, in another correspondence, this time with Lord Lifford. Here Newman delves even more into the real meaning of the differences between him and the Evangelicals. The main interest of this letter lies in the use it makes of the example of antiquity.

After repeating his firm conviction that he has nothing against persons but only their systems – «in my sermons nothing is written against individuals; but against their system»[28] – Newman immediately refers to the contrast that is evidenced from a situation where the question is put forward: «what must one do to be saved?» The diversity of the answers constitutes the difference that exists between his approach and that of the Evangelicals. The following long quote reveals this whole dilemma.

«If an awakened sinner asked an ancient believer what he must do to be saved, he would answer (I consider) look to the Word Incarnate, break off your sins, do good whereas you have done evil - But I conceive one of the modern school, without denying this would for the most part drop it and say instead, 'Your heart must be changed - till you have faith you have nothing - you must have a spiritual apprehension of Christ - you must utterly renounce yourself and your merits and throw yourself at the

---

27   *Id.*, p. 45.

foot of the Cross etc' Now the question is not whether this is not true. I have said expressly 'That such a spiritual temper is indispensable, is agreed on all hands'; but whether this is the way to make a man Christian. I would maintain, that if we take care of the Objects and works of faith, faith will almost take care of itself. This modern view says take care of the state of heart, and the Objects and works will almost take care of themselves. But I have been stating this modern view as judicious, pious, and moderate men put it forward abstractedly. But the mass of men develop it, and then what is in itself (as I conceive) a mistake, becomes a mischief».[29]

Not being content to show the defect of the Evangelical system itself, Newman further indicates how that same system, failing to promote the wholeness of the doctrine it professes to proclaim, succeeds, all the while, to prepare its own theological limbo.

«That system has become Rationalistic in Germany, Socinian in Geneva – Socinian among English Presbyterians and Arian among Irish – Latitudinarian in Holland – it tends to Socinianism among our own the Evangelical Party... In consequence the body will split into parts, some will go back to the Church's doctrine, others will proceed to an open disavowal of it».[30]

2.5. Idea and Function of a Sermon

The ground covered by these letters, in these essentially different approaches that Newman and the Evangelicals adopt, prepare the way for a better understanding of what is found in other letters regarding what a sermon should be in itself. In a letter to Samuel Wilberforce, Newman, in showing that he and Wilberforce are not of the same opinion about what ground a sermon should

---

28 *LD* VI, p. 129.
29 *Id.*, p. 130.
30 *Id.*, p. 133.

cover, affirms a basic belief that sermons cannot possibly be the end and all of the Christian teaching.

«I think good part of our difference in the idea of a Sermon, lies in this – that you think of it as much more of a totum and rotundum than I do... I lay it down as a fundamental Canon, that a Sermon to be effective must be imperfect. A second sermon will correct it... I feel this as a vital principle – viz till we consent to follow Scripture in abandoning completeness in our Sermons, we do nothing accurately... I mean I have already said it is my principle, not to bring in every doctrine every where».[31]

This being the basic format of a sermon, imperfect, incomplete, its function is related to its nature. Newman's insistence on incompleteness is related to the vision he has of the formation of the Christian. Sermons only fulfil one of the needs of Christian formation and cannot pretend to cater for the complete journey.

Six days later, Newman writes another letter, quite a long one, this time to a friend in London, James Stephen, whose friendship with Newman started through Samuel Wilberforce. In this letter, continuing the elaboration on the idea of the sermons, Newman produces further reflections in relation to function and style: «I cannot consider Sermons to be the principal Ministration under the Gospel. The necessary style of a Sermon is such as to preclude the minuteness and familiarity necessary for the profit of the hearer».[32] Then, he reiterates his belief that sermons need to be complemented. The mention of Butler at this point is a reminder how Newman is influenced by him not simply on the level of contents or method, but more importantly on the level of understanding preaching in the wider picture of religion.

«The peculiarity of Butler is this – that, while on the one hand he is reserved, austere, infrequent in the mention of Christian doctrine, in his writings, yet on the other hand he was very earnest

---

31 *LD* V, pp. 38-39.
32 *Id.*, p. 44.

for what he calls a Cheap External Religion, put up a Cross in his private Chapel, and was charged with Popery. I conceive his wonderfully gifted intellect caught the idea which had actually been the rule of the Primitive Church, of teaching the more Sacred Truths ordinarily by rites and ceremonies. No mode of teaching can be imagined so public, constant, impressive, permanent, and at the same time reverential than that which makes the forms of devotion the memorial and declaration of doctrine – reverential because the very posture of the mind in worship is necessarily such. In this way Christians receive the Gospel literally on their knees, and in a temper altogether different from that critical and argumentative spirit which sitting and listening engender».[33]

What he writes towards the end of the letter is perhaps the most clear description of what a sermon by Newman really is. In the following verses, there lies in a nutshell what Newman stands for in relation to his preaching; it contains what we may call, in modern terminology, his «mission statement». He recapitulates the main ideas and guiding principles and, indirectly, refers again to that approach, influenced by Butler, which gives unity and coherence to a vision which risks being mistakenly dismissed because of its imperfect and incomplete state.

«Merely I would say the general object of preaching is to enlighten the mind as to its real state – to dig round about the Truth – to make men feel they are sinners and lost – to make them understand their need of pardon and sanctification – and the difficulty of the latter, to hinder them from mistaking words for ideas, and going on in a formal way, (which I cannot but think does follow that style of preaching, called simple and elementary, which the Evangelicals adopt…) – and if I effect this great object in preaching, I am little sollicitous to inquire whether I have every where brought forward in the front those simple Truths -, towards which I labour, and which the Sacraments secure, or

---

[33] *Id.*, p. 46.

whether I have gone through the full series of Christian doctrines in detail, which is the business of the Catechist. Services and Catechising are both essential, and I do not see how Sermons can supply their place. I wish heartily there was more of Catechising and Exposition – and again I earnestly desire that the Sacrament was now such as it was in the Primitive Church… - the presence of Christ in the Church for doctrine and grace – a continual revelation of the Incarnation».[34]

2.6. Moral rather than Doctrinal

A final remark, in connection with the effect of Butler, touches on the moral aspect of the sermons and how this aspect is in continuity with the model that the Primitive Church provides. The following letter to John Keble confirms that the principles and basic guidelines that were his in 1835 are further deepened in 1840. What needs to be taken in consideration at this stage is an event previously looked into: that from the summer of 1839 Newman is undergoing the effect of the article by Nicholas Wiseman. Without going into the details of the whole scenario, it is worth recalling that Newman feels like someone infront of whom a whole new scene is taking shape. In one of his letters he writes: «there is an uncomfortable vista opened which was closed before».[35]

The following lines confirm how the approach he has taken, first, in relation to the moral contents and pastoral approach of his sermons and, secondly, in relation to the influence of the Primitive Church's model, although they seem to be two distinct and not directly related elements, they end up by joining together and leading to the same destination. «No one will deny that most of my Sermons are on moral subjects, not doctrinal; still I

---
34   Id., p. 47.
35   LD VII, p. 155.

am leading my hearers, to the Primitive Church if you will, but not to the Church of England».[36] The reason he gives to this is the following:

«I fear I must allow that, whether I will or no, I am disposing them towards Rome. First, because Rome is the only representative of the Primitive Church besides ourselves; in proportion then as they are loosened from the one they will go to the other. Next because many doctrines which I hold have far greater, or their only scope, in the Roman system – e.g. the principle of reserve, or the consequences of post-baptismal sin».[37]

Newman's own line of action ends up by effecting not only his hearers but also himself, the preacher. He is sincere enough to accept the reality that the effect he wanted his words to have on his hearers is returning back to him, to achieve the same result. The sincerity and clarity with which he employs himself to share his spiritual journey with his hearers is proven by the effect the whole experience is having on him.

The recognition that the model of the Primitive Church subsists in the Church of Rome is a slow development, the origins of which could also be detected in the preaching ministry. «It must be added that this very circumstance that I have committed myself against Rome, has the effect of setting to sleep men's suspicions about me, which is painful now that I begin to have suspicions about myself».[38]

Conclusion

Newman had a pastoral motive in his preaching ministry. Yet this attention towards his hearers was not disjointed from those inner forces that moved him in his own faith journey.

---
36 *Id.*, p. 417.
37 *Ibid*.
38 *Id.*, p. 418; L. Bouyer expresses himself in the following terms about the overall value of the sermons and the destination they are heading towards:

The advice by his mother, who rejoices in seeing her son being able to «enlighten, correct, support and strengthen»[39] others on their way of faith, is a first affirmation of his principles. This will be a trait of his methodological approach right through his preaching. The primacy does not belong to the intellectual. The sermons are considered by Newman as vehicles of moral truths, and since «moral truth is discovered, not by reasoning, but [by] habituation, so it is recommended not by books b[ut by] oral instruction».[40]

Thus the person who is listening is not much a receiver of information, but as the «locus» where the Holy Spirit is operating through and within him or her. Preaching facilitates the person to get enriched by the action of the Spirit who makes real the coming together of the divine and the human.

Besides the role of the Spirit, the understanding of the Church also features, in a fundamental way, in Newman's idea of the sermon. The model he adopts, follows the pattern which Newman himself later recalls to be that of the Primitive Church: «no one will deny that most of my Sermons are on moral subjects, not doctrinal; still I am leading my hearers, to the Primitive Church if you will, but not to the Church of England».[41]

«mais toutes ses idées, que Newman devait développer tout au long de sa vie et de son ministère, dans l'Église anglicane, puis dans l'Église catholique, nous les voyons pour ainsi dir naître dans ses *Sermons paroissiaux et simples Sermons*, prêchés dans son église de la Sainte Vierge Marie au moment où il devenait à Oxford le chef de file du renouveau catholique au sein de l'Église d'Angleterre. Nous y voyons tuotes ses idées s'entrecroiser subtilement, mais sans qu'il y ait la moindre trace de spéculation abstraite. Au contraire, chacune émerge et trouve sa place dans une structure organique, convoquée précisément par l'inévitable nécessité qu'un christianisme authentique soit vécu au milieu du chaos intellectuel et moral qui était en train de s'installer et qui devait bientôt devenir notre univers. C'est dans ces *Sermons* que nous voyons apparaître pour la première fois les intuitions de Newman et qu'elles s'organisent peu à peu en cet ensemble vivant qui devait l'entraîner irrésistiblement à la conversion», in L. BOUYER, 'Actualité de Newman', *Communio* 12/3 (1987) 121-122.

39 *LD* I, p. 277.
40 *LD* II, p. 255.
41 *LD* VII, p. 417.

CHAPTER 5

Analysis of the term 'Conscience'

The following pages venture into the direct analysis of the word «conscience» as used by Newman in his sermons. The chronological divide adopted in the previous *Chapters* serves as the framework within which the analysis develops. The chronological examination helps on two different, but related, levels: first it offers the chance of documenting the growth within the vocabulary itself; secondly, it brings forth the development of the idea of conscience that the same vocabulary contains. The analysis, concentrating on the linguistic aspect of conscience, is related to the overall identity of conscience as a subject. For this reason, the analysis is divided into three parts that will amply cover the spectrum of the whole reality. First, the role conscience is examined from its standpoint as subject: what conscience «is»; second, its role as an agent, what is its activity, what does it «do»; third, what are the attributes of conscience, what does it «have».

The three aspects are necessarily related. The approach of examining conscience from three different angles is intended to bring out in a more pronounced way its fundamental unity. The division, clear and distinct, is conceived to favour the understanding of the meaning of «conscience». The aspects are the facets of a reality that is one in itself.

Before we start the analysis, we give some preliminary information concerning the sermons themselves. Out of all the sermons, 191 in all, 113 of them contain one or more references on conscience. This does not mean, though, that all these 113 sermons contain a complete reflection on conscience. In some of them the reference to conscience is very superficial, a mere passing remark, and does not constitute a reflection in its own right. At times, it is not even part of a reflection. In our analysis we work on those sermons which treat the term conscience in a detailed way, as constituting an object of reflection. This chosen corpus is made up of 37 sermons. They are almost evenly divided between the two periods: 19 belong to the first period, 1825-1832, and 18 to the second, 1833-1843.

Another telling feature belonging to these sermons is that during the first period only half of the sermons treat the aspect of conscience as subject: 9 out of 19. While in the second period 15 out of 18 sermons treat the same aspect. At this point, only on the level of numbers, these figures furnish us, in their own way, with useful information. It is important to point to the shift, from the first period to the second, towards a reflection on conscience that is more concerned with its own identity, than with what it does or what are its attributes. This shift of importance will be further confirmed and explained when we go through the examination of the sermons themselves.

1. The Linguistic Meaning of Conscience: 1825-1832[1]

1.1. Conscience «Is»

In this first period, we notice that the great reflections on conscience within Newman's sermons are tied up with those

---

1 A reading guide for 1825-1832 and 1833-1843 is presented in the *Appendix*.

events, which have a definite influence on the course of his life. The correspondence with his brother Charles and his struggle with liberalism feature in a prominent way. In the nine sermons that contain a reference to what conscience «is», we find the four fundamental sermons to which reference has already been previously made.[2] These together, with the others,[3] provide us with enough matter for reflection.

The way Newman refers to what conscience «is» in these sermons is necessarily related to the intellectual journey he is himself going through, as witnessed in the correspondence. The introduction of the theme of conscience in the early part of his dealings with his brother is further explained by what we discover now in the language he used in those same sermons written at the time. Here, it is worth naming the role these sermons have in Newman's life: they are the so-called product of the whole spiritual journey and intellectual struggle.

1.1.1. «Enlightened Guide»

When the vocabulary of these four sermons is taken into consideration, we become aware of how important it becomes for Newman to sustain the identity of conscience on the level of principle. The emphasis has to be on conscience as being a «powerful enlightened guide». The reasoning of his brother Charles is mistaken because it has waved away all possibility for the person to transcend self, with the consequence that despite «his utmost efforts, and after his most earnest prayers, he still falls short of what he knows to be right, and what he aims at».[4]

---

2 The sermons are: *PS* VIII. 8. *Inward Witness to the Truth of the Gospel*; *PS* VIII. 7. *Josiah, a Pattern for the Ignorant*; *PS* I. 17. *The Self-Wise Inquirer*; *PS* I. 24. *The Religion of the Day*.
3 *PS* I. 15. *Religious Faith Rational*; *PS* VII. 15. *Mental Prayer*; *PS* II. 9. *St. Paul's Conversion Viewed in Reference to His Office*; *PS* I. 9. *The Religious Use of Excited Feelings*; *PS* VIII. 5. *Curiosity a Temptation to Sin*.
4 *PS* VIII. 8, p. 116.

It is through conscience, and this being respected, that it «will become a more powerful and enlightened guide than before; it will become more refined and hard to please».[5]

This respect towards conscience qualifies its presence as a «constraining force», an «inward sense», and a «law written in heart». The shift that Newman creates from recognition on the level of knowledge towards recognition on the level of acceptance is smooth. Taking the example of Josiah, he presents the person who has moved from knowledge to action.

«In the words of the text, "his heart was tender;" he acknowledged a constraining force in the Divine voice within him - he heard and obeyed... And further, amid all the various worships offered to his acceptance, this same inward sense of his, strengthened by practice, unhesitatingly chose out the true one, the worship of the God of Israel. It chose between the better and the worse, though it could not have discovered the better by itself»[6]

«Whether it be we read and accept His word in Scripture (as Christians do), or His word in our conscience, the law written on the heart (as is the case with heathens); in either case, it is by following it, in spite of the seductions of the world around us, that we please God»[7]

The knowledge that guides Josiah is considered as the «better knowledge», which is able to take on the challenges, both from without, and from within, from the world and from reason. «Then in proportion to the intellectual gifts with which God had honoured us, came the temptation of unbelief and disobedience. Then came reason, led on by passion, to war against our better knowledge».[8]

---

5   *Ibid.*
6   *PS* VIII. 7, pp. 96-97.
7   *Id.*, pp. 107-108.
8   *PS* I. 17, p. 220.

1.1.2. «Independent Arbiter of Actions»

In the fourth sermon, *The Religion of the Day*,[9] conscience is further explained as an «independent arbiter of actions» and a «stern, gloomy principle». The long quotation that follows does justice to the importance that this sermon holds in this first period under examination.

«Thus elegance is gradually made the test and standard of virtue, which is no longer thought to possess an intrinsic claim on our hearts, or to exist, further than it leads to the quite and comfort of others. Conscience is no longer recognized as an independent arbiter of actions, its authority is explained away; partly it is superseded in the minds of men by the so-called moral sense, which is regarded merely as the love of the beautiful; partly by the rule of expediency, which is forthwith substituted for it in the details of conduct. Now conscience is a stern, gloomy principle; it tells us of guilt and prospective punishment. Accordingly, when its terrors disappear, then disappear also, in the creed of the day, those fearful images of Divine wrath with which the Scriptures abound. They are explained away. Everything is bright and cheerful. Religion is pleasant and easy; benevolence is the chief virtue; intolerance, bigotry, excess of zeal, are the first of sins. Austerity is an absurdity; - even firmness is looked on with an unfriendly, suspicious eye».[10]

1.1.3. «Placed by Almighty God»

Together with these four sermons, there are other five sermons that contribute to the wealth of vocabulary. Three of them present conscience in relation to reason, which is the central aspect of the controversy with Charles. Conscience is, first, «as much a

---

9 *PS* I. 24.
10 *Id.*, p. 312.

part of themselves as their reason is; and it is placed within them by Almighty God in order to balance the influence of sight and reason»;[11] secondly, in relation to prayer, public and private, both «conscience and reason would lead us to practice them, if we did but attend to these divinely-given informants».[12]

In the third one Newman explains the identity of conscience, in its relation to reason, in a hierarchical fashion, putting in perspective the effect of both, on the personal decision of the believer: «Conscience, and Reason in subjection to Conscience, *these* are those powerful instruments (under grace) which change a man». Yet, Newman is quick to point out «that though Conscience and Reason lead us to resolve on and to attempt a new life, they cannot at once make us *love* it».[13] By calling conscience a powerful instrument, Newman ends up by further qualifying its activity, the «occasional compunctions», an instrument of «His Spirit».

«Surely you must still have occasional compunctions of conscience for your neglect of Him. Your sin stares you in the face; your ingratitude to God affects you. Follow on to know the Lord, and to secure His favour by acting upon these impulses; by them He pleads with you, as well as by your conscience; they are the instruments of His Spirit stirring you up to seek your true peace».[14]

1.1.4. «Inward Voice»

In the remaining two sermons, conscience is explained as a reality which could be a fallible, erring conscience. Yet this does not diminish its authority. Faithfulness to conscience means in the end the discovery of the truth towards which conscience gently

---

11 *PS* I. 15, p. 200.
12 *PS* VII. 15, p. 204.
13 *PS* I. 9, p. 115.
14 *Id.*, p. 122.

and gradually guides. The example of St. Paul, frequently used by Newman in his sermons, is one of a person who had an: «inward voice which could be feeble, mixed up and obscured with human feelings and human traditions; so that what his conscience told him to do, was but partially true, and in part was wrong. Yet still, believing it to speak God's will, he deferred to it, acting as he did afterwards when he 'was not disobedient to the heavenly vision', which informed him Jesus was the Christ (Acts 26,19). Hear his own account of himself:- 'I have lived in all good conscience before God until this day' (Acts 23,1)».[15]

«Who has not felt a fear lest he be wandering from the true doctrine of Christ? Let him cherish and obey the holy light of conscience within him, as Saul did; let him carefully study the Scriptures, as Saul did not; and the God who had mercy even on the persecutor of His saints, will assuredly shed His grace upon him, and bring him into the truth as it is in Jesus».[16]

This same notion of fidelity to conscience is not dependent only on the fact that it is through conscience that truth is arrived at, but also due to the delicate nature that conscience has: «if we do not listen promptly to this secret monitor, its light goes out at once, and we are left to the mercy of mere conjecture, and grope about with but second-best guides».[17]

At this stage of the analysis, we have to point to the fact that in explaining the essence of conscience, Newman is mainly concerned with conscience in its role of helping the person towards the discovery of the truth. Both situations of controversy, his brother and the liberals, in a certain sense condition the space within which Newman explores what conscience is. If we may put it in academic terms, we may say that the philosophical aspect of conscience is much more important here than the theological reality it entails. This does not mean that Newman overlooks the

---

15 *PS* II. 9, pp. 103-104.
16 *Id.*, p. 106.
17 *PS* VIII. 5, p. 68.

latter aspect. The references above give witness to it. The aspect of conscience that Newman insists on at this stage, that is, its role of an enlightened guide, a powerful principle of strength, an independent arbiter of actions, will be of further interest when the same analysis of the second part of his preaching ministry will be presented.

1.2. Conscience «Does»

The following analysis furnishes us with the actions of conscience. Nearly all the sermons, 17 out of 19, contain one or more phrases on the «doings» of conscience. The multiplicity of the verbs describing the actions of conscience form a varied and colourful tapestry. To facilitate the exposition of the same we divide the vocabulary into two groups: those that show conscience from a proactive perspective, what it promotes and encourages; and those which present conscience as prohibiting.

1.2.1. «Bears Witness»

The diverse actions of conscience, those that promote and encourage, are almost all of them in relation to the divine reality. The first reference of such a proactive role of conscience in one of the early sermons, immediately speaks of conscience as related to the divine mystery.

«When, then, even an unlearned thus trained - from his own heart, from the action of his mind upon itself, from struggles with self, from an attempt to follow those impulses of his nature which he feels to be highest and noblest, from a vivid natural perception (natural, though cherished and strengthened by prayer; natural, though unfolded and diversified by practice; natural, though of that new and second nature which God the Holy Ghost gives),

Analysis of the term 'Conscience'

from an innate, though supernatural perception of the great vision of Truth which is external to him... Here is a mystery; but his own actual and too bitter experience bears witness to the truth of the declaration; he feels the mystery of iniquity within him... He reads, that God is angry at sin, and will punish the sinner, and that it is a hard matter, nay, an impossibility, for us to appease His wrath. Here, again, is a mystery: but here, too, his conscience anticipates the mystery, and convicts him; his mouth is stopped».[18]

This relationship is referred to again few months later. This time conscience is that reality which testifies the necessity of holiness for salvation: «the whole history of redemption, the covenant of mercy in all its parts and provisions, attests the necessity of holiness in order to salvation; as indeed even our natural conscience bears witness also».[19]

In the same vein, when the theme of prayer is introduced, the dependence of conscience on the divine realities becomes even more clear. Conscience has the ability to approve what, later on, experience will. It bids prayer because the action itself is an expression of a mystery towards which conscience indicates. Prayer being «that work of faith, which, though bidden by conscience, and authorized by reason, yet before He revealed His mercy, is laden in every man's case who attempts it, with guilt, remorse and fear».[20]

«The advice to pray without ceasing, which once you laughed at as fit only for the dull, the formal, the sour, the poor-spirited, or the aged, will be approved by your own experience, as it is even now by your reason and conscience. Oh, that you could be brought to give one serious hour to religion, in anticipation of that long eternity where you must be serious!»[21]

---

18 *PS* VIII. 8, pp. 117-119.
19 *PS* I. 1, p. 1.
20 *PS* I. 19, p. 245.
21 *PS* VII. 15, p.214.

1.2.2. «Aiding, Guiding, Composing»

Conscience has also a role of intercession, «aiding... guiding and composing their minds upon those objects of faith which they ought to look to, but cannot find themselves».[22] Newman here puts a reference to the Holy Spirit as helping conscience to intercede with His power, «while nature can but groan and travail in pain!»[23] The presence of the Holy Spirit will be one of the central themes of the second part of his preaching ministry.

In the role of «telling», the general use of the verb in relation to conscience is normally in the positive sense. In the several quotations available regarding what conscience «tells», and here we include the verbs «suggest», «teach», «speak», and those verbs tied with «notions» and «truth», Newman's use is quite frequent.

In the sermon, *Faith and Obedience*,[24] Newman presents the two realities contained in the title as «states of the mind... altogether one and the same» and «to have faith in God is to surrender one's-self to God». Within this context Newman presents the role of conscience as suggesting the act of obedience, of surrender, as an answer to the holiness that permeates the whole. The telling of conscience is a recognition of the holiness.

«And he will find nothing better as an offering, or as an evidence, than obedience to that Holy Law, which conscience tells him has been given us by God Himself; that is, he will be diligent in doing all his duty as far as he knows it and can do it.[25]

---

22 *PS* I. 20, p. 267.
23 *Id.*, pp. 267-278.
24 *PS* III. 6.
25 *Id.*, p. 80.

1.2.3. «Naturally Teaches Obedience»

On the same theme of obedience, Newman compares obedience as demanded by conscience and that asked for in Scripture as not different one from the other: «accordingly Christ's service is represented in Scripture, not as different from that religious obedience which conscience teaches us naturally, but as the perfection of it».[26]

In close relation with the above, the sermons smoothly move from «obedience» towards «discovery»: obedience to a law becomes the condition of the discovery of truths. It is within conscience that the person is helped to make this discovery. What follows is a series of reflections all centred on the role of conscience where truth can be learnt. In the sermon on *Josiah, a Pattern for the Ignorant*,[27] Newman presents the man as an example of a person who was guided by the provisions of conscience: «At first, not having the Book of the Law to guide him, he took such measures as natural conscience suggested».[28] The same example forms the backbone of what Newman reflects on in the following sermons, all of them written, more or less within the same period:[29]

«Seek truth in the way of obedience; try to act up to your conscience, and let your opinions be the results, not of mere chance reasoning or fancy, but of an improved heart. This way, I say, carries with it an evidence to ourselves of its being the right way, if any way be right; and that there is a right and a wrong way conscience also tells us».[30]

«Clear-sighted as reason is on other subjects, and trustworthy as a guide, still in questions connected with our duty to God and man it is very unskilful and equivocating. After all, it barely

---

26 *PS* VIII. 14, p. 205.
27 *PS* VIII. 7.
28 *Id.*, p. 98.
29 September - October 1830.
30 *PS* VIII. 13, p. 198.

reaches the same great truths which are authoritatively set forth by Conscience and Scripture».[31]

1.2.4. «Suggests»

In these sermons, the connection between the workings of conscience and the aim of Scripture is very evident. Newman continues to confirm his grounded belief that the provisions of conscience are those that Scripture approves and builds on. This method of proceeding continues to be very much influenced by what is going on at this particular period of his life, in particular the correspondence with his brother Charles.

«Indeed, it would have been strange if the God of nature had said one thing, and the God of grace another; if the truths which our conscience taught us without the information of Scripture, were contradicted by that information when obtained. But it is not so; there are two ways of pleasing God; what conscience suggests, Christ has sanctioned and explained... indeed, all revelation is grounded on those simple truths which our own consciences teach us in a measure, though a poor measure, even without it. It is One God, and none other but He, who speaks first in our consciences, then in His Holy Word; and, lest we should be in any difficulty about the matter, He has most mercifully told us so in Scripture, wherein He refers again and again (as in the passage connected with the text) to the great Moral Law, as the foundation of the truth, which his Apostles and Prophets, and last of all His Son, have taught us: 'Fear God, and keep His commandments; for this is the whole duty of man' (Eccles. 12,13)».[32]

Another aspect of the «tellings» of conscience is its ability to guide the person by discriminating between right and wrong.

---

31 *PS* I. 17, pp. 218-219.
32 *PS* VIII. 14, pp. 202-203.

Yet, Newman is not carried too far in this assertion without immediately pointing out that this function of conscience is as fragile and delicate as it is true. In two sermons, preached one week one from the other, Newman reflects on this aspect of conscience – the fragility of the truth that conscience proposes and the importance of not treating lightly both its information and its impulses. «At first our conscience tells us, in a plain straightforward way, what is right and what is wrong; but when we trifle with this warning, our reason becomes perverted, and comes in aid of our wishes, and deceives us to our ruin».[33]

«But this is the difference between seizing or letting slip these opportunities; - if you avail yourselves of them for acting, and yield to the impulse so far as conscience tells you to do, you have made a leap (so to say) across a gulf, to which your ordinary strength is not equal; you will have secured the beginning of obedience, and the further steps in the course are (generally speaking) far easier than those which first determine its direction».[34]

The second part of this analysis about the actions of conscience is concerned with those actions that can be classified as negative, or prohibiting. The actions we present here are closely related to the ideas above. Their presentation helps us to formulate how Newman envisages the role of conscience when it has to pronounce itself against something. The presentation, chronologically exposed, follows a gradual progression of how the conscience functions and how the person behaves when its indications are refused.

1.2.5. «Warns»

The fragility referred to above, is what comes to the fore, initially, even when the action of conscience is one of admonishment.

[33] *PS* VIII. 5, p. 67.
[34] *PS* I. 9, p. 117.

The delicate conscience that promotes truth is also delicate in its warning.

«Conscience at first warns us against sin; but if we disregard it, it soon ceases to upbraid us; and thus sins, once known, in time become secret sins. It seems then (and it is a startling reflection), that the more guilty we are, the less we know it; for the oftener we sin, the less we are distressed at it».[35]

The presence of this warning is a safeguard: it promotes the good and prevents the evil. Its function of warning is subsequent to its function of informing and promoting the good within. «Whatever is the first time persons hear evil, it is quite certain that good has been beforehand with them, and they have a something within them which tells them it is evil».[36] In another sermon, two months later,[37] Newman returns again on this same function of conscience and the risks that exist if its warning is not taken seriously.

«Yet they will not attend to it; for a plain reason, - they love sin, - they love to be their own masters, and therefore they will not attend to that secret whisper of their hearts, which tells them they are not their own masters, and that sin is hateful and ruinous».[38]

1.2.6. «Condemns»

The progression that is necessarily present when the dictates of conscience are followed is the exact opposite of what issues when conscience is neglected. This idea is presented in another sermon that same year.

---

35   *PS* I. 4, p. 51.
36   *PS* VII. 4, p. 45.
37   *PS* VII. 4. was preached on 15th March 1829; *PS* I. 15. was preached on 24th May 1829
38   *PS* I. 15, p. 200.

«They gradually let slip from their minds the very idea of obedience to a fixed external law; then they actually allow themselves in things which their conscience condemns; then they loose the direction of their conscience, which being ill used, at length refuses to direct them. And thus, being left by their true inward guide, they are obliged to take another guide, their reason, which by itself knows little or nothing about religion; then, this inner blind reason forms a system of right or wrong for them, as well as it can, flattering to their own desires, and presumptuous where it is not actually corrupt».[39]

In the above quoted sermons, the aspect of prohibition is not presented in a cold impersonal way. As much as it is the person who ultimately decides, the role of conscience, both when it promotes and when it disapproves of something, is very much considered to be that of helping in the discovery. The person always takes the centre stage. Conscience fulfils its promises only if it is allowed to do so by the person concerned. It can never enforce its aims. Conscience helps create an environment where the depth of the person can be disclosed to self. This cannot be done independent of self. While its sensitive nature puts it in a privileged state of getting the right information first, its delicate function does not allow it to be more than a messenger, a whisper.

1.3. Conscience «Has»

In this section, we present those realities that conscience possesses. This aspect will complement the previous two with added valuable information. It is worth noting that only seven of the 19 sermons furnish us with some reflections. Among these seven, six contain some other phrases which deal with what conscience

---

39 *PS* I. 19. *Times of Private Prayer*, p.254; this sermon was preached on 20th December 1829.

«is» and «does». Only one contains a reflection not dealing with the previous two sections.

What comes out of this examination is that when writing about what conscience has, Newman generally thinks along the lines of «authority». This does not exclude the fact that there are other references to the objects of conscience, like «stirrings of conscience»,[40] «relentings of conscience»,[41] «visitings of conscience»,[42] «compunctions of conscience».[43] What we will concentrate on here is its authority which links directly with what we have previously exposed.

1.3.1. «Authority»

Conscience, being such a fundamental reality in the person, has authority. In the sermon *The Self-Wise Inquirer*,[44] Newman refers more than once to conscience as having authority. The context within which these lines are written, the second part of the correspondence with his brother, goes a long way to explain why for Newman unless conscience has authority nothing holds which concerns the divine. If «to trust them (the notions of conscience) is not the false wisdom of the world, or foolishness, because they come from the Allwise God»,[45] therefore it follows that: «clear-sighted as reason is on other subjects, and trustworthy as a guide, still in questions connected with our duty to God and man it is very unskilful and equivocating. After all, it barely reaches the same great truths which are authoritatively set forth by Conscience and Scripture; and if it be used in religious inquiries,

---

40 *PS* I. 15, p. 200.
41 *PS* I. 17, p. 225.
42 *PS* I. 9, p. 118.
43 *Id.*, p. 122.
44 *PS* I. 17.
45 *Id.*, p. 217.

Analysis of the term 'Conscience'

without reference to these divinely-sanctioned informants, the probability is it will miss the Truth altogether».[46]

The refusal of conscience as a reality that has authority leads to what Newman calls «judicial blindness».

«A murmuring against that religious service which is perfect freedom, complaints that Christ's yoke is heavy, a rebellious rising against the authority of Conscience, and a proud arguing against the Truth, or at least an endurance of doubt and scoffing, and a light, unmeaning use of sceptical arguments and assertions, these are the beginnings of apostasy».[47]

«As they proceed in their course of judicial blindness, from undervaluing they learn to despise or to hate the authority of Conscience. They treat it as a weakness, to which all men indeed are subject, - they themselves in the number, - especially in seasons of sickness, but of which they have cause to be ashamed».[48]

Together with the reflections in this sermon, which has the advantage of treating the subject of conscience in more detail, Newman offers other reflections on the same idea in different words and in different contexts. When speaking about *St. Paul's Conversion Viewed in Reference to His Office*,[49] referring to the example of the Pharisees and the Gentiles, Newman draws the following parallelism in regards to conscience: «The Pharisees, then, were breakers of the Law; the Gentile reasoners and statesmen were infidels. Both were proud, both despised the voice of conscience».[50] The contempt of conscience is at the heart of their mistake that ends up by favouring «pride [which] hardens the heart against repentance, and sensuality debases it to a brutal nature».[51]

---

46 *Id.*, pp. 218-219.
47 *Id.*, pp. 220-221.
48 *Id.*, p. 224.
49 *PS* II. 9.
50 *Id.*, p. 105.
51 *Ibid*.

1.3.2. «Innate Principles»

Another reflection that highlights the importance of the authority of conscience is the fact that, within it, there are to be found innate principles. These principles are part and parcel of conscience. Newman presents them as forming an essential part of conscience. It is only through experience that we arrive at a point where we are conscious of them. To strengthen his reasoning, Newman takes the example of the child, a frequent example in his sermons when he writes about the reality of conscience in the stages of its discovery.

«For consider how gently God leads us on in our early years, and how very gradually He opens upon us the complicated duties of life. A child at first has hardly anything to do but to obey his parents; of God he knows just as much as they are able to tell him, and he is not equal to many thoughts either about Him or about the world. He is almost passive in their hands who gave him life; and, though he has those latent instincts about good and evil, truth and falsehood, which all men have, he does not know enough, has not had experience enough from the contact of external objects, to elicit into form and action those innate principles of conscience, or to make himself conscious of the existence of them».[52]

---

[52] *PS* I. 8, p. 102; Newman also explains these principles as «suggestions» through which the child «would begin to have a character; no longer influenced by every temptation to anger, discontent, fear, and obstinacy, in the same way as before; but with something of a firm principle in his heart to repel them in a defensive way, as a shield repels darts... and so he would grow up to man's estate, his duties at length attaining their full range, and his soul being completed in all its parts for the due performance of them», in *id.*, pp. 102-103.

1.3.3. «Natural True Sense»

One last remark is based on two sermons[53] which were among the last Newman preached before the tour of the Mediterranean. It concerns an attribute of conscience which is much related to the authority it carries with it: conscience has a «natural true sense». The context is one where a person refuses to come to terms with the repentance that conscience calls for. Taking the situation of the young, who have not as yet come «to an age to be callous, or have formed excuses to overcome the natural true sense of their conscience»,[54] Newman considers adulthood as a possible stage where a person even though he or she recognizes this «natural true sense», still refuse to act on it.

«When, then, a man complains of his hardness of heart or weakness of purpose, let him see to it whether this complaint is more than a mere pretence to quiet his conscience, which is frightened at his putting off repentance; or, again, more than a mere idle word, said half in jest and half in compunction».[55]

Closely linked with the above is a reflection, preached a week later, in the sermon *The Religion of the Day*.[56] The substance of this reflection is that once the reality of conscience is lost, then something else has to be found as a substitute.

«Conscience is no longer recognized as an independent arbiter of actions, its authority is explained away; partly it is superseded in the minds of men by the so-called moral sense, which is regarded merely as the love of the beautiful; partly by the rule of expediency, which is forthwith substituted for it in the details of conduct».[57]

---

53 *PS* I. 3. *Knowledge Of God's Will Without Obedience*, preached on 19th August 1832; *PS* I. 24. *The Religion Of The Day*, preached on 26th August 1832.
54 *PS* I. 3, p. 36.
55 *Ibid.*
56 *PS* I. 24, a detailed analysis of the sermon is given in *Chapter Two*.
57 *Id.*, p. 312.

One cannot fail to notice how the two lines of action, the essential role of conscience in his brother's correspondence with the refusal that is implied, and the struggle against the liberal idea with the substitution they propose, converge in these two sermons. It is against this background that a study of the last university sermon preached immediately before the tour acquires its real worth. Although it is outside our own field of research, a reference to this sermon, *Wilfulness, the Sin of Saul*,[58] is, in a certain sense, a fitting conclusion to this examination.

Newman presents the danger of both attitudes as «wilfulness». Saul represents for Newman the person whose «temptation and his fall consisted in a certain perverseness of mind, founded on some obscure feeling of self-importance, very commonly observable in human nature, and sometimes called pride».[59] It follows that one's own ways take precedence. The refusal of conscience, as «an independent arbiter», eventually creates the space for a substitute. In resisting God, wilfulness produces «a natural principle of disorder… At length the proud heart, which thought it much to obey its Maker, was humbled to seek comfort in a witch's cavern».[60]

The concluding sentence of the sermon contains an opportune warning in Newman's own time as it does for us now.

«These remarks may at first seem irrelevant in the case of those who, like ourselves, are bound by affection and express promises to the cause of Christ's Church; yet it should be recollected that very rarely have its members escaped the infection of the age in which they lived».[61]

---

58   *US* 9, pp. 156-175.
59   *Id.*, p. 158.
60   *Id.*, p. 165.
61   *Id.*, p. 175.

2. The Linguistic Meaning of Conscience: 1833-1843

Some preliminary information before we enter into the second part of the analysis *per sé*, helps us to appreciate what line of development does the use of the term conscience take. Out of the 18 sermons that form the area of study belonging to this period, 15 of them contain one or more references on the identity of conscience. This contrasts sharply with the first period of the sermons where only 9 out of 19 contained the same type of references. Thus we can already conclude, at this initial stage, that while in the first part attention was more on the «doings» of conscience, 17 out of 19 sermons contained some type of reference, in the second period of the sermons the emphasis of the reflection is on what «conscience is».

2.1. Conscience «Is»

We have previously hinted that in the first period the concern on the «being» of conscience is rather from a point of view that we qualified as philosophical. Conscience was understood as an instrument of discovery and its workings were very much related to those events that made up that phase of his life. With the same reasoning we can say that the presentation of «what conscience is», in this second period of Newman's preaching ministry, goes a long way to confirm that the predominantly spiritual aspect, the theological dimension, of conscience is very much in relation to, and one may add the result of, those deep guiding principles which direct his life in this second period. Thus, we can also conclude that the search for truth has shifted into an arena that is theologically influenced. The idea of the Church, the importance given to the notion of the indwelling of the Holy Spirit, both previously explored, are fundamental tools to our understanding and appreciation of what follows.

The 15 sermons that contain one or more reflections on «what conscience is», are mainly presented in direct relation to the presence of God or His Spirit. In fact it becomes immediately evident that when Newman writes about the identity of conscience, his practical concern with God suddenly comes to the fore. It is also important to note here that sermons dealing with the identity of conscience but not in relation to the presence of God, are all written during and after September 1839. These reflections are directly related to the period when the appearance of the article by Nicholas Wiseman opened a whole «new vista» in front of him. The dilemma of conscience that was presented to Newman, and the process that that article helped to bring to maturation, with its eventual outcome, have already been examined before.

2.1.1. «Representative of Him»

The sermon *The Immortality of the Soul*, [62] written in Naples between 23rd and 24th February 1833, during the tour, contains three significant references to conscience in relation to God. It is conceived as «representative of Him», as «law of God written in the heart», and as a «secret voice of God». The way Newman unfolds his thinking within the sermon, is of essential importance to the reflections he presents on conscience. First, he starts by presenting the challenge that a person has in arriving to acknowledge that there is a soul within.

«To understand that we have souls, is to feel our separation from things visible, our independence of them, our distinct existence in ourselves, our individuality, our power of acting for ourselves this way or that way, our accountableness for what we do. These are the great truths which lie wrapped up indeed even in a child's mind, and which God's grace can unfold there inspite

---

62 *PS* I. 2.

of the influence of the external world; but at first this outward world prevails. We look off from self to the things around us, and forget ourselves in them».[63]

This «forgetfulness», sustained and encouraged by all that is visible, tends to carry the person at a point of denial of what he or she really is. This danger is juxtaposed with the fact that «we still crave for something, we do not well know what; but we are sure it is something which the world has not given us».[64] Newman points to the moment when «we are led to understand the nothingness of this world... (which) cannot hide the view of what is beyond it; - and we begin by degrees, to perceive that there are but two beings in the whole universe, our own soul, and the God who made it».[65]

What strikes the reader is how smoothly and effectively Newman builds his argument on that which can be called the deep truth contained in the heart of the person, the real. He gently leads his hearers from the acceptance of the fact that this world's nature, with all its strength, is a passing one, to the acknowledgement that this present experience, ultimately, has to deal with the beyond, the next world. It is, therefore, within a journey of discovery that Newman goes on to present the notion of conscience. Thus, the true awareness of the world, as being «nothing more than a show»,[66] becomes closely, and essentially, related, almost in a necessary reciprocal dependency, to the discovery both of oneself and of God: «the clear vision we have, first, of our own existence, next of the presence of the great God in us, and over us, as our Governor and Judge, who dwells in us by our conscience, which is His representative».[67]

The reality of conscience, then, can ultimately be nothing more, and nothing less, than an experience of the divine supposing

---

63   *Id.*, p. 19.
64   *Id.*, p. 20.
65   *Ibid.*
66   *Ibid.*
67   *Id.*, p. 21.

and superseding the passing nature of this world. Within these parameters, we find ourselves already equipped with enough knowledge of the world to know «what is meant by this world's *not* living for ever»,[68] and provided with enough wisdom to arrive to recognize a «law of God written in our hearts (which) bids us serve Him, and partly tells us how to serve Him».[69]

At this point, Newman presents Christ, «as our visible Lord, (who) takes the place of the world as the only begotten of the Father».[70] It is a fundamental characteristic in Newman's reflections that the temporality of the Christian calling instead of being pushed aside or underestimated, is taken in all its implications. It is the place where redemption takes place. The importance of the mystery of the incarnation within his theology is in the order of necessity. The «visibility» of God made Man is central to the whole idea of redemption: it contrasts the «visibility» of the world, while at the same time offering to humanity the possibility to be «drawn forward by all manner of powerful influences to turn from things temporal to things eternal».[71] The Christians, then, «who, through grace, obey the secret voice of God, move onward contrary to the world's way, and careless what mankind may say of them, as understanding as they have souls, which is the one thing they have to care about».[72]

This sermon is of fundamental importance in this second period of his preaching ministry. It sets a pattern for other sermons which are considered of great significance: for their timing and the events they are related to; for the subject they treat which has its very source here.[73] What follows in the rest of the sermons is very much a development of what has been exposed so far.

---

68 *Ibid.*
69 *Ibid.*
70 *Id.*, pp. 21-22.
71 *Id.*, p. 22.
72 *Ibid.*
73 PS IV. 6. *The Individuality of the Soul*; PS IV. 14. *The Greatness and Littleness of Human Life*; PS IV. 22. *Watching*; PS V. 22. *The Thought of God, the Stay of the Soul*.

Conscience is further presented as an «original endowment».[74] Referring to the development that takes place in the child and how the dangers of temptations assail the person as he or she advances in life, the danger is that yielding to them, one can loose, «through sinning, a guide which they originally had from God».[75]

2.1.2. «Rule»

Revisiting the theme of the sermon *The Immortality of the Soul*,[76] the sermon *Faith without Sight*[77] continues to develop the relation between God and conscience, the latter being presented as a rule:

«which is born with him, which he did not make for himself, and to which he feels bound in duty to submit… conscience immediately directs his thoughts to some Being exterior to himself, who gave it, and is evidently superior to him; for a law implies a lawgiver, and a command implies a superior. Thus a man is at once thrown out of himself, by the very Voice which speaks within him; and while he rules his heart and conduct by his inward sense of right and wrong, not by the maxims of the external world, still that inward sense does not allow him to rest in itself, but sends him forth again from home to seek abroad for Him who has put His Word in him…»[78]

Conscience, in this sense, is not reduced to a function but, more importantly so, it is envisaged as containing experience, where the divine is accessible from within. Here Newman recalls another reflection from the first period of his preaching ministry where he presents faith and conscientiousness almost on the same level.

---

74 *PS* II. 6, p. 65.
75 *Id.*, p. 66.
76 *PS* I. 2.
77 *PS* II. 2.
78 *Id.*, p. 18.

«It is no matter whether we call it faith or conscientiousness, they are in substance one and the same: where there is faith, there is conscientiousness - where there is conscientiousness, there is faith; they may be distinguished from each other in words, but they are not divided in fact. They belong to one, and but one, habit of mind - dutifulness; they show themselves in obedience, in the careful, anxious observance of God's will, however we learn it».[79]

2.1.3. «Voice of God»

In the next four sermons[80] there runs an identical theme that centres on the metaphor of the «voice» which reflects, like a mirror, the «intimations» of God. In the first one, the Holy Spirit has the role of eliciting this «voice of Truth in the hearts of all rational beings, tuning them into harmony with the intimations of God's Law».[81] Thus conscience, which for the «narrow religionist… is not the voice of God at all, - or is a mere benevolence, according to the disciple of Utility, - or, in the judgment of the more mystical sort, a kind of passion for the beautiful and sublime»,[82] for the faith person it:

«assures us that there is something higher than earth. We cannot analyze, define, contemplate what it is that thus whispers to us. It has no shape or material form. There is that in our hearts which prompts us to religion, and which condemns and chastises sin. And this yearning of our nature is met and sustained, it finds an object to rest upon, when it hears of the existence of an All-powerful, All-gracious Creator. It incites to a noble faith in what we cannot see».[83]

---

79 *PS* VIII. 7. *Josiah, a Pattern for the Ignorant*, p. 107.
80 *PS* II. 19. *The Indwelling Spirit*, and *PS* II. 23. *Tolerance of Religious Error*, both written in November/December 1834; *PS* VI. 23. *Faith without Demonstration*, written in 21st May 1837 and *PS* IV. 22. *Watching*, written in 3rd December 1837.
81 *PS* II. 19, p. 218.
82 *PS* II, 23, pp. 288-289.

Analysis of the term 'Conscience'

In the last sermon of this group, conscience is fittingly presented as a mirror. Newman makes use of this example by connecting it with the first subject we touched in this section: the seduction of the visibility of the world. The use of the example is all in the negative sense. It is like showing the bad to highlight in an indirect way the force of goodness.

«The breath of the world has a peculiar power in what may be called rusting the soul. The mirror within them, instead of reflecting back the Son of God their Saviour, has become dim and discoloured; and hence, though (to use a common expression) they have a good deal of good in them, it is only in them, it is not through them, around them, and upon them».[84]

2.1.4. «Throne»

In the next two sermons,[85] very much in a developmental line with what has been so far presented, Newman presents conscience as a place where God dwells. The image of the «throne» is presented in the first one and it is further enriched with other images in the second. The first reflection speaks about God as coming «to us as a Law, before He comes as a Lawgiver; that is, He sets up His throne within us, and enables us to obey Him, before we have learned to reflect on our own sensations, and to know the voice of God».[86] In the second Newman reflects on the nature of the true Christian:

«who is in a state of acceptance with God... has faith in Him, as to live in the thought that He is present with him, - present not externally, not in nature merely, or in providence, but in his innermost heart, or in his conscience. A man is justified whose

---
83 *PS* VI. 23, pp. 339-340.
84 *PS* IV. 22, p. 328.
85 *PS* IV. 21. *Faith and Love*; *PS* V. 16. *Sincerity and Hypocrisy*.
86 *PS* IV. 21, p. 312.

conscience is illuminated by God, so that he habitually realizes that all his thoughts, all the first springs of his moral life, all his motives and his wishes, are open to Almighty God... He alone admits Christ into the shrine of his heart; whereas others wish in some way or other, to be by themselves, to have a home, a chamber, a tribunal, a throne, a self where God is not, - a home within them which is not a temple, a chamber which is not a confessional, a tribunal without a judge, a throne without a king; - that self may be king and judge».[87]

In concluding this section on the identity of conscience in relation to God, we present the last three reflections that slightly vary between themselves. The first one contains the idea that «to have a good conscience... (is) to ever be reminded of God by our own hearts, to have our hearts in such a state as to be led thereby to look up to Him, and to desire His eye to be upon us through the day?»[88] Good conscience is, therefore, a reminding source of the discovery it has made and for this reason it is a force which asks to be reckoned with.

The invitations that come out of this discovery are directly related to Him who, simultaneously, animates and participates in this experience, made up of «our own soul, and the God who made it»;[89] and, finally, this presence of God develops into a situation where choices have to be made. The choice is the moment of self-determination. Obedience or disobedience are actions which are as necessary as much as they are unavoidable, since they express the person's own self: «whether He commands by a visible presence, or by a voice, or by our consciences, it matters not, so that we feel it to be a command. If it is a command, it may be obeyed or disobeyed».[90]

---

87 *PS* V. 16, p. 226.
88 *PS* V. 22, p. 322.
89 *PS* I, 20.
90 *PS* VIII. 2, pp. 24-25.

2.1.5. «Inward Incommunicable Perception»

We need to remind ourselves that the moment he is writing this last reflection and the following one, Newman is going through that delicate period in his life after the appearance of the article by Nicholas Wiseman. The quotation that follows captures the essence of a conscience, in harmony with reason, which is in search of the truth and is ready to accept the challenges God proposes.

«He goes by a law which others know not; not his own wisdom or judgment, but by Christ's wisdom and the judgment of the Spirit, which is imparted to him, - by that inward incommunicable perception of truth and duty, which is the rule of his reason, affections, wishes, tastes, and all that is in him, and which is the result of persevering obedience».[91]

The vocabulary adopted, which is not related directly to God, is very much the same, or similar, to the one explored in the first period of the preaching ministry: that is conscience as inward sense,[92] as more acute than reason,[93] invisible guide,[94] law,[95] and inward feeling.[96] The return to the original vocabulary is not much to be considered as a retreat to the first phase. It is more to be seen as the involvement of the whole personality, both from a theological and philosophical perspective, in a moment so important in his life. The pages in the *Apologia* which deal with this period[97] are a witness to the unified approach. The frequency of themes such as conscience and truth, consistency and certitude, all indicate to the involvement of the whole personality.[98]

---

91   *PS* VI. 18, p. 267.
92   *PS* II. 2, p. 18.
93   *Id.*, p. 19.
94   *Ibid*.
95   *PS* V. 11, p. 147.
96   *PS* VI. 3, p. 35.
97   *Apol.* pp. 147-237.
98   *Id.*, pp. 206, 209, 215-216, 222, 228, 229, 231, 235-236.

2.2. Conscience «Does»

In this part of the study, we examine the area Newman develops in connection with the actions of conscience. It is important to note that out of the nine sermons which contain one or more reflections on the action of conscience, eight of them form part of the fifteen sermons examined in the previous analysis on «what conscience is». Therefore it necessarily follows that the centrality of God is very much the key here, as it was in the last section just examined.

We need to recall here two important conclusions reached previously; first, in our analysis on «what conscience does» in the first period, the positive actions of conscience favour the approach to God; secondly, we have also confirmed that the context of the analysis of «what conscience is» in the second period, does favour, as well, the mystery of God. This has an effect on what we discover in this part of the analysis. In actual fact, this effects the contents of the actions in such a way that the need of dividing the verbs into positive actions and prohibiting ones is not necessary here. Out the twenty reflections we have, only three can be considered to be negative.[99]

2.2.1. «Tells»

The action that mostly features in this part is that of «telling». Besides the actual verb itself, we also include with it those verbs which convey a similar meaning, that of conveying knowledge or encouraging towards action. Conscience «tells us, or bids us, how to serve Him», while it informs us that «we are answerable for what we do, and that God is a righteous Judge».[100] Conscience,

---

[99] «Does not allow him to rest in itself», in *PS* II, 2, p. 18; «forebodes ill to the sinner», in *PS* II. 23, p. 288; «condemns and chastises sin», in *PS* VI. 23, p. 339.
[100] *PS* I. 2, p. 21.

similarly, offers us «suggestions»[101] and helps in telling «the difference between right and wrong».[102]

Besides the actions of conscience related to knowledge and information, Newman also highlights the role of conscience in favouring that tension of the human towards the divine. This aspect already came to the fore in the analysis of «what conscience is» in the second period and finds an echo here as well. Conscience, as an experience of the discovery of truth, has this unambiguous role of moving the human experience towards the mystery. The verbs Newman employs are consistent with this sense of urgency and movement. Conscience «directs thoughts to some being»[103] and does not allow the person to rest in self, «but sends him forth again from home to seek abroad for Him who has put His Word in him».[104] The movement in itself becomes the confirmation «of the presence of God, originally certified to them by the inward voice of conscience».[105]

The theme of the visibility of the world and the «visibility of the Son of God made Man» gives to the role of conscience a particular aspect that is so dear to Newman. Christ has bridged the gap between the human and the divine and fulfilled the yearnings of all that conscience tends towards. The fact that within conscience we find the way to Christ, «the mirror within them... reflecting back the Son of God their Saviour»,[106] is in not alien to its workings but rather explains and justifies all that conscience stands for.

---

101 *PS* I. 5, p. 58.
102 *PS* II. 6, p. 65; also *PS* II. 2, p. 18; *PS* VI. 3, p. 35; *PS* IV. 21, pp. 313-314.
103 *PS* II. 2, p. 18.
104 *Ibid*.
105 *Id.*, p. 19; see also *PS* VI. 23, pp. 339-340.
106 *PS* IV. 22, p. 328.

2.3. Conscience «Has»

The detailed examination that we presented on the same topic in the first part of the sermons, in a certain way, has covered enough ground in this area. We do not discover here any significant contribution regarding that which concerns the attributes of conscience. The four sermons that contain the reflections, present the fact that conscience «has a claim to be followed in matters of conduct».[107] Even though «it has no shape or material form»,[108] still there are persons who try «to beat down the risings of conscience»[109] because their heart is not Christ's. Finally in one particular sermon[110] Newman has quite a complete reflection about the feeling of a good conscience as different from the bad one. The style is Newman at its best. The time he wrote it, May 1840, was the time when he himself was not sure what road to take. It is the typical case of a personal reflection that has more of the person than at first appears.

«Is there anyone who does not know how very painful the feeling of a bad conscience is? Do not you recollect, my Brethren, some time or other, having done something you knew to be wrong? and do you not remember afterwards what a piercing bitter feeling came on you? Is not the feeling of a bad conscience different from any other feeling, and more distressing than any other, till we have accustomed ourselves to it? Persons do accustom themselves and lose this feeling; but till we blunt our conscience, it is very painful. And why? It is the feeling of God's displeasure, and therefore it is so painful. Consider then: if God's displeasure is so distressing to us, must not God's approval and favour be just the reverse; like life from the dead, most exceedingly joyful and

---

107 *PS* II. 2, p. 19.
108 *PS* VI. 23, p. 339.
109 *PS* V. 17, p. 246.
110 *PS* VII. 14. *Religion Pleasant to the Religious*.

transporting?... From the pain of a bad conscience, believe in the unspeakable joy and gladness of a good conscience».[111]

Conclusion

The main aim of this analysis has been to search within Newman's own sermons what are the particular riches that lie behind the reflections on conscience. The examination from a linguistic perspective has the advantage of unearthing and putting together the plurality of words and their meaning therein.

The division of the sermons proposed here, initially motivated by the historical event of the tour, has been further justified through this analysis. In both groups, the analysis followed a tripartite division: the being, the doing and the having. These three views on conscience cover a wide spectrum of the whole reality: identity of conscience; activity of conscience; attributes of conscience. This pattern has been advantageous in helping to gather and classify the richness of the vocabulary and the reflections contained in the sermons.

Simultaneously, we endeavoured to discover the internal relationship that these reflections have with the rest of Newman's journey. The sermons are a reflection of his intellectual and spiritual journey. The events that surround them, in a certain sense, have the dual role of effecting and being effected by his fundamental beliefs. The study has helped us, in this way, to discover how the two periods of the sermons highlight the reciprocity that exists between the notion of conscience and the events.

The first period is very much concerned with the «doing» of conscience, which we qualified as philosophical. Situations of controversy, his brother and the liberals, in a certain sense

---

111 *Id.*, pp. 199-200.

condition the space within which Newman explores what conscience is. Conscience is understood as an instrument of discovery and its workings have a philosophical connotation about them. It comes across that the intellectual, philosophical, aspect of conscience is much more to the fore than the theological reality it explores later on.

The aspect of conscience Newman insists on at this stage, its role as an enlightened guide, a powerful principle of strength, an independent arbiter of actions, proves essential in the second part of his preaching ministry. «What conscience does» in the first period, the positive actions of conscience which favour the approach to God, is complemented by what we have discovered in the analysis of «what conscience is» in the second period. Conscience favours the tension of the human towards the divine. As an experience of the discovery of truth, it has the unambiguous role of moving the human experience towards the mystery of God. The movement in itself, ultimately becomes the confirmation «of the presence of God, originally certified to them by the inward voice of conscience».[112]

This difference between the two periods helps to unearth not only what are the events that had a crucial role, but, more importantly, it helps appreciate how, in moving from one aspect to the other, there is development and, as a result, enrichment. In other words, the so-called «philosophical» aspect, so prominent in the first phase, does not disappear when the «theological» aspect is developed in the second one.

We also believe that favouring a chronological reading of the sermons has advantaged our findings for two reasons. First, we witnessed even more the bond that exists between the events of Newman's life and his sermons. This served as the guiding theme all along. Secondly, in employing the chronological method, we noticed that the actual development taking place is very much

---

112 *PS* II. 2, p. 19; see also *PS* VI. 23, pp. 339-340.

in line with that gradual growth that is witnessed within the moral experience of the person. Studying Newman, therefore, becomes a study of his moral journey, as reflected in his life and preaching.

The method that has been adopted here does not claim any exclusiveness in the conclusions it reached. What it claims, though, is that it helped us to contextualize, *ad intra* and *ad extra*, the reflections that John Henry Newman shares in his *Parochial and Plain Sermons*.

Conclusion

The guiding question with which we began our inquiry, was «How is Newman's understanding of conscience within the *Parochial and Plain Sermons* related to his personal life story?» Within this question are contained the traces of the journey we have taken. In trying to understand the meaning of the word conscience we have visited the events which made and sustained his life experience.

1. The Man and His Journey

The discovery of the inner self, in Newman's case, is not a refuge disjointed from outside reality. It rather serves as a pre-condition of, and for, conscience. This inwardness is the privileged place wherefrom Newman is able to identify the force of a guide, that of conscience, which translates itself into an invitation calling for a personal commitment. «Myself and my Creator»[1] is the synthesis of this experience.

The journey of faith, the quest for holiness, becomes a deep concern within him. He moves on in this direction not irrespective

---

1   *Apol* . p. 4.

of what is happening around him, but in relation to it. The challenges he meets, with their related risks, are characterized by a sense of equilibrium. In his contact with liberalism, he succeeds in not sacrificing reason on the altar of religion. In him there is constant awareness not to relegate the moral by letting it be preceeded by the intellectual.

The Oriel period, with its potential danger to Newman's future development, turns out to be a most beneficial phase. It helps him take the distance from Evangelicalism through liberalism. It gives him confidence in his intellectual powers. It equips him with the right intuitive abilities that turn out to be as useful in affirming his stand against liberalism.

His controversies with Charles further promote conscience as the experience where attitudes are decided, where the frame of mind is formed. Newman presents truth to self as the starting point of any inquiry. And this starting point happens to be within the heart, the latter being the forum within which the person lives an attitudinal respect towards conscience. In presenting the concept of person as dependent on a «superior being», Newman contemplates this dependency as being lived through the guide of conscience.

This is profoundly connected with his unequivocal stand against liberalism. By promoting conscience Newman clarifies the role of reason. While Newman is never short in accepting and appreciating the value of reason, he is also clear about the fact that in matters which touch the depth of our being, reason cannot claim to be the best of guides. The relationship between «myself and my Creator» cannot depend on the primacy of reason, being this limited in its nature and function. It is rather founded upon conscience as the moral core of our being.

Presenting the experience of the heart as the space where the demands from conscience are dealt with, Newman sees liberalism as favouring a line of thought and action where both, conscience and the space of the heart, are refuted. The intellectual mind, with

Conclusion

its rational strength, relegates religion as something relative to self, while trust of self takes the place of God. Knowledge becomes a substituting principle, sustaining a vision where things can be put right by scientific knowledge.

As his life goes on, spiritual realities tend to have a more predominant role. The understanding of the reality of the Church encourages him to come in closer contact with the Fathers. Through them he strengthens his basic belief that the Church is more than a mere institution, it is an experience where the divine enters into a privileged relationship with humanity. Newman, after the tour of the Mediterranean, channels his energy to safeguard the ecclesial experience from being left to the mercy of the currents of the day.

The other theological theme related to that of the Church, as the place where the experience of the divine takes place, is that of the «indwelling of the Holy Spirit». We have seen how «the promise of the indwelling of the Holy Spirit in the soul, and through him, of the Father and the Son, was the culminating point of the Christian revelation».[2] It is a belief that is not limited to a purely theoretical aspect but «is primarily and essentially *personal*. God takes possession of man and is present in him».[3]

The Church and the Spirit, therefore, these two fundamental beliefs, focus even more Newman's struggle against liberalism. In philosophical rationalism, as represented by R. D. Hampden, Newman detects the exact antithesis of both the supremacy of the divine, as experienced within the Church, and the possible enriching experience of divine revelation within the soul, through the action of the Holy Spirit.

---

[2] C.S. Dessain, 'The Biblical Basis of Newman's Ecumenical Theology', in *Rediscovery*, p. 102.
[3] *Ibid.*

2. The Meaning of Conscience

Newman is clear to himself as to the pastoral motive of his preaching. The primary driving force was not the intellectual. The sermons were meant to be vehicles of moral truths. The listeners and the readers were the «locus» where the action of the Holy Spirit takes place, the action of the Spirit that makes real the coming together of the divine and the human.

Besides the role of the Spirit, the understanding of the Church features deeply in Newman's idea of the sermon. The model he adopts follows the pattern which is later qualified by Newman as that of the Primitive Church: «no one will deny that most of my Sermons are on moral subjects, not doctrinal; still I am leading my hearers, to the Primitive Church if you will, but not to the Church of England».[4]

The analysis of the sermons had followed a tripartite division: «what conscience is», «what conscience does» and «what conscience has». These three views on conscience have provided us with a wide spectrum of the whole reality both within the sermons and, simultaneously, with the fundamental relationship that these reflections have with the rest of Newman's journey. Even in this exercise, the events came across in their dual role of effecting and being effected by his fundamental beliefs.

---

[4] *LD* VII, p. 417; «the peculiarity of Butler is this – that, while on the one hand he is reserved, austere, infrequent in the mention of Christian doctrine, in his writings, yet on the other hand he was very earnest for what he calls a Cheap External Religion, put up a Cross in his private Chapel, and was charged with Popery. I conceive his wonderfully gifted intellect caught the idea which had actually been the rule of the Primitive Church, of teaching the more Sacred Truths ordinarily by rites and ceremonies. No mode of teaching can be imagined so public, constant, impressive, permanent, and at the same time reverential than that which makes the forms of devotion the memorial and declaration of doctrine – reverential because the very posture of the mind in worship is necessarily such. In this way Christians receive the Gospel literally on their knees, and in a temper altogether different from that critical and argumentative spirit which sitting and listening engender», in *LD* V, p. 46.

3. A Personal Journey

The study of the background of Newman's spiritual and intellectual journey, has the benefit of rooting the reflections on conscience in the daily realities of life. E.J. Sillem, in the following reflection, captures what we felt throughout the development of this work: «as one feels one's way gradually step by step, into Newman's way of seeing things and of thinking, one realises that he himself stands partially revealed in the vast vision of reality which is his own, and that he could not speak of it without speaking of himself».[5]

In contact with Newman's sermons, we have realised how «this vision shines alike in Newman's writing, in his character and in the ideals by which he shaped the conduct of his life... In him alone do his ideas form a system, and in him alone do they seem at first to be real».[6] Besides, Sillem anticipates as well what any reader is left with after meeting Newman in this manner: «we soon discover that it is not Newman alone who stands revealed in the great vision he imparts to his readers; Newman only seems to be revealing himself so as to reveal the reader to himself, as a new vision of man's life in the world gradually takes shape in his own mind».[7]

We have to acknowledge that the same process has occurred in our case. The discovery of Newman has been constantly complemented by the discovery of our own self to us. Although this note is very personal in nature, its importance lies in the fact that Newman does not ask to be met, and cannot be explored, solely on a purely intellectual platform; this is only one dimension of the process. Newman involves the person in his or her totality, as much as he himself comes across, through the sermons, with his intellectual, spiritual and human dimensions.

---

5   E.J. SILLEM, *John Henry Newman - The Philosophical Notebook*, vol.1, p. 5.
6   *Ibid.*
7   *Ibid.*

4. Future Tasks

Being this, therefore, a journey of revelation, and self-revelation, we are also aware that the journey has to go on, and this for various reasons. From varied standpoints, this work asks to be complemented and enriched. The period we dealt with encompasses other publications, amongst which the *Fifteen Sermons Preached before the University of Oxford*. They need to be looked into so as to complement and, surely, enrich our findings. This eventual study, although it will benefit from our findings, will undoubtedly produce and unveil other interesting discoveries.

Another area of study that will complement our work, and which is endowed with more publications and letters, is the whole Catholic period. We have to keep in mind that the ideas, which we examined here, got enriched and further developed in his later years. The *Essay in Aid of a Grammar of Assent* has a history that needs to be discovered not only on the level of ideas, their origin and development, but also on the level of his own life. Standing by what we have discovered, we are convinced that this area of study is as intrinsically tied up with Newman as the one we examined here.

While so far we mentioned areas that concern Newman from an *ad intra* perspective, his life and the publications he produced, we are also aware that there are other areas of further study *ad extra* to Newman himself. We name two in particular. The first one would be a possible comparative study between Newman and other contemporary Anglican authors, to see how far or how near Newman's own understanding of conscience was shared within Anglican theology. This study would shed more light on the whole question on how Newman influenced or was influenced by the ideas of his time.

A second area of further research would be the analysis of Newman's influence on the development of post-Vatican II moral theology, with special attention to the understanding of conscience. This ultimate area of research necessarily supposes that the whole of Newman corpus would be studied and analysed in its entirety. In view of this eventual research, we feel that the present study has given a contribution in this direction.

Newman's influence on theology today is an accepted fact. Yet, after this experience of working on the primary sources, one is tempted to ask whether enough use is made of the sources available. The literature that is produced on Newman is not small. The methodology that these same publications adopt or follow leaves several unanswered questions. One is struck by the lack of use of *The Letters and Diaries* in recent articles or books that treat Newman and his message.

One cannot also fail to notice that at times Newman's own ideas, from different periods of his life, are put together to support or to confirm certain pre-determined conclusions. Newman's worth cannot be asserted, or otherwise, by quoting and collating references from primary sources without situating those same sources.

We hope that the effect of this work, if there should only be one, would be to understand how Newman, in his search for truth, was able to bring in not only his intellect but also all the other dimensions of his personality. The quest for truth was not a mere quest for knowledge or certainties. His quest for truth was one which was concerned with his whole personal experience and interpreting that in the light of the divine.

5. The Essence of Our Study

By way of closing this part of our journey with John Henry Newman, we would like to make reference to a reflection by Maurice Nédoncelle on Newman. Nédoncelle, who studied Newman from a philosophical perspective, winds up one of his studies by naming two principles that can guide us in understanding the foundations of Newman's edifice. He calls them implicit principles, and they are: «la doctrine d'une intentionnalité de la conscience» and that of the «personnalisme moral».[8] Nédoncelle, referring to Newman's journey of faith, offers these two principles within a clear framework of a relationship between the human and the divine: «Newman est un philosophe essentiellement religieux qui envisage tous les problèmes humains dans leurs rapports avec Dieu. Et le seul Dieu qu'il reconaisse, c'est celui de l'Evangile, qui offre à la raison la plus éminente sagesse, parce qu'il lui donne les lumières et les forces de la foi».[9]

In studying Newman's sermons from a conscience perspective, we recognize that this statement by Nédoncelle offers in a nutshell the essence of our study. The intentionality of conscience, while completely refusing any superficial approach in being simply limited to «intending to do», is reflected not only in the willingness it contains but also in the experience of moral growth that it gradually produces. This experience becomes the experience of the person, where the latter is encouraged to go forward. Morality, therefore, does not end up being an experience of exteriority. Morality becomes a search for the truth that is within, which can only be discovered in the experience of conscience and the living out of conscience.

---

[8] M. NÉDONCELLE, *La philosophie religieuse de John Henry Newman*. (Sostralib, Strasbourg 1946) p. 289.
[9] *Id.*, p. 292.

Appendix

Reading guide (I) - 1825-1832

Conscience IS		Conscience DOES		Conscience HAS	
VIII.8:	law	I.4:	warns, up raids	I.15:	stirrings
VIII.8:	powerful enlightened guide	VIII.8:	anticipates mystery	I.17:	authority (a)
				I.17:	authority (b)
VIII.8:	a match	VIII.8:	enjoins	I.17:	relentings
I.15:	part of self as reason	I.1:	bears witness	II.9:	voice
		I.1:	reproaches	I.8:	innate principles
VII.15:	divinely given informant	VII.4:	tells them evil	I.9:	visitings
		I.15:	to balance the influence of sight and reason	I.9:	compunctions
VIII.7:	constraining force			I.3:	natural true sense
VIII.7:	inward sense	I.15:	tells them they are not their own masters, and that sin is hateful and ruinous	I.24:	authority
VIII.7:	law written in heart				
I.17:	better knowledge				
II.9:	inward voice	VII.15:	approves		
II.9:	light within	I.19:	bids work of faith		
VIII.5:	secret monitor				
VIII.5:	power in the heart	I.19:	condemns		
		I.19:	refuses to direct		
VIII.5:	principle of strength	I.20:	aiding to say, guiding, composing, interceding minds on objects of faith		
I.9:	powerful instrument				
I.9:	instrument of His Spirit				
I.24:	independent arbiter of actions	III.6:	tells Holy Law as given by God		
		VIII.7:	suggests measures		
I.24:	stern, gloomy principle	VIII.13:	tells there is a right and a wrong		

231

Conscience in *Parochial and Plain Sermons*

Conscience IS	Conscience DOES	Conscience HAS
	I.17: gives notions	
	I.17: sets great truths authoritatively	
	VIII.14: teaches truth	
	VIII.14: suggestions sanctioned and explained by Christ	
	VIII.14: teach simple truths	
	VIII.14: teach religious obedience	
	I.8: suggestions of conscience	
	I.8: God and conscience approve	
	VIII.5: tells what is right and wrong	
	VIII.5: resists temptation	
	VIII.5: saves from spiritual death	
	I.9: leads us to a new life, does not make us love new life	
	I.9: tells impuls for action	
	I.24: tells of guilt and punishment	
	I.24: loudly speaks of God's wrath	

Appendix

Reading guide (II) - 1833-1841

Conscience IS		Conscience DOES		Conscience HAS	
I.2:	representative of Him	I.2:	bids us serve Him	II.2:	claim to be followed
I.2:	law of God written in our heart	I.2:	tells us how to serve Him	VI.23:	no shape or material form
I.2:	secret voice of God	I.2:	tells us we are answerable	V.17:	risings of conscience
II.6:	original endowment	I.5:	suggests	VII.14:	feelings of bad conscience
II.6:	guide originally from God	II.6:	tells difference between right and wrong	VII.14:	pain of bad conscience
II.2:	rule	II.2:	directs thoughts to some being	VII.14:	joy and gladness of good conscience
II.2:	born with him	II.2:	speaks within		
II.2:	voice within	II.2:	rules heart with inward sense		
II.2:	inward sense				
II.2:	more acute than reason	II.2:	does not allow him to rest in itself		
II.2:	inward voice	II.2:	sends him forth to Him		
II.2:	leadings of God's Spirit within	II.2:	inward sense certifies presence of God		
II.2:	invisible guide				
II.2:	Divine Voice within issues into His existence	II.23:	forbodes ill to the sinner		
II.19:	Voice of truth in hearts	VI.23:	assures		
II.23:	testimony	VI.23:	prompts us to religion		
VI.23:	voice within us	VI.23:	condemns and chastises sin		
IV.22:	mirror within	VI.23:	finds an object to rest upon God		
IV.21:	inward law				
V.16:	home, chamber, tribunal, throne, self	VI.23:	incites to a noble faith		
V.22:	good conscience is being reminded of God in our hearts	IV.22:	reflects to the Son of God		
		IV.21:	inward voice speaking		
VIII.2:	channel of God's voice	VI.3:	tells us what we have a right to do, and what we have not		
V.11:	law				
VII.13:	bad conscience is torment				
VI.18:	inward incommunicable perception of truth and duty				
VI.3:	inward feeling				
VI.3:	inward voice				

233

Bibliography

WORKS BY JOHN HENRY NEWMAN
(alphabetical order with date of uniform edition)

Anglican Difficulties, 2vols. 1879, 1876
Apologia 1873
Arians of the Fourth Century 1871
Callista 1876
Development of Christian Doctrine 1878
Discourses to Mixed Congregations 1871
Discussions and Arguments 1872
Essays Critical and Historical 3vols 1871
Grammar of Assent 1870
Historical Sketches 2vols 1872
Idea of a University 1873
Lectures on Justification 1874
Loss and Gain 1874
Meditations and Devotions 1893
Oxford University Sermons 1872
Parochial and Plain Sermons, 8vols. 1868
Present Position of Catholics in England 1872
Select Treatises of St. Athanasius, 2vols. 1881
Sermons bearing on Subjects of the Day 1869
Sermons preached on Various Occasions 1870
Tracts Theological and Eclesiastical 1874
Via Media, 2vols. 1877
Verses on Various Occasions 1874

Books and Articles Quoted in this Work

BARFIELD, O.,	*What Coleridge Thought* (London 1972).
BLEHL, V.F.,	'The Intellectual and Spiritual Influence of J.H. Newman', *The Downside Review* 111 (1993) 251-257.
BOEKRAAD, A.J.,	'Conscience in the Vision of John Henry Newman', *Divus thomas* 82 (1979) 233-249.
BOUDENS, R.,	'*Growth*: A Key Concept in understanding Newman', *Ephemerides theologicae lovaniensis* 69 (1993) 335-353.
BOUYER, L.,	'Actualité de Newman', *Communio* 12/3 (1987) 115-122.
BOUYER, L.,	*Newman: His Life and Spirituality.* (Burns & Oates, London 1958).
CAMERON, J.M.,	'Newman and the Empiricist Tradition', in COULSON, J., - ALLCHIN, A.M., (eds.), *The Rediscovery of Newman: An Oxford Symposium* (Sheed & Ward - SPCK, London - Melbourne 1967) pp. 76-96.
CHADWICK, O.,	*Newman.* (Oxford University Press, Oxford 1986).
CHADWICK, O.,	*The Mind of the Oxford Movement* (Adams and Charles Black, London 1960).
COULSON, J., - A.M. ALLCHIN, A.M. – TREVOR, M., (eds.),	*Newman: A Portrait Restored.* (Sheed & Ward, London - Melbourne - New York 1965).
COULSON, J., - ALLCHIN, A.M., (eds.),	*The Rediscovery of Newman: An Oxford Symposium* (Sheed & Ward - SPCK, London - Melbourne 1967).
CULLER, A.D.,	*The Imperial Intellect.* (New Haven 1955).
DE BERRANGER, O.,	'Des paradoxes au mystère chez J.H.

	Newman et H. de Lubac', *Revue des sciences philosophiques et théologiques* 78 (1994) 45-79.
DENIS, Y.,	'Les mécanismes mentaux du développement doctrinal d'aprés *L'Essai sur le développement de la doctrine chrétienne* de Newman', *Bulletin de litterature ecclésiastique* 80 (1979) 179-194.
DESSAIN, C.S.	'The Biblical Basis of Newman's Ecumenical Theology,' in COULSON, J., - ALLCHIN, A.M., (eds.), *The Rediscovery of Newman: An Oxford Symposium* (Sheed & Ward - SPCK, London - Melbourne 1967) pp. 100-122.
DESSAIN, C.S.,	*John Henry Newman* (Adam and Charles Black, London 1971).
DESSAIN, C.S.,	'Newman's First Conversion', *Newman Studien* 3 (1957) 37-53.
DESSAIN, C.S.,	'Newman's Philosophy and Theology', in DE LAURA, D.J. (ed.) *Victorian Prose - A Guide to Research* (The Modern Language Association of America, New York 1973) pp. 166-184.
EVANS, G.R.,	'Newman's Letters to Charles', *The Downside Review* 100 (1982) 92.
FABER, G.,	*Oxford Apostles. A Character Study of the Oxford Movement.* (Pelican Books, Harmondsworth - Middlesex 1954).
GILLEY, S.,	'The Ecclesiology of the Oxford Movement: a Reconsideration', in VAISS, P. (ed.), *Newman: From Oxford to the People.* (Gracewing, Herefordshire 1996) pp. 60-75.
GUITTON, J.,	*La philosophie de Newman: Essai sur l'Idée de Développement* (Paris 1933).
HOLLIS, C.,	*Newman and the Modern World* (The Catholic Book Club, London 1967).
HUMMEL, T.C.,	'John Henry Newman and the Oriel Noetics', *Anglican Theological Review* 74 (1992) 203-215.

Bibliography

JANSSENS, A., *Newman: Inleiding tot zijn geest en zijn werk.* (N.V. Standaard Boekhandel, Brussles 1937).

KER, I., *John Henry Newman* (Oxford University Press, Oxford - New York 1988).

KER, I., *Newman and the Fullness of Christianity.* (Clark, Edinburgh 1993).

LOSSKY, N., 'The Oxford Movement and the Revival of Patristic Theology', in P. VAISS, (ed.), *From Oxford to People*, pp. 76-81.

MERRIGAN, T., '*Numquam minus solus, quam cum solus.* Newman's First Conversion: Its Significance for His Life and Thought', *The Downside Review* 103 (1985) 99-116.

MURRAY, P. – BLEHL, V.F. (eds.), *John Henry Newman: Sermons 1824-1834. Volume I: Sermons on the Liturgy and Sacraments and on Christ the Mediator; Volume II: Sermons on Biblical History, Sin and Justification, the Christian Way of Life, and Biblical Theology.* (Clarendon Press, Oxford 1991, 1993).

MERRIGAN, T., *Clear Heads and Holy Hearts: The Religious and Theological Ideal of John Henry Newman.* 'Louvain Theological & Pastoral Monographs, 7'. (Peeters, Louvain 1991).

NÉDONCELLE, M., *La philosophie religieuse de John Henry Newman.* (Sostralib, Strasbourg 1946).

NEWSOME, D., 'The Evangelical Sources of Newman's Power', in COULSON, J., - ALLCHIN, A.M., (eds.), *The Rediscovery of Newman: An Oxford Symposium* (Sheed & Ward - SPCK, London - Melbourne 1967) pp. 11-30.

O'CONNELL, M.R., *The Oxford Conspirators. A History of the Oxford Movement 1833-1845.* (University Press of America, Lanham/New York – London 1969)

PARKER, T.M.,	'The Rediscovery of the Fathers in the Seventeenth-Century Anglican Tradition', in COULSON, J., - ALLCHIN, A.M., (eds.), *The Rediscovery of Newman: An Oxford Symposium* (Sheed & Ward - SPCK, London - Melbourne 1967) pp. 31-49.
ROBBINS, W.,	*The Newman Brothers* (Heinemann, London 1966).
ROWELL, G.,	'Newman and the Anglican Tradition: Reflections on Tractarianism and the Seventeenth-Century Anglican Divines', *Louvain Studies* 15 (1990) 136-150.
SHAIRP, J.C.,	*Studies in Poetry and Philosophy* (Edinburgh 1872).
SHERIDAN, T.,	*Newman on Justification.* (New York, 1967).
SILLEM, E.J.,	*John Henry Newman. The Philosophical Notebook.* 2vols. (Nauwelaerts Publishing House, Louvain 1969).
TREVOR, M.,	*Newman, the Pillar of the Cloud. Newman, Light in the Winter.* 2 volumes (Macmillan, London 1962).
VAISS, P., (ed.),	*Newman: From Oxford to the People.* (Gracewing, Herefordshire 1996).
VARGISH, T.,	*Newman: The Contemplation of Mind.* (The Catholic Book Club, London 1973).
WALGRAVE, J.H.,	*J.H. Newman: His Personality, His Principles, His Fundamental Doctrines: Course Delivered by Professor J.H. Walgrave, Katholieke Universiteit Leuven 1975 - 1976 - 1977.* (Printed Manuscript, K.U.L., Leuven, Belgium 1981).
WALGRAVE, J.H.,	*Newman the Theologian: The Nature of Belief and Doctrine as Exemplified in His Life and Works.* (London, Geoffrey Chapman 1960).

ZENO, P., 'Newman's Inner Life up to His Election as Fellow of Oriel College», *The Irish Ecclesiastical Record* 78 (1952) 255-275.

General Index

Contents vii
Acknowledgements ix
Abbreviations xii
Introduction xiii
1. The main question xiii
2. Why the *Parochial and Plain Sermons?* xiv
3. The Reason of the Present Work xvii
4. The Structure of the Work xix

THE DISCOVERY OF CONSCIENCE 1816-1825 3
1.   Ealing: Conversion and Inwardness 4
1.1.   Myself and My Creator 5
1.2.   Relatedness with the Invisible 6
1.3.   Uniqueness and Distance 8
1.4.   Conscience as Guardian 11
1.5.   The Seeds of Evangelicalism 12
1.8.   The Importance of Ealing 15
2.   Oxford: Student at Trinity 16
2.1.   Aloneness 16
2.2   The Talented Mind 18
2.3.   Reasonableness of Religion 20

2.4.	Graduality as Basis for Development	26
2.5.	Meeting of Opposites	29
3.	Oxford: Fellow and Tutor at Oriel	33
3.1.	Whately and Hawkins: Thinking and Tradition	34
3.2.	Butler: Analogy and Probability	40
3.3.	The First Encounter with Liberalism	42
3.4.	The Devotion to the Fathers	47
Conclusion		51

ADVOCACY OF CONSCIENCE: 1825-1832		**55**
1.	Controversy with Charles – 1825	56
1.1.	Analogical Argument	58
1.2.	The Notion of Conscience	59
1.3.	External and Internal Evidences	60
1.4.	The Heart	61
1.5.	Pride and Prejudice	63
1.6.	The Conscientious Inquirer	65
1.7.	Secret Faults	67
1.8.	*Inward Witness to the Truth of the Gospel*	68
1.9.	The Indications of Conscience	69
1.10.	The Obedient Heart	70
2.	Peel Affair	71
3.	Grave College Questions	74
3.1.	The Tutorial System	74
3.2.	The Obligation of Higher Duties	78
4.	Controversy with Charles: 1830	80
4.1.	Certainty and Probability	81
4.2.	Josiah, a Pattern for the Ignorant – Memorandum	84
4.3.	Faith or Conscientiousness	87
4.4.	Temptation of Sight: Preconceived Notions	88
4.5.	The Self-Wise Inquirer	89
5.	The Spirit of Liberalism	96
5.1.	Benevolence	97
5.2.	God's attributes	99

5.3.	*The Religion of the Day*	101
5.4.	Knowledge and Improvement of Morality	105
5.5.	*Sins of Ignorance and Weakness*	107
Conclusion		108

ADVOCACY OF CONSCIENCE: 1833-1843 ... 111

1.	A Work to do	112
1.1.	Primitive Christianity	114
1.2.	The Fathers as Precedents	115
1.3.	Precedents and Trial	118
1.4.	The Clergy	120
1.5.	The Church Visible and Invisible	121
1.6.	Church and State	125
2.	Truth – According to Light	131
3.	The Indwelling of the Holy Spirit	134
3.1.	The Indwelling Spirit	134
3.2.	Spiritual Influences in the Heart	136
3.3.	The Gift of the Spirit: Contemplation and Action	138
3.4.	The Law of Conscience	140
4.	Spiritual and Intellectual Controversies	143
4.1.	Evangelicalism	144
4.2.	R. D. Hampden: The Theory of Rationalism	145
4.3.	R.H. Froude: Metaphysical and Practical	146
5.	Francis W. Newman	148
5.1.	The Church	149
5.2.	Latitudinarianism	150
5.3.	The Ethos of the Christian and the Dissenter	152
6.	Lights of the Uncomfortable Vista	154
6.1.	The Return to the Fathers	155
6.2.	Truth and Light	156
6.3.	*Divine Calls*	160
Conclusion		162

THE REASON BEHIND THE SERMON 165
1. Correspondence before 1834 166
1.1. Truth and Holiness: Scope of Sermons....................166
1.2. Danger of Vanity and Love of Literary Pursuit 168
1.3. Intellect Servant of Moral Sense...............................169
1.4. Divine guidance 171
1.5. Preparation, Study and Calm 172
1.6. Unwritten Memory...173
2. Correspondence after 1834 173
2.1. Ministers as Protesters 174
2.2. The Heart and the Holy Spirit 175
2.3. The Evangelicals 178
2.4. Ancient and Modern (Evangelical) School 179
2.5. Idea and Function of a Sermon................................180
2.6. Moral rather than Doctrinal 183
Conclusion 184

ANALYSIS OF THE TERM 'CONSCIENCE' 187
1. The Linguistic Meaning of Conscience: 1825-1832 ...188
1.1. Conscience «Is» 188
1.1.1. «Enlightened Guide» 189
1.1.2. «Independent Arbiter of Actions» 191
1.1.3. «Placed by Almighty God» 191
1.1.4. «Inward Voice» 192
1.2. Conscience «Does» 194
1.2.1. «Bears Witness» 194
1.2.2. «Aiding, Guiding, Composing» 196
1.2.3. «Naturally Teaches Obedience» 197
1.2.4. «Suggests» 198
1.2.5. «Warns»...199
1.2.6. «Condemns» 200
1.3. Conscience «Has»...201
1.3.1. «Authority» 202
1.3.2. «Innate Principles» 204

243

1.3.3. «Natural True Sense» 205
2. The Linguistic Meaning of Conscience: 1833-1843 .. 207
2.1. Conscience «Is» 207
2.1.1. «Representative of Him» 208
2.1.2. «Rule» 211
2.1.3. «Voice of God» 212
2.1.4. «Throne» 213
2.1.5. «Inward Incommunicable Perception» 215
2.2. Conscience «Does» 216
2.2.1. «Tells» 216
2.3. Conscience «Has» 218
Conclusion 219

CONCLUSION 223
1. The Man and His Journey 223
2. The Meaning of Conscience 226
3. A Personal Journey 227
4. Future Tasks 228
5. The Essence of Our Study 230

Appendix 233
Bibliography 236
General Index 242